ntering 1878 -79
CIRCLE
River
Lena
LAPTEV
SEA
U. S. S. R.
Cape Chelyuskin
Yenisei River
Dickson
Novaya
KARA
SEA
Zemlya
Ob
River
BARENTS
SEA
Tromsö
NORWAY
SWEDEN
0
500
kilometers

North-east passage

GEORGE KISH

North-east passage

Adolf Erik Nordenskiöld, his life and times

NICO ISRAEL / AMSTERDAM

1973

Published with the support of the Royal Swedish Academy of Sciences.

Printed in the Netherlands

ISBN 90 6072 720 7

For Vin and Susie

A man in coat of ice arrayed
  Stood up once by the Arctic Ocean
  The whole earth shook with proud emotion
And honor to the giant paid.

from 'Post Festum'
by Björnstjerne Björnson

PREFACE

Adolf Erik Nordenskiöld was one of the great public figures of the late 19th century: at the time of his death brief sketches of his life appeared in scores of newspapers throughout Europe, the Americas, and Japan, and scientific journals the world over printed obituary notices, paying tribute to his work. Two biographies were published in Sweden, one by the distinguished geographer-explorer Sven Hedin, entitled *Adolf Erik Nordenskiöld,* in 1926, the other by Henrik Ramsay, *Nordenskiöld Sjöfararen* (Nordenskiöld the Navigator), in 1950. The only partial biography in a language other than Swedish, published prior to the present work, appeared in London, in 1879: *The Arctic Voyages of Adolf Erik Nordenskiöld, 1858-1879;* it was written by Alexander Leslie, who later translated the *Voyage of the 'Vega'*.
To the specialist concerned with Nordenskiöld's scientific contributions, the sole serious attempt to evaluate his work was published as a special issue of *YMER,* the Journal of the Swedish Society for Anthropology and Geography, in 1902. It consists of a brief biographical sketch, and four articles describing the work of Nordenskiöld as an Arctic explorer, geologist, mineralogist, and historian of geography and cartography. A full bibliography of Nordenskiöld's writings, numbered in chronological order, concludes the issue; another bibliography, arranged by topics, is part of the memorial address delivered to the Finnish Scientific Society by Wilhelm Ramsay, and published in Helsingfors in 1903.
In writing this, the first full-length biography of Nordenskiöld to be published outside Scandinavia, the author relied principally on the 'Nordenskiöld papers', a large collection of documents and correspondence, preserved in the Library of the Royal Swedish Academy of Sciences. Quotations in the text represent translations from the Swedish originals, but responsibility for their interpretation lies entirely with the author. Considerable use was made of contemporary printed sources, published in Scandinavia and elsewhere; quotations from Nordenskiöld's own writings are translations from the original text. In establishing a chronology of Nordenskiöld's life, the author found Ramsay's biography most useful; Hedin's book, written by a contemporary of Nordenskiöld's older son and a lifelong admirer of the great explorer, provided eyewitness accounts not found anywhere else.
To the National Science Foundation of the United States, the author is deeply grateful for continuing and generous support, making possible a

year's stay in Sweden and travels throughout Scandinavia, from southern Denmark to Spitsbergen, and for time at home to get the book started. In ways just as generous, the Royal Swedish Academy of Sciences lent its support to this venture, welcoming the author to its house, opening its treasure of documents, providing assistance up to the very moment of publication.

Equally important and truly indispensable was the warm welcome offered to a newcomer to Sweden by Swedish friends. The author's thanks are due first and foremost to the Head Librarian of the Royal Swedish Academy of Sciences, Dr. Wilhelm Odelberg, gracious and generous host, who helped to make a dream come true; and to Dr. Olof Arrhenius and his wife, Eva Nordenskiöld Arrhenius; their enthusiasm for this project never faltered and they helped the author to see Nordenskiöld as the man behind the statue. Mrs. Birgit Högbom, the author's Research Associate, provided invaluable assistance in deciphering documents, interpreting difficult texts, looking after innumerable yet important details.

Profesors William-Olson and Gunnar Alexandersson, of the Stockholm school of Economics, and Ulla Ehrensvärd, Head of the Division of Maps and Prints of the Stockholm Royal Library, not only offered working space in their departments, but gave generously of their time to help a visitor get acquainted with Swedish ways and Swedish values. Members of the Nordenskiöld family: Baron Erik Nordenskiöld, General Bengt Nordenskiöld, Miss Margareta Nordenskiöld provided original photographs, family documents, and precious details about their distinguished ancestor.

1967-1968 was 'our year in Sweden' to the author, and his wife and daughter. They shared with him the long darkness of winter days, the exciting white nights of a Nordic summer, the months of library research and those of writing, the excitement of finding new information, the long wait for completing the book. Their love and their loyalty made this work possible.

TABLE OF CONTENTS

The ilustrations at the end of the chapters are chosen from *A. E. Nordenskiöld:* Vegas färd kring Asien och Europa – jemte en historisk återblik på föregående resor längs gamla verldens nordkust. Stockholm, F. & G. Beijers Förlag. (1881-2) 2 vols.

LIST OF ILLUSTRATIONS

(between pages 140 and 141)

INTRODUCTION

It was a grey, cold August afternoon on Bering Island, a small and lonely spot in the North Pacific, buffeted by wind and rain much of the year. Columns of smoke spiralled from the wooden shacks of the settlement, strung out along the open harbor. Though it has been Russian territory since its discovery by the great Arctic explorer Bering, in 1741, the colony on Bering Island received support and income from an American corporation, the Alaska Commercial Company of San Francisco, that had leased the island as a base for sealing in the Bering Sea nearby. Besides a small group of native Aleuts, and a few Russian officials, the people on Bering Island in that year of 1879 were a typical group of American immigrants, from all of Europe. But Scandinavians were the most numerous among them.

Few ships ever touch on Bering Island. On August 14, 1879, a minor sensation was created by the appearance of a low-slung, black ship approaching the harbor from the northwest. The ship had a brig-type rigging, with two tall masts; a small smoke stack indicated it had a steam engine as well. The men standing on shore, watching the ship maneuver its way toward the settlement, soon noticed the flag: it was the yellow and blue standard of Sweden, well known to most of them. One, a Finnish carpenter, jumped into a small rowboat, and as he came near the ship, he yelled: 'Is this Nordenskiöld? This is Andersson, from Kimito. Welcome! I am the only fellow from Kimito on this island.'

The carpenter from south Finland was the first European to meet and greet the Swedish ship, *Vega*, upon its completion of one of the great sea voyages of all time. Starting from Norway the year before, *Vega* had sailed along the northern coasts of Europe and of Asia, and thus made an old explorers' dream come true: the Northeast Passage, the seaway from Europe through the waters of the Arctic Ocean to the Pacific and the Far East. *Vega's* commander, Adolf Erik Nordenskiöld, had accomplished the voyage without mishap, only to be frozen fast in Arctic ice, less than a hundred miles from his goal, Bering Strait. There, while the whole of the civilized world sought news about *Vega's* whereabouts and the welfare of the men aboard her, they had spent the winter of 1878-1879, set off once more when the pack ice broke up, crossed Bering Strait, and now were touching at Bering Island on their way homeward.

Isak Andersson, the carpenter from Finland, knew of the disappearance of *Vega* in the mists of the Siberian Arctic the year before. Being from Finland, he knew the name of *Vega's* commander, and knew him as a fellow Finn. For Nordenskiöld was a native of Finland, one of that small band of Swedes whose ancestors had settled there centuries earlier, and who had preserved their language and their ties with the old country. Andersson, the carpenter, and Nordenskiöld, the scholar-explorer, shared a deep love for the woods and lakes and streams of Finland, the myriad rocky islands offshore, the long winter nights and the endless summer days. They shared the dialect they spoke and the memories of childhood, the fierce independence and the singleminded drive toward a goal set early in life, that is part of the Swedes of Finland. They had both left their homeland, the carpenter to earn a better living than the meager resources of Finland could offer, the scholar, to seek freedom of inquiry, and a chance to pursue knowledge and widen man's geographical horizon.

Adolf Erik Nordenskiöld's forebears had moved to Finland in the late seventeenth century, and for three generations had served both the old country and their new, adopted one with great distinction. Adolf Erik Nordenskiöld, born in 1832, followed in the family tradition, and distinguished himself as a young man in his chosen field of work, mineralogy. Had it not been for an unusual series of coincidences, pitting the young Finn, fiercely independent in spirit, against the Russian autocracy ruling Finland, he may have lived out his days in the quiet and comfortably obscure academic world of the small University of Helsingfors. Instead, deprived of any chance of appointment, let alone advancement, at the university by Russian decree, he returned to the land of his ancestors, to Sweden, to find a better, freer, more congenial atmosphere. He found there fame and fortune, and became not only the best known citizen of his adopted Sweden, but one of the great figures of the century.

Adolf Erik Nordenskiöld's world now appears to us staid, stolid, Victorian. But the nineteenth century inherited an earth from its forerunner that was still incompletely known. There were new horizons of unknown seas and islands. The poles were yet to be conquered, the highest mountains to be climbed. Nordenskiöld made his contribution to the nineteenth century, and to posterity, by completing the conquest of one of the last great mysteries, the Northeast Passage. He is also, and justly, regarded as the man who introduced science into polar exploration, and at the same time made the practical use of discoveries respectable. And to the very end of his life, he kept his spirit of adventure, ready to plunge into new undertakings, to formulate new theories, to argue with his contemporaries, to push forward and encourage the young men around him. The story of Adolf Erik Nordenskiöld's life is the story of a man, of a land reborn, Sweden, and of a time of change, the nineteenth century.

I. YOUTH IN FINLAND

The countryside of southern Finland is a mosaic of forest and meadow, of lakes and streams. Each farmstead lives in a little world of its own, its horizon limited by rocky outcrops, woods of pine and fir and birch, a narrow road its only link with its nearest neighbor, with nearby village and town. There are only two seasons that count: summer and winter, and the rhythm of life adjusts itself to the deep contrasts that separate these.

Winter is harsh in Finland. The cold is intense, and a deep snow hides every dip and rise in the ground. Mornings, a fog often settles over rivers and lakes, and the sun rises late and low over the south. The sun gives light but no heat, and that only for a few hours. Shadows are long, and only the masses of fir and pine break the monotony of the snow-covered landscape. Men have to bundle up to be outside, even for the shortest time, frostbite is an ever-present danger. But the houses are kept warm by wood fires in open fireplace or tiled stove, men carve wooden bowls and spoons and tool handles, women spin and weave, until the winter passes, the days begin to lengthen, and the breakup of ice promises spring.

On summer days, there is never complete darkness. There are no stars visible; the northern sky is always light. The land turns green, and the dark of the evergreens contrasts sharply with the bright green of meadow and cropland, and the white trunks of the birches. Men work long hours in the open, birds abound, fish frolic in the water, and the blessed light from the sun keeps all living things awake all day. The earth may be stony, the soil poor, but after the long, dark winter everything comes to life.

In Mäntsälä township, in southern Finland, an old house stands on the edge of a meadow, overlooking a small stream. A wide lawn once stretched from the front steps of the house to the water, but there is only a meadow now, where geese and chickens wander about. There are fields nearby of rye and oats and potatoes. No one lives in the old house now; it is empty, yet there remains an air of elegance about it, a sense of spaciousness. Frugård is the name of the house, 'the lady's estate'. For two centuries it was the home of the Nordenskiölds. It was here Adolf Erik Nordenskiöld spent the years of his childhood, on a gentleman's farm.

The Nordenskiölds called themselves 'Finland Swedes'. Ever since the early 1200's, the 'Finland Swedes' lived in a conquered land; their ancestors had crossed the narrow Baltic Sea and brought Christianity and alien rule to the people of Finland. Finnish farmers, fishermen, and hunters continued to speak their own tongue under Swedish rule, a language completely different from Swedish. But the language of church and state was Swedish. The Swedes were the officials, the merchants and craftsmen, the land owners and aristocrats. The Finns remained hard-working peasants and lumbermen.

For seven hundred years, the Finland Swedes lived in their conquered land, always looking westward, across the sea, to the old country, Sweden, the source of kingly power and authority. They served the Swedish crown and for their services were rewarded with Swedish titles and honors. Yet when Sweden's rule over Finland came to an end, in 1809, only a handful of them chose to return to the home of their ancestors. Most of them accepted the new ruling power, Russia, because they felt that, though separated by their speech and by their social position from their Finnish neighbors, they shared with them their love for the rocks and woods and lakes of Finland. It was a Finland Swede, Runeberg, who wrote Finland's national anthem. The words of its original version were written in Swedish, they spoke of love of country to all who dwelt there.

In 1832, the year Adolf Nordenskiöld was born, Finland had been under Russian rule for more than twenty years. Finland had been a battlefield more than once in preceding centuries, coveted by Sweden as well as by Russia. After gradually encroaching on Finland from the east, Russia carried out a quick and successful campaign in 1809, overran the country, and incorporated it in the Russian Empire. Finland became a Grand Duchy, with the Tsar acquiring that new title, and Finnish fears of Russian rule were quieted by the Tsar's solemn assurance to respect ancient liberties and established laws.

At the time, one out of every six people living in Finland spoke Swedish, but it was that small minority that ran the country. The Finnish 'diet' or parliament was made up of four estates: three of these, the church, the aristocracy, and the burghers were represented by persons speaking Swedish, only the fourth estate, the farmers, numbered Finnish speakers among them. Education, business, the civil service were manned by Swedish-speaking people, who were well acquainted with German and French, some spoke Russian too, but few could speak Finnish, the language of the majority of Finland's population.

The upper class of Finland consisted of a small group of families closely acquainted with each other, related by speech, social standing, and marriage. They were landowners, civil servants, ministers of the Lutheran church, businessmen; some served with distinction in the Russian Army. Education was held in high esteem and so were good manners. The upper class families usually had a town house or apartment either in the capital, Helsinki, then known only by its Swedish name of Helsingfors, or in the old capital, Turku, called Åbo in Swedish. Most families owned a country estate, too, and it was on those estates they spent most of their time.

Frugård, the Nordenskiöld country estate, had been in the family since 1709. Their first known ancestor, one Johan Nordberg, came to Finland at the end of the 17th century, as administrator of the estates of a Swedish nobleman. He prospered in Finland, acquired holdings in the countryside east of Helsinki, and enjoyed high standing in the Swedish community. Both his elder sons entered the Swedish army, became engineering officers, and were rewarded for their services to the crown by being ennobled in 1751. The family was henceforth known as *Nordenskiöld*, and the family device conforms to that name, 'shield of the North', by showing a sword and a star-studded shield in its upper portion.

Both Anders Johan and Carl Fredrik Nordenskiöld had been also interested in science, in mineralogy, botany, and zoology, and were among the first to be appointed to the newly formed Academy of Sciences in Stockholm, in 1739. The first men to bear the Nordenskiöld name thus established the family tradition of interest and devotion to science, while serving their country as army officers or as civil servants.

The two brothers married sisters, and it is from the younger, Carl Fredrik, that all Nordenskiölds descend. They have been, and remain, a remarkable family, displaying a bewildering variety of talents: they served in the army, the navy, later in the air force, distinguished themselves as scientists, or as public servants. In every generation since the mid-eighteenth century, at least one Nordenskiöld became a national figure, and one, Adolf Erik, a world-known personality.

Science and public service have always been foremost among the goals of the Nordenskiölds. But there was another, less known characteristic among the members of this remarkable family: mysticism. Nowadays, there is a public image of Swedes as matter-of-fact, no-nonsense, well-organized, rational beings. Yet for centuries there have been mystics among Swedes, who wanted to explore the mysteries of the universe, the depths of human existence, the enigma of a supreme Being. St. Bridget of Vadstena, the medieval mystic nun, was one of these; so were Emmanuel Swedenborg, the 18th century theologian, and Dag Hammarskjöld, Secretary-General of the United Nations in our time. They share a sense of dedication to the well-being of mankind, as well as the search for ultimate answers.

There was one Nordenskiöld among these seekers of truth, one of Carl Fredrik's sons, August. He started his career by taking a degree in mineralogy in 1772, the first in the family to complete a university education. But mineralogy soon faded into the background, as August Nordenskiöld devoted all his time and energy to the search for gold. Only by being able to make gold, said he, was mankind to be delivered from the tyranny of gold, and he received royal support in his labors. King Gustav III, fascinated by alchemy, gave the young man a position in the administration of Finland's mines, to support his work, and later gave him laboratory space in the charming royal palace of Drottningholm, on the outskirts of Stockholm.

But gold eluded the alchemist, and as pressure from the court to produce results increased, Nordenskiöld decided to quit. He had always been attracted to the mystic teaching of Swedenborg, and there was suddenly an opportunity to offer his services and skills for the benefit of mankind. The anti-slavery movement was gathering momentum then in England, and Sierra Leone, in west Africa, was chosen to become a haven for freed slaves. Nordenskiöld sailed there and was killed in a skirmish in the African bush, in 1792.

The year August Nordenskiöld died in Africa, Nils Gustav Nordenskiöld, Adolf Erik's father, was born in Finland. By the time he grew to manhood, the ties between Finland and Sweden had been cut, but he chose to remain in Finland, and completed his legal studies at Åbo University. Law was the proper field of study for a young man in his family, unless he chose to follow a military career, but Nils Gustav Nordenskiöld was far more interested in science, especially in mineralogy and chemistry. After graduation, he went to Sweden, where he became a student, and later a close personal friend, of the great chemist, Jöns Jacob Berzelius. He did well enough in his studies to receive a degree in mining engineering in 1817.

Gustav Nordenskiöld then decided to make mineralogy his life's work. After studying in Sweden, he went on to visit Germany, France, and England, to become acquainted with the great chemists and physicists of his time, with Davy and Faraday in England, with Rose and Mitscherlich in Germany. When he returned home, in 1823, his qualifications were recognized by the state and he was appointed chief of Finland's mining administration.

But Gustav Nordenskiöld was no bureaucrat; he spent little time in his office and preferred, with geologist's hammer in hand and a pack on his back, to look for new metals and minerals. There was always a 'wanderlust' in him.

Frugård, the family estate, was inherited by Gustav Nordenskiöld, and after his marriage in 1829, he made his home there. There had been a good library in the house, and he added to it continuously, and brought samples of metals and minerals, of flowers and insects and birds, home from his wanderings. It was a good place for a youngster with a bent toward science to grow up, in a small museum of natural history.

Gustav Nordenskiöld married Margareta Sofia von Haartman, daughter of a distinguished professor of medicine at Åbo. Adolf Erik was the third child of his parents, born in Helsingfors on November 18, 1832. The family had an apartment close to the center of town, but Frugård was home; there, in the manor, the children played and studied.

Among the homes of the Swedish aristocracy in southern Finland, Frugård is one of the oldest. The estate was originally given by royal decree in 1606 to the widow of Henrik Wrede, and its name, 'the lady's estate', is due to its original owner. The first, and rather modest home on the estate, built by Colonel Carl Fredrik Nordenskiöld in the 1730's, is still standing. It is a low building, with a steep pitched roof, a large central living room, kitchen, and several small rooms grouped around it, The family seldom lived at Frugård then; it was one of several estates that made up the Nordenskiöld patrimony.

It was in the early 1780's that a younger Nordenskiöld, who had inherited Frugård, decided to move there with his family. This was Adolf's grandfather, Colonel Adolf Gustav, who followed the family tradition and served as an engineering officer in the Swedish army. His engineering training included work in architecture, and it was according to his design that the manor house at Frugård was built, between 1802 and 1805.

Colonel Nordenskiöld was well read, acquainted with the architectural trends of his time, and the manor house he designed shows an individuality that sets it apart from most contemporary buildings in Finland and in Sweden. The heart of the house is a large living room, some fifty feet long by twenty feet wide. Above it there runs a gallery, with windows on all sides, and above that a steeply pitched roof. Colonel Nordenskiöld suffered from the cold Finnish winters, and designed his house to be comfortable. There are huge tiled stoves at both ends of the living room, and all other rooms, including bedrooms, small sitting rooms, and kitchen, are built around the central core, thus insulating it from the outside. In spite of its great height, the ceiling being two stories above the floor, the living room is the warmest room in the house, and its great height gives it grandeur and elegance.

Building a manor house at Frugård meant also providing it with the proper perspective for the approaching traveller. This was achieved by leaving a wide lawn in front, that ran to the river's edge. The bridge, carrying the road from Helsingfors, faces the manor, but then the road turns, and leads to a side entrance, so as not to spoil the effect achieved by carefully planned landscaping. The old, low house is now balanced by stables and barns, and sets off the manor in a spacious and elegant frame.

Adolf Erik spent the years of his childhood at Frugård, and returned there often during his parents' lifetime. After his father died, in 1866, one of his younger brothers took over the mangement of the estate, and lived there until he sold it in 1912. In 1964, descendants of the family purchased buildings and grounds from the owners, and turned them over to the National Museum of Finland. It is being renovated, to be furnished in 19th century style, and shown as an outstanding example of a manor house of the time. Hidden in a nearby group of trees is the tiny cemetery where Nordenskiölds had been buried for some seventy years; that, too, is now part of Frugård manor.

There were seven children at Frugård in Adolf Nordenskiöld's childhood, four boys and three girls, and the manor and its grounds resounded with their noise all summer long. The father was on the go much of the time, visiting mines in Finland and abroad, spending some days at his office in Helsingfors, little time at home. It was the mother who looked after the children's upbringing.

When Adolf Nordenskiöld was in his forties, he was asked to prepare a brief biographical sketch. In it, he spoke of his mother with warmth and affection. She was, he said, a woman of good judgment, generous, simple in her ways. She disliked idle hands and always found something for her brood to do. She was impartial and honest, and there was a feeling of trust and understanding in the family circle at Frugård. It was Margareta Nordenskiöld who saw to it that a young tutor came to live at Frugård, to look after the children's schooling until they were old enough to leave home for boarding school.

Adolf Nordenskiöld speaks little of his father in his autobiography. But the few passing references to Gustav Nordenskiöld are filled with admiration, for in his son's eyes he could do no wrong. Gustav Nordenskiöld was indeed an outstanding mineralogist, widely read, at home in field and laboratory alike. He taught his son Adolf about searching for minerals and collecting samples, and he showed him simple and effective methods of chemical analysis in the laboratory. Father and son travelled together during the summer holidays, collected minerals, stayed in country inns, talked endlessly about the world of nature. All his life, Adolf Nordenskiöld was as happy outdoors, chipping a rock with his hammer, making observations and writing them down in his notebook, as he was when experimenting in his laboratory. His career, in his own words, was predetermined from childhoods days.

In 1845, at the age of thirteen, it was time for young Nordenskiöld to enter secondary school. The nearest school was in the town of Borgå, twenty miles from Frugård. Borgå was, and still is, one of the principal Swedish settlements in southern Finland; it was in Borgå, in 1809 ,that the Tsar pledged to respect Finland's ancient laws and freedom. As was customary with well-to-do Swedish families when time came to put children to school, Margareta Nordenskiöld moved to Borgå with her two sons, Adolf and Otto, rented an apartment, and hired a private tutor to supervise the boys' studies.

When the report card for Adolf Nordenskiöld's first term at school arrived, it made dismal reading. He distinguished himself, in the words of the principal, 'by being completely lazy', and failed in nearly all his subjects. The parents' reaction to Adolf's performance was quite unexpected. Instead of increasing parental control, they decided to let the two boys, aged 13 and 11, shift for themselves. Their mother returned home; their tutor was dismissed; the boys boarded in a simple home and were left to their own devices. The trick worked, and within a year Adolf became one of the best students at school.

Being a high school student in Finland meant belonging to the upper class. Children of poor parents, after completing elementary school, became apprentices. Though there was no serfdom in Finland, the upper class felt it their right to order others about. The young students, secure in their social standing, would not merely engage apprentices in street fights and tavern brawls, they would go so far as to appear at a wedding held by one of the poorer families, and demand that bride and groom appear at the door, to receive their 'approval'. On one such occasion, the groom refused to obey the summons, and the students literally fought their way into the room where the wedding party was having a festive meal. There were insults and threats, and the matter was reported to the school authorities.

This breach of school discipline was punished. The ringleaders were expelled, others were given a caning, administered by the principal in the presence of the whole school, all according to rules. But the year was 1848, when revolutions swept across Europe, when young men demanded liberty and fought on the barricades in France and Germany, in Italy, Austria and Hungary. The 'Marseillaise', greatest of all revolutionary songs, was sung, with Swedish words, on the streets of Finnish cities, and the students at Borgå high school felt that their freedom was in peril. In protest against the punishment of their comrades, half of the students quit school.

Adolf Nordenskiöld, and his brother Otto, were among the protestors, though they had not taken part in the fight. They left school, and obtained their parents' permission to stay in Borgå, study on their own. The following fall, 1849, Adolf Nordenskiöld passed his final high school examinations, and at the age of seventeen entered the university at Helsingfors.

The Borgå episode ended in his leaving high school, in protest against school rules and the authority of the principal. But this clash of wills applied only to the formal matters of school attendance, for the principal of Borgå high school continued, in spite of the open rebellion of one of his best pupils, to consider him as a friend and to invite him to his home. Johan Ludvig Runeberg, the principal, was an unusual man, and made a deep impression on his students. He was the son of a sea captain, who, after graduation from the university, lived for several years in the Finnish countryside, as tutor to a wealthy family. He became deeply attached to the forests and lakes and scattered farms of Finland, and listened, at peasant firesides, to tales of the last great war, the battles of 1809 fought between Russian and Swede on Finnish soil.

Runeberg was in his early forties when Adolf Nordenskiöld entered as a student at Borgå high school. It was in those years that Runeberg wrote 'Vårt Land', 'Our Land'. It was set to music and sung for the first time in May 1848, year of revolutions, and became Finland's national anthem.

Its opening stanza sets theme and spirit:

Our land, our land, our fatherland
Sound loud, O name of worth!
No mount that meets the heavens' band,
No hidden vale, no wave-washed strand,
Is loved as is our native North,
Our own forefathers' earth.

'Our Land' later became the prologue to a cycle of poetry by Runeberg, 'Ensign Stål's Stories'. Under Russian rule, Finland had precious little freedom, and "Ensign Stål's Stories', telling of the war of 1809, the fight against Russia, was soon invested with a political significance seldom given to a work of poetry. Though he wrote in Swedish, Runeberg became Finland's national poet.

During his years at the university, Nordenskiöld often returned to Borgå, to spend an evening at Runeberg's home, to listen to the stories and yarns swapped by the host and his young guests, occasionally to hear a poem, as yet unpublished, read at the fireside. Runeberg was a man of great dignity, a poet and a patriot. To the young men around him, he set an example by his love of country, by his refusal to bow to tyranny, by his insistence on honesty toward his fellow men. To return from Runeberg's home, where freedom and honesty were valued above all things, to the bureaucratic atmosphere of Helsingfors, where petty officials made daily decisions concerning the lives of men, was not an easy transition to make.

In 1849, when Adolf Nordenskiöld first entered the University in Helsingfors, the city had been Finland's capital for less than forty years. During the centuries of Swedish rule, Åbo, in southwesternmost Finland, only a short sail from Sweden, was the seat of government, of the university, and of the church. Russia, anxious to break with the past, picked Helsingfors, closer to the Tsar's capital, St. Petersburg, to become the center of Finnish life. In 1808 much of the city, then still consisting of wooden houses, was destroyed by fire, and there was thus an opportunity to build a capital in the imperial image.

Ehrenström, a distinguished Army engineer, formerly in Swedish service and Engel, a German architect, were commissioned to design the layout and building of the center of the city. Around a large square, full of light from the sky, Ehrenström and Engel built the three structures that symbolize the community: the cathedral, the senate house, and the university. The heart of Helsingfors is dominated by these three buildings, grouped around Senate Square, harmonious in their proportions, elegant in their simplicity. Students who tired of reading under the skylighted dome of the university library could go out into the dazzling spring light of Senate Square, wander the short block south to the harbor to the open air market, or walk around the quiet streets of the neighborhood, where the great families had their town homes.

But on a hill only a few short blocks away, overlooking the harbor and dominating it, stood the Russian cathedral, symbol of the alien power that ruled Finland. It was the Russia of Tsar Nicholas I, a true autocrat who brooked no interference in the rule of his widespread domain by anyone, least of all by upstart young revolutionaries. It was the task of the Governor-General, the Tsar's personal representative in Finland, to enforce his absolute authority.

During the years when Adolf Nordenskiöld attended the university in Helsingfors and, later, when he became a young researcher, Count F. W. R. von Berg sat in the Governor-General's palace. Count von Berg was a career army officer, a member of that handful of German families that had for centuries ruled on the eastern shores of the Baltic, and now served the new order, in the person of the Tsar, with great devotion.

Von Berg fitted well into the autocratic form of government Tsar Nicholas I maintained over his subjects. He was a moody person, given to arbitrary decisions based solely on personal likes and dislikes, distrustful of his subordinates, and convinced that the fire of rebellion was smoldering in every Finn. He was particularly prejudiced against what he considered the two strongholds of disloyalty and revolution, the press and the university. It was customary for the Governor-General to order editors of the Finnish papers to appear in his office to be dressed down for their past mistakes and advised on their future actions. As for the university, the Governor-General considered it a creation of the devil. As a place of inquiry and free discussions, the label was certainly well deserved.

When Adolf Nordenskiöld entered the University of Helsingfors, in 1849, it was organized along traditional lines inherited from Sweden. The student body was divided into 'nations', uniting students from a given area or region for purposes of study and of welfare. The 'nations' enjoyed considerable self-government: the administrative officer of each group, the curator, was elected by the members. Each 'nation' had its own funds to make loans to its members; each had its own quarters, with a small library, where the students met, at least once a week, to attend to their own affairs and to discuss current matters, mostly politics. Occasionally the discussions were quite violent, and free speech certainly prevailed.

The existence of these debating societies, as the Russian administration thought of them, certainly did not fit into an autocratic order, and in 1850 the 'nations' were abolished. The student body was organized into 'faculties', groups uniting all students in a given field of study. Theology, law, medicine, mathematics and physics, and history and philology were the new groups. There was no faculty of philosophy since, in Tsar Nicholas' view, it was the philosophers who planted dangerous ideas in young people's minds and thus were responsible for the revolutions threatening the established order.

Having studied chemistry, physics, and mineralogy the young Nordenskiöld obtained excellent marks and received his first degree, candidate in the natural sciences, in the spring of 1853. During summer vacations he continued to travel throughout Finland, visiting mines, acquiring a knack for spotting metals and minerals in the landscape. Following graduation, he went on his first long journey, in the fall of 1853, travelling with his father to the Ural Mountains, in the far reaches of European Russia.

The low ranges of the Urals are a mineralogist's paradise. Few places on earth are endowed with a similar wealth and variety of metals and minerals, and many of the locations were already well known in the mid-nineteenth century. The Nordenskiölds, father and son, spent the winter of 1853-1854 at Tagil, in the eastern Urals, at the iron and copper mines of the Demidov family.

Adolf Nordenskiöld visited mines, collected samples, and filled notebook after notebook with observations. His father was involved in metallurgical experiments, and Adolf was often put in charge of the laboratory. On one such occasion a large metal cylinder, filled with oxyhydrogen gas and sulphuric acid, exploded. The young man remained unharmed, even though the entire laboratory was splashed with sulphuric acid.

Early in 1854, the elder Nordenskiöld was leaving the mines, to return to his duties in Finland. His son, undecided about his own plans, had earlier met a young French mining engineer and the two decided to await the spring in the Urals and then travel to Siberia, to the east. The vast, little-known world of Siberia, the northern part of Asia, meant adventure to the young men.

But the exciting plans came to naught. When the elder Nordenskiöld was about to return to Finland, startling news came from Europe. Three months earlier, France, England and Turkey had declared war on Russia. This was not the time to travel around in the company of a suspect enemy, a Frenchman, and Adolf Nordenskiöld, disappointed in the failure of his plans, packed his bags and followed his father back home.

There was plenty to do in Helsingfors, though, for a young man aspiring to a university career. There was work in laboratory and library to complete and a thesis to defend. These took up most of the year 1854, and in February, 1855, Adolf Nordenskiöld completed his second university degree, in mineralogy. His thesis, dealing with crystalline forms of the minerals graphite and chondrodite, was accepted by the university and, rather an unusual distinction for a young man of twenty-two, it was also published in the leading German journal for chemistry and mineralogy.

Shortly afterwards, Nordenskiöld published a handbook on Finland's mineral deposits, that became the standard reference work on the subject. Having travelled since his childhood across his native land, in the company of his father, having visited every important mineral deposit, he was exceptionally well qualified to write such a book, and it was received with considerable acclaim. Success fired him to continue his work, and within two years he presented five papers to the Finnish Scientific Society and was elected to membership at the age of twenty-four.

This impressive record of research and publications was duly noted by the authorities of the state and of the university. He was appointed to a junior post in the state mining administration, that required few hours of work, yet represented a first step toward a possible career in that direction. At the same time he was appointed 'curator', administrative officer, of his university group, the faculty of mathematics and physics. He wrote to his father: 'As you may well realize, this delighted me, for to be curator is the highest honor a young member of the university can attain.'

Adolf Nordenskiöld was now in the enviable position of having two titles, two salaries, and plenty of free time to continue his research in mineralogy and earn his final university degree, his doctorate. But he had barely begun to enjoy his newly won honors, when he ran afoul of the authorities.

It was October, 1855. Russia had been at war for a year, and though the main actions had been fought fifteen hundred miles south of Finland, on the Crimean peninsula, there was constant danger of an English-French attack from the west, from the Baltic. Lord Palmerston, the British Prime Minister, did threaten just such an attack, and British and French men-of-war entered the Baltic, destroyed a Russian fortress in the islands off the Finnish coast, and, in August, 1855, made an attack on the harbor of Helsingfors itself.

The Governor-General of Finland, von Berg, entrusted with the administration and safe-keeping of that exposed part of the Russian Empire, doubled his efforts to keep his subjects under control. Yet, in spite of the strictest censorship, dangerous ideas seeped in, especially from Sweden.

Nearly half a century had passed since Sweden had to give up its rule over Finland, yet there were people in both countries who wanted a return to the old order. 'Scandinavism' was the name given to this political idea, especially popular among young Finland Swedes: Sweden should liberate Finland and the two countries would then form a personal union. The king of Sweden would become a common monarch, and a close alliance would also be concluded with Denmark, thus creating true Scandinavian unity. The Swedish press gave considerable publicity to the idea, and emphasized it by publishing anonymous letters from Finland that reviled Russia and supported Sweden.

The Governor-General, convinced that the letters in the Swedish newspapers were written by students in Finland, decided to plant a spy among them. He persuaded a student to go to Stockholm, find out who were the authors of the letters and articles from Finland and then, on his return, unmask them to the authorities. But the Governor did not reckon with the fact that his own subordinates might find the scheme so repugnant and so much against Finnish traditions that they would give the game away. One of the officials in the Governor-General's office alerted student leaders, and suggested that they should drive the spy out of the University.

The student leaders, including Nordenskiöld, met in an apartment, and the young spy was invited to join them. As soon as he arrived, the door was locked, and he was confronted with the statement: 'You are a spy and we have proof of it!' After he confessed that he was hired by the Russian administration, he was ordered to withdraw from the university and leave Helsingfors. When the Governor-General found out what had happened, he was furious but there was not much he could do, for, as Nordenskiöld wrote later, 'not even the almighty Governor-General could protect a spy who had been found out'. Von Berg, however, obtained the names of all who were members of the student 'court' and swore vengeance.

He did not have to wait for long. On November 30, 1855, Andrew's Day, a group of students, Nordenskiöld among them, met at Tölö inn, on the outskirts of Helsingfors. It is customary in Scandinavia to celebrate one's name day, and the party was in honor of several students named Andrew. Inn and garden were decorated with lanterns for the occasion, there was a choir, and a Navy band. Food and drink, and songs contributed to the success of the party, everybody was in a mood for fun, even if it was to be at the expense of the authorities.

One of the group, a young poet, wrote a special skit for the occasion, poking fun at Russia and its inept conduct of the war. There were toasts, in scarcely veiled terms, to the western powers, and when the party broke up, everyone marched round the room, singing that most dangerous revolutionary anthem, the *Marseillaise.*

The students could scarcely have picked a worse time for their party. Marshal Canrobert, special representative of the French Emperor, was then in Stockholm on a double mission. Officially, he was there to present French decorations to the king and crown prince of Sweden, but his real task was to persuade Sweden to join the western powers, attack Russia, and thus free Finland. It was a time for tact and diplomacy, but the students at Tölö never thought of that. It was just a prank, all in good fun.

According to old custom, the band at the Tölö party scored each toast with a blast of horns and trumpets. It was a Navy band, and the non-com in charge felt it was his duty to report on the party to his commanding officer, but he insisted in his report that the students were merely enjoying themselves. The naval officer called in the student leaders, whom he knew well. He berated them for not having had enough sense to choose a Russian band, that would not have understood anything that went on, told them that he had to let the report go on through channels, and advised the group to explain the whole thing away as merely a joke.

At first, this seemed good advice, but quite a few of the students who were at the party had dabbled in politics, and the authorities did not believe their story. And when the report on the party finally reached the Governor-General's desk, there was no doubt as to the outcome.

'Well, these are all old acquaintances!' exclaimed von Berg, as he saw the report, and the names of those present. This was his chance to revenge himself for the humiliation he had suffered earlier in the year, when these young men uncovered the spy he tried to plant in their midst.

Undergraduates who had been at the Tölö party were suspended from the university for a term, but Nordenskiöld, the senior student leader present, was fired both from his University post and from his appointment in the mining administration.

There was little point in staying in Finland for Nordenskiöld. His research was going well, he could continue somewhere else for the next few months, and he had always wanted to travel westward, and become acquainted with western Europe. He went home, to Frugård, for the Christmas holidays, then, having borrowed funds from friends, set out in February, 1855 for Berlin.

II. A 'DANGEROUS RABBLEROUSER': NORDENSKIÖLD RUNS AFOUL OF RUSSIA

Travel in eastern Europe was an adventure in the 1850's. To reach Berlin, a Finn had two possible routes: either across the Baltic to Stockholm, a time-consuming business in mid-winter, when ferries were subject to the hazards of ice and snow; or overland to the Russian capital of Saint Petersburg first, and thence across the Baltic countries to Germany. Adolf Nordenskiöld chose the safer route, and left the family estate of Frugård on February 8, 1856, for Saint Petersburg.

It was a three-day journey across the wintry landscape of Finland, and there were friends to meet in the Russian capital, while waiting for the departure of the stage coach to Germany. Young Nordenskiöld was riding in a hired sleigh down Saint Petersburg's most elegant boulevard, Nevsky Prospekt, when he saw his father strolling along the sidewalk. Gustav Nordenskiöld had left home some months earlier, for yet another trip to the Ural mines, and was on his return journey when the unexpected meeting took place.

The elder Nordenskiöld was truly surprised to find his favorite son in Saint Petersburg, instead of pursuing his research in the university laboratory at Helsingfors. But when he found out what had happened at Tölö and afterwards, he approved of his son's plans to lie low until the storm blew over. He even provided Adolf with letters of introduction to the leading German scholars in mineralogy, and wished him godspeed as he left, on February 26, for the west.

Wrapped in fur coats and hats, huddling in their travel rugs, the passengers in the stage coach rode across the snowy fields of the Russian empire. Narva, on the Gulf of Finland, was the first stop, where Nordenskiöld's ancestors had fought Russia a century and a half earlier; then the Esthonian university town of Dorpat; Riga, the capital of the province of Livland was a short stop, time to transfer to another coach; then, coastal towns and ports on the Baltic and, five days out of Saint Petersburg, the travellers crossed over into Prussia. There were short halts in Tilsit and Königsberg, hurried meals at inns, a few hours of sleep on the road. After seven days of uninterrupted travel, the weary Nordenskiöld arrived in Berlin, the Prussian capital.

Prussia was one of the leading powers of mid-nineteenth century Europe, and Berlin, Germany's largest city, not only a political center but noted for its cultural life as well. The university boasted men of great distinction on its faculty, and the letters of introduction Nordenskiöld's father had given him proved to be invaluable.

On the very day of his arrival, the young Finn was received by Eilhard Mitscherlich, one of the founders of modern chemistry and mineralogy. The next day, Mitscherlich took Adolf Nordenskiöld as his guest to the meeting of the German Geological Society, and introduced him to the brothers Rose, leaders in mineralogy and crystallography. Nordenskiöld's name was already known to these scholars. He was invited to work in Professor Gustav Rose's laboratory. There he had a chance to learn the most up-to-date methods of chemical and mineralogical analysis. He met and made friends with geologists and geographers, attended the theater and the opera, and thoroughly enjoyed life in the German metropolis.

June came, and it was time to return home. This time it was an easier and much more pleasant journey: Nordenskiöld sailed across the Baltic to Sweden, visited Stockholm for the first time, and returned to Finland in mid-summer, 1856.

The war between Russia and the western powers had ended some months earlier, all was quiet in Finland, and the Tölö incident seemed to have been forgotten. Nordenskiöld was only thought of now as a most promising young scientist, one who had already made his mark. He spoke several times before the leading scientific society of Finland, his work on Finland's minerals had won wide critical acclaim, and during the summer of 1856 he had been awarded a university prize for an essay on Finnish molluscs, that he prepared in collaboration with his friend, the zoologist Nylander. His chances of getting back in the university's good graces were excellent.

There was no chair in the earth sciences at Helsingfors, and only introductory courses in these subjects were taught, mostly by Professor Adolf Arppe, a chemist, who had directed Nordenskiöld's first independent research. The university senate had given its consent to the establishment of a chair of geology and mineralogy, but the post remained vacant for lack of a qualified person. Arppe, convinced that his prize pupil, Adolf Nordenskiöld, was the natural choice, asked him whether he would want to be considered for the appointment.

But Professor Arppe knew his student well and realized that Nordenskiöld would like a final fling at travel, before settling down to university routine. He suggested that this might be possible through a university travel grant, and early in 1857 Adolf Nordenskiöld was notified that he was awarded a prize plum: the 'Alexander' travel stipend. In his application, he had proposed a journey across Siberia all the way to the Pacific, and the letter of award stated that the project had received full approval, and that, it was hoped, the experience thus gained would make young Nordenskiöld eligible for appointment to the chair of mineralogy and geology.

All was well in the spring of 1857. Nordenskiöld completed his studies with high honors, and, in late May, the graduation festivities commenced. Though the season was well advanced for travel to Siberia, he postponed his departure, so as to be able to take part in graduation. This was a solemn occasion: each new doctor received a laurel wreath, a special top hat, and a gold ring, and at that solemn moment a battery of guns, on the nearby waterfront, fired a salute. There were speeches, and a choir sang a special cantata composed for the occasion.

Once the formal graduation ceremony was over, it was time to sit down at the banquet, an indispensable part of the proceedings. There was plenty of food, and lots to drink. Faculty were present, so were the newly graduated doctors and their friends and relations. There were foreign guests as well, two professors, two graduate students and two undergraduates from Swedish universities.

Graduation dinners at Swedish universities are always punctuated by speeches, and the dinner held on May 30, 1857, conformed to custom. There were speeches by professors and replies from graduates, and it was only natural that Adolf Nordenskiöld, who received his degrees with distinction, should be called upon to speak.

Not many present at the banquet realized that a complete transcript of the speech pronounced by Nordenskiöld was made, but the text was found, seventy years later, in the secret archives of the Russian police. One of the leading Finnish newspapers reprinted parts of the speech, and Nordenskiöld himself saved his notes from that occasion. Reconstructed from these sources, this is what he said:

> Gentlemen!
>
> Many toasts had been proposed these last happy days, toasts that came from our very hearts: toasts to our memories, toasts to our guests from the free and sane land of Sweden, toasts to all the noble thoughts and ambitions of our own country. Let me now propose one more toast, a toast to the future, to Finland's uncertain future.
>
> Men have at all times thought of the future in the rosy color of

> hope. The sick man, with but a few days left to live, hopes for long years of good health. The slave, who had been bought and sold as far back as he can remember, dreams of freedom. Should we not allow hope to color a few streaks of light on the dark sky of our own future? Yes, we can hope, because since early times there has always been a powerful, indomitable urge to freedom within our souls, because that band which was broken fifty years ago is beginning to reassert itself, and because we are thus assured that in our fight against darkness we never need be alone.
>
> Let us drink a toast to all our memories, to old times and to the days to come, if only they do not bring an end to Finland, a toast to memory's bygone days, and to the hope that lingers on!

To our ears, this is not the discourse of an agitator. Rather, it is a speech full of nostalgia for the good old days of Swedish rule, a protest against Russian thought control delivered in a mild manner, expressing only a faint hope for more freedom of speech and press and political activity. Nordenskiöld, writing twenty years later, said that 'it was an after-dinner speech, embellished with what reasonable and practical people call "rhetoric". Phrases such as these are natural to a speaker on such an occasion, as indispensable to him as salt is to meat.'

He may have struck a responsive chord in the audience, or people might just have become bored with the whole long, drawn-out affair. Whatever the reason, a storm of applause greeted the speech. The young people thought that Nordenskiöld painted Finland's future as it really was. But to the senior faculty present, the speech was just too forward, to some downright dangerous.

The war between Russia and the western powers had come to an end more than a year earlier, but tempers were still tense in Finland. Younger men believed that Finland's best hope was reunion with Sweden, while the older generation had made its peace with Russia and looked forward to a softening of Russian attitudes toward Finland. It was one of the senior professors present, Fredrik Cygnaeus, who rose to speak when the applause for Nordenskiöld died down, and he tried to pour oil on the troubled waters.

Cygnaeus, aware that whatever was said at this official university function was likely to be reported to the police and to the Russian administration, said that things in Finland were really not as bad as they seemed to some observers. There were difficulties, to be sure, but the Finns wanted no compassion. Not content with these words, however,

Cygnaeus went on to counterattack. He singled out a poem, written by a young Swede a year earlier, that described Finland as 'a gilded cage of serfdom'. The poem was read at a student festival in Stockholm, and, said Cygnaeus, no one rose against this abominable attack and defended Finland.

There were Swedish guests at the banquet, and to most of those present, Cygnaeus' attack on Sweden was in the worst taste. Courtesy to the guests and Finnish hospitality had become the issue, and Nordenskiöld, incensed by this breach of good manner, went up to the head table and shouted: 'He does not speak for us!'

What had started as an evening of good fellowship had become a political event. J. V. Snellman, one of the leading Finnish newspaper editors, expressed strong disapproval in the Helsingfors *Literaturbladet*:

> Dr. N., the last of the younger men to propose a toast, expressed himself in the usual terms of a bragging liberal. But because of the occasion, and because of the presence of foreigners, his words were disparaging to his own country.

Rebuke in the press was one thing, a police report a much more serious matter. A full report on the banquet, on Nordenskiöld's speech, and his heated words spoken against Cygnaeus, was made to Governor-General von Berg the next morning. He sent for the presiding officer of the university, the rector, and demanded an explanation of the disgraceful behavior of a member of the university community.

The rector, Professor Rein, had known Nordenskiöld well and called him into his presence. 'What in the name of the Lord did you say?' asked the rector. Nordenskiöld reached into his pocket and handed him the text of his speech. After reading it, Professor Rein's frown disappeared. 'There does not seem to be anything particularly offensive here,' he said. 'It might be best if I showed your notes to the Governor. May I do so?' Nordenskiöld doubted the wisdom of such a step; he knew that he was considered a radical by the Governor; but he could hardly say no to the rector's request.

When Professor Rein returned to the Governor-General's office, and presented the text of the speech, von Berg made it quite clear that it was nothing less than high treason and an attack on the person of the Emperor himself. A full report on the affair was immediately sent to Saint Petersburg. Nordenskiöld, in the meantime, believing that nothing much was to be gained by staying in Helsingfors, went home to Frugård. But in his absence, the wheels of bureaucracy ground on.

This was the third time that Adolf Nordenskiöld had run afoul of the authorities. Unmasking the Governor-General's personal spy was bad enough. Being present at the Tölö dinner, in 1855, when Russia was openly mocked, was worse. But making a subversive speech on a solemn, formal occasion, in the presence of foreign guests, was unforgivable. In a police state, such a man was bound to be marked as a dangerous troublemaker.

On June 10, 1857, eleven days after the graduation banquet, the Vice-Chancellor of Helsingfors University, Count Alexander Armfelt, pronounced judgment on the offender. He informed the University that 'Doctor Nordenskiöld committed a serious offense on May 30, and thereafter behaved in a deplorable manner'. The Chancellor had no choice but to notify the University that Nordenskiöld must lose his travel grant and be expelled from the University. The Chancellor pointed out that Nordenskiöld received his education at the University, that he was twice honored for his outstanding record, and that, by awarding him a travel grant, the University gave him the highest recognition and support at its disposal. He also noted with deep sorrow that these offenses were committed in the presence of foreigners, a further aggravating circumstance held against the offender.

By the time the Chancellor's letter was sent to the University, Nordenskiöld had left the country. A family friend who occupied an important post in the Governor-General's office warned him that serious troubles lay ahead. Stay home and bluff it out, ran his advice, say that it was a misinterpretation of an innocent speech. Or leave Finland at once, and stay away until tempers cooled down and a rational explanation might be accepted.

In his youthful enthusiasm, Adolf Nordenskiöld was certainly impulsive. But he was also an honest man, and it was inconceivable to him that he should lie, even if it meant safeguarding his career. Better to leave Finland once more, work abroad in peace and quiet, until he could return, salvage his reputation with the authorities and patch up his relations with the University.

This time, Sweden was the logical choice. He had visited Sweden the previous year, made friends, was well received by his father's contemporaries, and felt very much at ease. To Nordenskiöld, as to many Finland Swedes, Sweden was a second homeland, and so once more he made the quick trip across the Baltic and arrived in Stockholm, in June, 1857, eager to work, a temporary refugee, yet one who had not burned all bridges behind him.

III. FIRST JOURNEY TO THE ARCTIC - 1858

It is only one hundred and sixty miles from Åbo in southern Finland to Stockholm, a long day's journey in the small steamships that plied between the two cities in the 1850's. But it is a fascinating trip, as the ship twists and turns between the thousands of islands that dot the Baltic and form a land bridge from Finland to Sweden.

Some of these islands are large enough to allow farming, and support villages and small towns. Others barely provide standing room for more than a dozen sheep. The wake of a ship crossing here is an endless zig-zag of twists and turns; on a sunny day, the brilliant blue sky, the deep blue waters, the dark green of pines and firs and the grey-brown of bare rock form a striking symphony of color.

As the steamer approached Stockholm, winding its way through the labyrinth of offshore islands, the passengers would crowd the deck, hoping to catch a first glimpse of the city. Rounding the last island, Djurgården, the old royal deer park, they could see the tall towers of the cathedral and the German church, and as the ship turned into the inner bay, the immense stone mass of the royal palace loomed on the hill above Skeppsbron, the quay where the steamer from Finland would end its journey.

The 'Old Town', the island that was the cradle of Stockholm, has changed very little in its appearance since that day, in June, 1857, when Adolf Nordenskiöld stepped ashore from the mail steamer. A stately row of seventeenth-century houses still stands on the embankment, narrow alleys lead to the labyrinth of streets in the interior of the 'Old Town', inns and taverns welcome the weary traveller from across the Baltic.

By the middle of the last century, the city of Stockholm had already expanded beyond the narrow confines of the island, across the waters of Lake Mälar to the hills that lie north and south of the 'Old Town'. The southern suburb, as it is still called, became a crowded, uninspiring residential area. It was to the north shore that the people of means had moved, there the principal business district had come into being.

In the 1850's Stockholm was a city of stone houses, sturdily built to defy the bitter cold of winter days. The houses were well heated and, according to foreign visitors, clean enough inside. But streets were poorly paved and sidewalks were either non-existent or so narrow that people had to walk in the street. Stockholm was not at all the clean, well-kept city present-day visitors admire so much, and there was a far greater contrast between the few of wealth and position and the masses of the poor than one finds today.

Sweden in the mid-1800's had not yet realized the full extent of its natural resources. The majority of its people were farmers, tilling poor soils, coping with a harsh climate, using only the simplest of tools, growing rye and potatoes to eke out a meager existence. Part of the grain was distilled to make brandy, and alcoholism was rampant. The great forests of northern Sweden, now one of the bases of the Swedish economy, were barely touched as yet, the primitive sawmills produced more sawdust than lumber. When spring planting was delayed by a long winter, or when an early frost destroyed the harvest, the peasants were on the verge of starvation. A few hardy souls, unwilling to face the future on home grounds, were beginning to emigrate, but they were considered traitors to Sweden.

The mining of iron and copper, long an important source of income, was declining as the mines of Central Sweden were nearing exhaustion. Industry offered as yet little employment, and those who tried to escape from the countryside found little hope in the cities. The industrial revolution was yet to come as far as Sweden was concerned.

Swedish politics was as backward, compared with Western Europe, as the economy. Royal power was no longer absolute, but the king still had a strong voice in national affairs. Parliament was organized by 'estates': nobility, clergy, town burghers, and farmers, and the right to vote was restricted to a tiny part of the population.

But, in spite of its backward economy and outmoded political system, Sweden offered one incomparable advantage over Russian-dominated Finland: freedom of speech and freedom of the press. To a man who had fled from the oppression of the Tsar's government, it was a blessing to be able to speak freely without fear.

To a young scientist, the center of Sweden's intellectual life was Stockholm. The Swedish Academy of Sciences, the Royal Caroline Medical-Surgical Institute, the National Museum of Natural History were staffed with fine scholars, there was laboratory space available, and a strong interest in research. True, facilities and equipment were modest, and the staff had to fight for better quarters, modern research tools, more generous funds, trying to keep up with their more fortunate colleagues in western Europe. It was to these institutions that Adolf Nordenskiöld turned, using both his own contacts, and the name of his father, known and respected in the Swedish scientific community. He was well received, and given a desk and space to work, in the chemical laboratory of the Caroline Institute, the 'Karolinska' as it is called to this day.

It was mid-summer, 1857, and Nordenskiöld, always eager to be outdoors whenever the rigors of Scandinavian climate allowed, took off for a tour of central Sweden, to become familiar with the structure of the Swedish earth, and the minerals hidden under its surface.

On his return in the fall, he went to work in the laboratory. He gave several papers on mineralogy and chemistry at the meetings of the Academy of Sciences, and one that caused quite a stir, on the phenomenon of rising shorelines in the area of Stockholm. That paper was awarded a special prize by the Academy, and he became known as a young scholar of promise.

His host in the chemical laboratory, where he carried out his researches and experiments, was one of the distinguished Swedish scholars of the time, Carl Mosander. Mosander held the chair of chemistry, but his real passion was the study of minerals. Although seriously hampered by cataracts, his sight was still good enough to allow him to continue his work, and he found the quick mind and the excellent theoretical and practical background of the young Finlander much to his liking.

Mosander was conservative in his politics, he supported the established system, believed that the old ways were the best for the country, and opposed change. Nordenskiöld, never one to hide his own views, was a liberal, heart and soul. He believed that a parliament elected by popular vote was essential for progress, that free trade improved the lot of peasant and working man and made the economy expand and flourish, and that education was of the highest value in building a new and better social order. As he tells it in his autobiography, the old gentleman indulged from time to time in violent arguments with the liberal views of his younger colleague, but this did not in the least affect the close relationship of the two.

By the fall of 1857 Nordenskiöld had made himself a place, albeit a temporary one, in Stockholm. Living in a hotel was expensive, and not very comfortable, and he was forced to look for other quarters. He wrote his father that he had found a room in the district of Kungsholm, within easy walking distance of the laboratory where he was working. It was on the second floor, well heated, and there was a maid to clean the room and keep the tile stove going. Walking from his room to the Caroline Institute laboratory, Nordenskiöld's eyes would sweep across the wide expanse of Lake Mälar to the steep cliffs on the opposite shore, the tall spire of the church of Mary Magdalen, and in the distance, the roofs and turrets of the 'Old Town'.

At first, the young scientist felt lonely and homesick for his family and friends. On Christmas Eve, 1857, he wandered about downtown, when he saw a small plaster bust of Garibaldi in a store window. Here was a fellow spirit, a man who fought tyranny and oppression, thought Adolf Nordenskiöld, and bought the little statue for his desk to be a companion in his loneliness. But this feeling of isolation did not last long. There were young men of his age in Stockholm who had read about his 'rebellion' against the Russian authorities, and sought him out to offer him their friendship. Two of them became his close friends: Harald Wieselgren, writer and librarian, and Christian Lovén, fellow scientist.

Through his friends and through his Swedish relatives, Adolf Nordenskiöld was quickly admitted to the small circle that was Swedish high society. He described in a letter the Sunday afternoon receptions held at the Stockholm observatory by the director of the institution, Professor Solander and his wife. Madame Solander had been one of the great beauties of Sweden in her youth, and she loved to entertain young people. The observatory stands on a high hill, and the receptions were held in the charming oval 'salon' of the director's apartment. Drinks were served on a mahogany table, gleaming in candlelight, and one was always certain to meet a bevy of charming and beautiful young ladies on these occasions.

There were balls in the winter months, and many dinner invitations for a handsome, eligible bachelor. A photograph of Adolf Nordenskiöld, taken at the time, shows him serious, even solemn, dressed in a frock coat, with just a corner of a satin waistcoat showing, holding the top hat that was the mark of a Stockholm man-about-town. His contemporaries spoke of his grey-blue eyes, with heavy eyelids, that sometimes gave him a dreamy, far-away look. The story of his outspoken opposition to the Russians was well known in Stockholm, and gave him an aura of a hero.

It was on such an occasion, during the winter of 1857, that he met a striking, dark-haired girl from his native Finland, Anna Mannerheim. Her brother Carl was one of Nordenskiöld's classmates and close friends in Helsingfors, and it was probably due to that friendship that the two young people met. Five years later, Adolf Nordenskiöld was to journey to Finland, to ask for Anna Mannerheim's hand in marriage.

Spring came, and Nordenskiöld's thoughts turned once more eastward across the Baltic, to Finland. He did finally receive an official transcript of his dismissal from Helsingfors University, but as yet he was unwilling to accept the sentence as final. His father kept his hopes alive by insisting that there was still a place for him on the university faculty, and former teachers kept writing letters on his behalf to the authorities. But in late April, he received an invitation to join the Swedish zoologist, Otto Torell, in an expedition to the Arctic island group called Spitsbergen.

Men who study the earth, geologists, mineralogists, geographers, are the wandering kind. For them, nothing can replace the first-hand look, the close contact, the experience of living in a faraway place. They live by the sailor's motto: It is necessary to travel, more than it is to live! To Adolf Nordenskiöld, his first summons to visit the Arctic was irresistible.

Otto Torell, the organizer of the voyage, was Nordenskiöld's senior by only four years. He trained as a zoologist under Sven Lovén at the university of Lund. Lovén was the first Swedish scientist to venture to the Arctic: in 1837 he had spent the summer in the archipelago of Spitsbergen, known until then only as a rich hunting ground for fishermen and for whalers. While in Spitsbergen, Lovén studied molluscs dragged from the bottom of the bays in the archipelago, and found that they were identical to species found in the gravels of Sweden's west coast.

The fact, that during the ice ages vast glaciers covered much of North America, Northern Europe and North Asia, is well known today. But in the first half of the last century, this was not the case, and Lovén's discovery stimulated his student Torell to continue the search for more evidence of widespread glaciation. Dragging the sea bottom off Sweden's west coast, Torell found more specimens of Arctic marine life, in the form of mussels, and travelled to Iceland in 1857, looking for more evidence to support his theory. Not yet content with his findings, Torell then resolved to go to Spitsbergen, in the footsteps of his teacher, and look not only for specimens found live in the waters off those islands, but for evidence of a fossil fauna.

Otto Torell was anxious to have one or two fellow scientists with him, and asked his old teacher, Sven Lovén, for advice. Adolf Nordenskiöld was a close friend of the professor's son, Christian Lovén, and was thus well known to the household. Professor Lovén suggested that an earth scientist should be part of the expedition to Spitsbergen, and that Nordenskiöld certainly was well qualified for the post. There was just one difficulty: Torell, the leader of the expedition, did not have funds to cover the travel and living expenses of anyone wishing to join him; they would have to look elsewhere for financial support.

Once more Adolf Nordenskiöld fell back on his father's reputation. He called on the distinguished physician Anders Retzius, a friend and contemporary of his father, explained his needs, pointing out that he needed funds in a hurry, for Torell had already left for Norway, on his way to the Arctic. Doctor Retzius loaned him a substantial sum and managed to get the rest of the amount needed by asking his friends for contributions. With his help, Nordenskiöld got ready for his first trip to the polar regions.

At home, in Finland, his impending voyage created quite a sensation, his mother wrote in a letter from Frugård. 'All of your friends are delighted that you are thus honored,' wrote Margareta Nordenskiöld. But as mothers will do, she worried about the many difficulties he had to face, and regretted that he would have to forego his favorite drink, milk.

It was a week's journey by stagecoach from Stockholm to the Norwegian port of Trondheim. The road followed the north shore of Lake Mälar at first, affording glimpses of its blue waters and numberless bays and inlets. The countryside northwest of Stockholm is still among the most fertile in central Sweden, well settled, with towns and villages and single farmsteads spread across low-lying land, that was regained from marsh and bog and put under the plough.

The stage coach took two days to Falun, the heart of the copper country, where copper ore has been mined since the Middle Ages. Once past Falun, the road enters the evergreen forest of pine and fir that covers most of the countryside. The coach rolled along the gleaming waters of Lake Siljan, the heart of the 'Land of the Valleys', Dalarna. Past picturesque villages, each with a handsome church, the travellers rattled on, until the coach finally stopped for a few hours' rest at Mora.

Mora is a town famed in Swedish history. It was in Mora churchyard, in the early sixteenth century, that Gustav Vasa, founder of Sweden's last national ruling house, rallied the farmers of the district to the defense of Swedish independence. The coaches used to stop at an inn a stone's throw from church and churchyard, and offered a chance to the travellers to visit these hallowed places.

From Mora, the road plunges into a rough and remote region of mountains, forests, and steeply cut valleys. There are isolated hamlets on the valley floor, surrounded by small fields where farmers harvest meager crops of hay, oats and potatoes. Most of the land is covered by endless evergreen forests, carefully managed and presenting a 'mani cured' appearance.

Gradually the road rises toward the Norwegian border. Even though Sweden and Norway maintained a personal union throughout the nineteenth century, and the king of Sweden ruled in Norway as well, the two nations maintained their separate existence, each carefully guarding its rights and privileges. And among these privileges, that of levying customs duties was important enough to justify a customs office in this lonely and remote wilderness. At Lillebu, the coach stopped, Norwegian officials examined and stamped documents, and Norwegian replaced the Swedish language.

It took three more days of travel, across steep mountain passes, along deep lakes filled with the icy water of melted mountain snows, past small, quiet villages, until the journey finally ended, in the old Norwegian royal city, Trondheim.

Once a week a small steamer left Trondheim throughout the spring and summer months, to carry passengers, mail and freight along the coast of Norway, far beyond the Arctic Circle, to the Russian-Norwegian frontier. Nordenskiöld boarded the steamer in late May for the journey to Hammerfest, Norway's northernmost city.

There is no darkness in those high latitudes during the summer months, only twilight, and if the weather is clear, the fortunate traveller may be treated to the spectacle of the midnight sun. A contemporary of Nordenskiöld, the American writer Bayard Taylor, described it in these words: 'The sun hung low between the islands of Fuglöy and Arnöy, rising like a double dome from the sea; the islands resembled immense masses of transparent purple glass, gradually melting into crimson fire at their bases. The glassy, leaden-colored sea was powdered with a golden bloom, and the tremendous precipices at the mouth of the fjord behind us were steeped in a dark red, mellow flush, and touched with pencillings of pure, rose-colored light, until their naked ribs seemed to be clothed in imperial velvet.'

Other times, the sky might be of a depressingly uniform grey, clouds hanging low over nearly invisible mountains, a driving wind whipping the dark water into spume-capped waves, and the small steamer would roll and pitch, even as it sought protection behind the innumerable islands that screen the coast from the open Atlantic. Adolf Nordenskiöld was a poor sailor all his life, and on stormy days he would have to concentrate all his energy into surviving the hours of violence at sea.

Northward the little steamer puffed its way, steering a winding course through the labyrinth of offshore islands. Every few hours, it would tie up at a small settlement, discharge mail and passengers, take on others, and continue on its way. From the sea, the traveller could only see vast mountains, that appeared to rise, often vertically, straight from the waves. But whenever the ship turned into a sheltered bay, there would be farms along the shore with fields of potatoes and barley, vegetable gardens, meadows of lush grass, and rows upon rows of pine and fir trees on the lower slopes of the mountains. Though this part of Norway lies near, or even to the north of the Arctic Circle, the warm offshore waters of the Gulf Stream allow man to sow and harvest in these small areas between snow-capped mountains and the sea.

Gradually, the forests would thin out as the ship continued northward, to be replaced by bushes, until even these could survive only in protected hollows. Instead of the long string of small hamlets and individual farms, there were only isolated, lonely houses, hidden in a cove, with a small patch of a garden, a tiny meadow where a few sheep grazed, and a boat tied up to a landing.

The rocks of Finnmark, the northernmost part of Norway, are barren, and as the coastal steamer passes from brilliant sunlight into deep shadows thrown by spectacular mountains, there is a sharp drop in temperature. A breath of the Arctic passes across the deck. The signs of human occupance are few and far apart. The uplands are snowbound, rugged, theatrical. When seen against the sun, they seem giant, two-dimensional stage sets for a 'Twilight of the Gods'. Man is a stranger in Finnmark, even if he has lived there for five thousand years. He is always overshadowed by wind and water and mountain.

At the end of a long week, the steamer reached the town of Hammerfest. Huddled against the protecting slopes of mountains, the long rows of its houses follow the outline of the waterfront. It was here that Otto Torell was waiting for Nordenskiöld and for his other companion, Quennerstedt, a young zoologist. Torell had chartered a *jakt*, a small Norwegian fishing vessel, called *Frithjof*. It had a single mast, with a large square sail, and though it leaked and was at times clumsy to handle, it was well adapted to sailing in those northern seas. Torell also secured the services of a Norwegian skipper and a half-dozen crewmen, and on June 3, 1858, the *Frithjof* sailed from Hammerfest, bound for Spitsbergen.

The young scientists were eager to reach Spitsbergen as early in the season as possible, but their progress was slowed down by drifting ice floes even before they reached the half-way point between Norway and Spitsbergen, Bear Island. The *Frithjof* moved slowly and cautiously among the blue-green ice floes, trying to land on Bear Island, a paradise for birds. Hundreds of thousands of birds nest on Bear Island, and the guillemots and arctic gulls fill the air with their cries, and the sound of their wings. Skimming low over the water, they would approach the ship, wheeling around it at the last moment, swooping down again as they fished for food.

This was Nordenskiöld's first encounter with the birds of the Arctic. During the next twenty-five years, as he led expedition after expedition northward, he was always fascinated by the variety and the immensity of the bird population. Though no ornithologist, he studied birds and their habits and was able, decades later, to remember on what day and in what year he had observed a particular bird in Spitsbergen or Siberia or Greenland.

The ice surrounding Bear Island was too heavy for the small *Frithjof* to tackle, and it turned northward instead, cautiously feeling its way across the ice, until, almost a fortnight out of Norway, the jagged skyline of Spitsbergen hove into view.

Peak after serrated peak, the mountains of South Spitsbergen filled much of the northern horizon. They looked grim and desolate, without a trace of life, their steep slopes falling directly into the sea, a soft, grey mist rising along the invisible line where mountains and water met. A few gulls, white with black wingtips, followed the wake of the ship, always hoping for some tidbit from the galley; their raucous cries were the only sound heard, except for the creak of the rigging and the sound of the wind in the sails.

On they sailed northwestward, along the inhospitable shores of the islands, until suddenly the entrance to Isfjord, one of the great inlets on the west coast, opened up before them. To their north, the long plateau of Prince Karl's Foreland, with its twin peaks at either end, barred the view, but to the east they could catch a glimpse of masses of snowy mountains. The sky was clouded and a dark grey light fell upon the mountains as the small ship eased its way into the fjord.

All around the *Frithjof*, as it slowly advanced into the bay, there were barren stony slopes, but patches of snow still remained at the bottom of gullies. The peaks were covered with low clouds, the sea was an angry green-blue, flecked with white ice floes. As the low clouds scudded across the sky, there would occasionally be a rift and a travelling beam of sunlight would pick out a valley or a slope in bright white-grey.

Then, as it often happens in those high latitudes, a sudden shift of the wind would completely change the scene. The low clouds torn apart by the wind, replaced by a few patches of fluff floating high, the sky a brilliant hue of light blue, sunlight would bring out small patches of green on the brown slopes, and the waters of the bay would turn a bright indigo blue. The travellers were in the midst of a vast amphitheater of snow, ice, rocks, and sky.

Later, in their explorations, Torell, Nordenskiöld, and Quennerstedt investigated the immense valley glaciers that are among the characteristic features of Spitsbergen. They cover much of the interior of the western part of the achipelago, their immense tongues of ice stretch as far as fifty miles, clear across the land, from shore to shore. Like vast rivers of ice, burning in the sunlight, the glaciers move slowly toward the sea, forming a wall of ice sixty to eighty feet high, stretching as much as six miles along the shore. Though in the summer their surfaces are streaked with brown dust, from a short distance they appear immaculately white, their uniformity interrupted only by small, jagged, light blue openings, where pieces of ice fell into the sea, to begin their journey as ice floes. The water at the base of the great glaciers is a muddy brown, where the sand and gravel, suspended in the ice and carried by the glacier down slope, dissolves. The temperature of the sea water is only a few degrees above freezing, kept perpetually cold by the masses of ice constantly tumbling down from the glaciers: a man who fell into the water could not survive for more than ten to twelve minutes.

The young scientists landed on shore wherever a small inlet would allow anchoring their sailing vessel. Nordenskiöld looked for rock samples and was delighted to discover a whole fossilized flora, imprisoned in the sandstone that forms much of the western parts of Spitsbergen. Quennerstedt was more concerned with the world of living plants and, often joined by Nordenskiöld, he would spend many hours collecting specimens.

The first impression upon landing in Spitsbergen is that of a desert, of a world of slopes covered by scree, loose stones that would start small avalanches under a man's feet, and make walking across the moutainsides difficult, dangerous, and sometimes downright impossible. The sharply incised valleys show an accumulation of softer sand and gravel, but this too, could be difficult to traverse, and in the wider, U-shaped valleys the bottom is often covered by muskeg, waterlogged and incapable of supporting a man.

But on closer inspection, the seemingly barren soil displays a variety of plant life that, especially when the sun is out, is astonishingly varied and brilliant. Plants in the tundra, the Arctic desert of western Spitsbergen, hug the ground closely, thus escaping the icy winds that sweep across the land. Much of the ground is covered by grey lichen, its convoluted branches penetrate every crack in the rocks, slowly splitting them apart, and at the same time affording protection for the flowers of the tundra. These are tiny, a clump of flowering plants seldom measures more than three inches in diameter, and rises not more than an inch above the surface. That close to the ground, the plants get full benefit of the long hours of summer sunlight, and manage to survive, to bloom, and to produce spores and seeds to propagate their species. The strong green of their tiny leaves, the vivid pink, sulfurous yellow, bright white and gold of the blossoms form a striking contrast to the browns and greys of the surrounding mountainsides.

Spitsbergen is above all a paradise for migratory birds, and their cries fill the air throughout the summer. Small rodents, too, are part of the fauna, and the seas, offering a wide variety of plant foods, teem with life ranging from tiny succulent shrimp to sea bass and arctic char. Torell, Nordenskiöld, and Quennerstedt did not lack fresh food as long as they were willing to hunt and fish.

Spitsbergen represents the northernmost extension of the world of Europe; it lies at the same latitude as northern Greenland and the northern islands of the Canadian Arctic. During the summer months, from mid-June to mid-August, the sun never sets, and days and nights merge without any perceptible difference in the intensity of light. At midnight, the sun is still far above the horizon, its slanting rays emphasizing each peak and crest of the mountains. Each glacier shines, dazzling white, throughout the night; when the sky is clear, its reflection in the sea is like melted gold, and even under a cloudy sky wave crests retain a silvery glow.

The results of some ten weeks' wanderings along the west coast of Spitsbergen were thoroughly satisfactory. The three young scientists gathered a rich harvest of zoological, botanical, and geological specimens. Nordenskiöld brought back a number of fossil plants, as well as samples of the carboniferous rocks so abundant in the area. The fossil plants were later described in detail by Oswald Heer, a Swiss geologist, one of the founders of palaeobotany, the study of plant life in earlier geological periods.

In the 1850's, people went to the Arctic either to fish and to hunt whales and seals, or to attempt to reach a higher latitude, closer to the North Pole, than anyone was ever able to do. Torell's and Nordenskiöld's expedition did neither of these. Their purpose was solely scientific, to study the plants, animals and geological formations of Spitsbergen. Their journey was the first in a series, lasting for nearly a century, that brought scientists from all over Scandinavia to the Arctic, and resulted in a vast mass of scholarly treatises, making Spitsbergen the best known part of the far North.

The *Frithjof* landed the three scientists in Hammerfest on August 28, and by mid-September they were back in Stockholm. Now that he had seen the Arctic, Nordenskiöld's thoughts returned to his own future: could he return to Finland, and receive a university appointment? His father assured him that all was not lost at home. The elder Nordenskiöld was convinced that if Adolf would only state in writing that he regretted his hasty speech at the time of the graduation banquet, in May of 1857, the way would be open to a university career in Finland.

While Nordenskiöld was returning from Spitsbergen, his old teacher and friend, Professor Arppe, was busy in Helsingfors trying to convince the authorities that Nordenskiöld should be given a university appointment. Arppe became rector, leader of the faculty, at the university of Helsingfors, and on September 21, 1858, addressed an eloquent appeal on Nordenskiöld's behalf to Count Alexander Armfelt, Secretary of State for Finland in Saint Petersburg.

'Under the 1852 Act, reorganizing the university, a chair for mineralogy and geology was established. That chair is still vacant. In the meantime, a young man of unusual talents and irreproachable habits has dedicated himself to the study of these sciences, and as a writer and researcher has made truly impressive progress in them. He has been expelled from the university for reasons well known to your Excellency, which I am not about to excuse. But one must also realize that he is young and that it is too hard a punishment to be deprived of what could be a lifetime career, because he forgot for one moment what he owed his government and his country. It was with this in mind that I did not give up hope to secure for our university the services of this exceptionally talented young man: having known him and worked with him in close, daily contact, I know him better than anyone else...' Arppe closed his appeal by suggesting that Nordenskiöld be allowed to receive his travel grant, that he should complete the research project he had originally proposed in his application for the grant, and that, on his return in a year's time, he be allowed to apply for the chair of mineralogy and geology at the university.

In his reply to Professor Arppe, Count Armfelt expressed his hope that a pardon for Nordenskiöld could be obtained. It was necessary, however, that Nordenskiöld declare in writing his apology for what had happened, and state his desire to apply for a position in Finland. But Nordenskiöld, fiercely independent, was not about to retract his words spoken at the graduation banquet. He wrote to his father on September 9, 1858, while aboard ship on his way back from Spitsbergen: 'I have a very strong wish to return home, but only on condition that all that happened is to be forgotten, without any further fuss.'

What had troubled Nordenskiöld was the refusal of the University administration to let him see the text of the decision expelling him from the university and withdrawing his travel grant. Earlier in the year, on February 2, 1858, he had written to the rector of the university, and requested a copy of his 'sentence'. 'The right of every condemned person to obtain a copy of his sentence,' wrote Nordenskiöld, 'is one of the most important rights in our land. Perhaps this is the only guarantee against sentences of which even the judges must feel ashamed. It seems to me that the university, guardian of our culture, has created a precedent by violating this right. As I was condemned without any investigation, without the least attempt to offer me the opportunity of an explanation, it ought to have been a moral obligation to inform me of the reasons for this sentence, since it will result in my leaving my country and going into exile.'

The letter did have an effect, and Nordenskiöld received a certified copy of that section of the minutes of the faculty meeting pronouncing his disgrace and expulsion. But it certainly did not soften Nordenskiöld's attitude toward the Finnish authorities, since he was never given a chance to state his own case. In the meantime, while Finland dangled the possibility of a pardon and of an appointment, hedged with conditions that Nordenskiöld was not too eager to meet, a real opportunity arose in Sweden.

In early October, 1858, shortly after Nordenskiöld's return to Stockholm, Professor Mosander died. He was head of the division of mineralogy at the National Museum, and held the courtesy title of Professor; it was in his laboratory that Nordenskiöld had worked during the previous winter. The position that had thus become vacant was as important as any in Scandinavia, and it offered prospects of a bright future. The choice of the authorities fell on the young Finn, and Nordenskiöld, barely twenty-six years old, was informally approached by his friend and supporter, Christian Lovén, who sounded him out. Since it was customary to have qualified persons compete for this appointment, Lovén wanted to know whether Nordenskiöld was interested.

It was a difficult choice for Nordenskiöld. It was not only flattering to be offered a position of such importance in Sweden, it also meant financial security, the possibility of building an important mineralogical collection, in a word, a promising career. Yet there remained the tantalizing possibility of getting a university appointment at home, in his beloved Finland, and Nordenskiöld decided to return to his parents' house, before giving a final answer.

Shortly after his return, a telegram from Lovén arrived formally asking whether he would accept the position of chief of mineralogy at the Stockholm museum, if it were offered. Nordenskiöld's reply was brief: 'I await the decision, and am ready to accept.' On December 8, 1858, Lovén's triumphant telegram was delivered at the homestead of the Nordenskiölds: 'Complete success – They await your answer all day and all night.' By then, Nordenskiöld's mind was made up; he would go to Sweden.

But a passport was necessary if he was to leave Finland, and Nordenskiöld applied to the authorities for one. A year and a half earlier, in the spring of 1857, he had obtained a passport, while planning for his research journey, and had used it to go to Sweden after the incident of the graduation banquet. Ever mindful of the past, the Helsingfors authorities now stalled, and Nordenskiöld was advised to wait upon the Governor-General in person, before his request would be granted.

The residence and offices of the Governor-General of Finland were in an elegant, early nineteenth century house, overlooking Helsingfors harbor. When Nordenskiöld was ushered in, von Berg, the Governor-General, received him in a friendly way. He spoke in his native German, a language that Nordenskiöld spoke fluently, as did a senior official, a Finn, who was present at the interview.

Von Berg was in a good mood, and as he glanced out over the harbor and the lively scenes of the market under his window, he called Nordenskiöld to account for having travelled abroad without a valid passport, some eighteen months earlier. Nordenskiöld replied that he was not familiar with passport rules and regulations, and that it was up to the Governor-General's employees to enforce them. 'Well, you must at least admit that those who allowed you to leave Finland with an expired passport were wrong!' said von Berg. 'With the greatest of pleasure, your Excellency.' This reply was obviously gratifying to the Governor-General and he began to speak in a perfectly sensible way about what he called the 'graduation catastrophe'. He assured Nordenskiöld that everything could be straightened out and that he would be better off than before. Nordenskiöld, encouraged by the mild and pleasant attitude of a man he knew to be an unforgiving martinet, replied in a meek tone of voice. He felt that, even if he had committed an offence in his speech at the graduation banquet, by now he had suffered so much annoyance and even loss of money for the affair, that he thought the whole matter could be forgotten.

At this point, von Berg, who had obviously expected an abject apology, turned to the official present at the interview, intending to make Nordenskiöld feel his own insignificance, and said: 'It is not enough to admit one's mistakes, one must be sorry for them!' Without a moment's hesitation, Nordenskiöld snapped his answer, 'That I shall never do!' The Governor-General, furious at the independent-minded young Finn, pronounced sentence on him on the spot: 'You shall have your passport, but you may say good-bye to Finland. I shall see to that!' The interview was ended, Nordenskiöld returned to Frugård to spend the Christmas holidays with his parents, received his passport, and at the end of December started out on his journey to Stockholm.

Winter days are short in Finland, and by four o'clock in the afternoon it is pitch dark. Adolf Nordenskiöld left the stagecoach on the main road from Helsingfors to Åbo, confident that he could find his way to Björkboda, a small iron works owned by his distant cousin, Anders Ramsay. But he lost his way, and it was the sound of hammer striking iron in the forge that led him to the foundry, where the red tongues of flame were reflected on the snow outside. The engineer in charge of the foundry, Birger Anderson, remembered years later the weary traveller, stumbling to the door, and asking for directions to the owner's home. Soon, he was sitting by the great tiled stove, talking about student days, for Anders Ramsay was one of the young men whose health was toasted at Tölö inn, the day when Nordenskiöld's Finnish misadventures started.

The next day, December 31, dawned bright and sunny, and Adolf Nordenskiöld set out with his cousin to look at some interesting rock formations near the foundry. In a quarry he discovered a rare mineral, tantalite, at that time known to occur in only five places in all Europe. His outing was a success, and within a few week's time he wrote a short report on his discovery.

On January 1, 1859, he started on his way to Sweden. Winter travel across the narrow seas between Finland and Sweden was quite an adventure then, and Nordenskiöld was much too impatient to wait for a ferryman willing to face the dangers of those icy waters. Instead, he put on skates, and started on his way. Three times he missed his footing and fell into the icy water up to his neck, according to his own story of the crossing. At long last he reached Eckerö, on the west side of the Åland Islands, and in a small boat was rowed over to Sweden.

As the first day of 1859 ended, Adolf Nordenskiöld left his native Finland behind him. Though he returned there many times, it was in Sweden that he settled, it was to his adopted land that he brought fame in the years ahead.

IV. SETTLING DOWN IN SWEDEN – 1859-61

Early in January, 1859, Adolf Nordenskiöld began to work in the Mineralogy Division of the National Museum of Natural History. He remained head of the division for forty-three years, and during those years he built it into one of the great collections of rare – and often beautiful – specimens of minerals in all Europe. Many of the samples added during those years when Nordenskiöld was in charge of the collection came from the excursions he undertook every summer within Scandinavia, excursions that took him to every district of Sweden, Norway, and Finland. The 'extraordinary riches of the Scandinavian peninsula in rare and remarkable minerals', as he put it is his autobiography, enabled him to look for new and different samples on every trip; besides, his constant helper and assistant, Lindström, as well as students from Stockholm University, kept bringing in new treasures. He was in touch with dealers throughout Europe and the United States, and his voluminous correspondence with them, and with fellow curators of similar collections abroad, bear witness to his unflagging efforts to make the Stockholm mineralogical museum one of the best in the world.

His first summer on the new job was dedicated to one of these 'collecting' trips: it took him to north central Sweden, to the provinces of Dalarna and Jämtland. There he wandered through the months of July and August, with his knapsack, his geologist's hammer and his note book, pausing only long enough to mail his samples back to the museum. For once, though, the summer was not without its problem: Adolf Nordenskiöld became seriously ill with a sudden intestinal infection, and was confined to bed, with a high fever, in the home of a peasant. For several days his life seemed in danger, but his robust constitution overcame the infection, and he does not seem to have known another day of ill health for the rest of his life.

Once the worst of the fever was past, Nordenskiöld sat for nearly two weeks in the garden of the homestead, overlooking the deep blue waters of Storsjön, 'The Great Lake', watching the passing clouds, listening to the constant singing of birds, enjoying the long hours of summer sunshine. Back in good health once more, he returned by stagecoach and train to Stockholm and to work in his laboratory and collections.

In the fall of 1859 he had company: his classmate from Helsingfors University, the chemist Johan Chydenius, 'Hannes', came to spend several months with him in Stockholm. Chydenius and Nordenskiöld had known each other for years; they were together at Tölö and on the day of the graduation banquet. They thoroughly enjoyed the hours they spent together in the laboratory, the long evenings of talk over wine and cigars.

In the meantime, Nordenskiöld kept his pen busy, reporting his first journey to Spitsbergen to the 'newsletter' of European geography, published by Dr. August Petermann in Jena, Germany, and published papers dealing with his studies in mineralogy and chemistry in German as well as in British journals.

Early in 1860, sad news came from Finland. His mother, ailing for some months, died on January 26 at the family estate of Frugård. Adolf Nordenskiöld, banned by Finland's Governor-General from returning home, was not able to see his mother before she died. In vain did he apply for a passport to go to her funeral: five months later, he wrote to his father that not even the support of Prince Oscar (later King Oscar II), and of the Swedish Minister for Foreign Affairs, could help him. As long as his old adversary, Count von Berg, sat in the Governor's palace in Helsingfors, Nordenskiöld 'the rabble-rouser' would find the gates of his homeland closed to him.

Never one to waste his energy battling obstacles that, in his view, could disappear later, he turned to more practical matters. For the first time, he showed his talents as a fund raiser, applying, and receiving, help for his friend Chydenius for a field trip to Norway. The two spent the summer tramping around the mines and quarries of south Norway, and Chydenius returned to Helsingfors University laden with valuable additions to the local collections.

While Nordenskiöld worked in his museum-laboratory, his companion Otto Torell had bigger, more promising schemes in mind. Excited by the results of the summer tour in 1858, when Torell, accompanied by Nordenskiöld and another young scientist, had spent some ten weeks visiting the Arctic archipelago of Spitsbergen, he resolved to continue his researches, but on a more serious basis. He planned to return to Spitsbergen with a staff of scientists from several fields, to study not only the land but the sea as well, and he went looking for funds.

At the beginning of the 1860's, England led the world in Arctic exploration. After years of search, the tragedy of Sir John Franklin and his men was solved, and the Arctic specialists of the British Navy and of the Royal Geographical Society of London were the undisputed authorities in polar matters. In the summer of 1860, while Nordenskiöld tramped through southern Norway, Otto Torell journeyed to London, consulted such leading figures as Sir Leopold McClintock and Sir Roderick Murchison, and was encouraged by their interest in a scientific survey of Spitsbergen.

But these were times for discovery, too, and Torell professed to have other things in mind besides collecting scientific data, making observations, and bringing home specimens. In his application for funds from the Swedish government, which he submitted to the Academy of Sciences for prior approval, Torell was quite explicit about his hopes of pushing northward. He proposed to land his scientific staff on the northern coast of West Spitsbergen, and then push still further north, with a small crew consisting of himself, Nordenskiöld, and not more than five others, using dogsleds to penetrate the polar ice.

'When one finds oneself at latitude 80° North, barely six hundred miles from the North Pole, the question is: are the obstacles on the way to the Pole insuperable, or is it possible to overcome at least a few of them? After all, many an authority on polar matters feels that man will reach the Pole some day.' Torell went on to say: 'It is easy to explain – and to excuse – the fact that the two of us, Nordenskiöld and I, who went to the Arctic with scientific aims in mind, were seized by the same desire that caught so many before us, that we too want to make an attempt to push as far north as possible, and thus allow Swedish science to take part in this effort.'

Torell's eloquent appeal convinced the cautious scholars of the Academy of Sciences to approve his plan. Early in 1861, the Swedish parliament made him a grant of 20,000 riksdaler, the equivalent of about five thousand dollars, U.S., at the time. Prince Oscar, heir to the throne, contributed another 4,000 riksdaler; several people made smaller donations; and in order to save funds, it was agreed that members of the expedition's scientific staff should pay their own expenses.

Torell chartered two sailing vessels in Tromsö, *Aeolus* and *Magdalena.* These were small ships, about the size of a harbor tug of today, slow sailors, but also easy to maneuver, a matter of some importance when searching for a channel through pack ice, or slipping through narrow passages in the offshore islands of Spitsbergen.

The crew and scientific staff represented all of Scandinavia. Besides the two leaders, Torell and Nordenskiöld, there were geologists, botanists, physicists, an astronomer, and a medical man, from Finland and Sweden. From Denmark came Karl Petersen, a veteran of Arctic explorations, who had gone to the far North with Parry and McClintock of Britain, with Kane and Hayes from the United States, had spent nearly twenty years in Greenland, and was considered an oracle on Arctic life and survival. *Aeolus*' commander was a Swedish naval officer, while the man in charge of *Magdalena* was an officer from the Norwegian merchant marine. The crew was made up mostly of Norwegians, but the harpooners and hunters were Quanes, a group of Finns whose ancestors had settled in northernmost Norway some two centuries earlier.

Whenever Nordenskiöld had to assemble a crew and a scientific staff for his later expeditions, he followed the same pattern, and sought the best men throughout Scandinavia, regardless of their home or their speech. The three languages, Swedish, Danish and Norwegian, while differing in many particulars, are closely related, and men speaking any one of the three tongues never have too much trouble understanding the others. 'We understand each other,' seems to be the linguistic, if not the political, motto of Scandinavia. As for the Finns, though their speech is totally unrelated to the Scandinavian languages, they, too fitted in, through their understanding – and speaking – either Swedish or Norwegian.

Disparate in language, these small groups were held together by a common allegiance to their leader. As early as the expedition of 1861, one notices the recurrence of names from Nordenskiöld's earlier journeys among the participants. Time and again, whether skilled scientists or simple seamen and whalers, these men returned to the Arctic under Nordenskiöld's leadership. He was able to inspire them with his own contagious enthusiasm, to exact from them the same devotion to the objective of the expedition that he professed. Adolf Nordenskiöld was truly a leader of men.

The original plan for 1861 was to sail from Tromsö in mid-April, to reach northern Spitsbergen as early as possible, and take off on the attempt to reach the North Pole. But a strong northerly-northwesterly wind blew steadily for three weeks, and there was nothing for it but to wait.

Tromsö was the largest town of northern Norway, the center of the fishing and whaling fleet, and the townspeople opened their homes to the group of young scientists stranded in their midst. The men Nordenskiöld met then, merchants, shipowners, seacaptains, became his lifelong friends. He relied on them in the years to come for help to find ships for his polar expeditions, to hire crews, to equip the vessels for the long and hard journeys in polar waters. Most important, listening to the skippers, steersmen, harpooners, in port and on deck at sea, he learned much about the lore of the Arctic. They told him about the 'ice blink', the strange light on the horizon that tells of a solid mass of ice ahead, about the behavior of birds when a storm is imminent, as well as stories about their experiences in the waters north of Europe.

The men who sailed with Nordenskiöld in later years never failed to be impressed by the 'sea sense' of their chief. Not that he was a good sailor: he suffered from sea sickness all his life. But even when he had put on a good deal of weight, he would still climb the crow's nest to have a good look at the sea ahead, and he could 'smell' and tell an icefield as well as any Norwegian sailor. This was one of the ingredients of Nordenskiöld's success, that he combined the training of a scientist with a profound respect for the hard-gained practical knowledge of seafaring men. Planning his voyages, he would read every printed account of the experiences of his predecessors. But at the same time he also contacted every whaler and every captain of a fishing vessel who sailed the waters he was about to enter; he would go out of his way to acquire the logs of their ships, and extract from those terse accounts information that was both practical and accurate.

On May 7, a coastal steamer put in at Tromsö, and its captain offered to tow the ships to the northern entrance of Tromsö fjord, enabling them to get a start on their voyage. After another two days' waiting, the wind finally veered, the local pilot accompanying the ships was dropped, and as he called out to the crew, 'May God protect you,' *Aeolus* and *Magdalena* set sail for Spitsbergen.

It is hard to realize that when they were travelling in these two ships, Nordenskiöld and his companions lived aboard in conditions as crowded and primitive as those prevailing three centuries earlier. In fact, it is safe to say that the larger of the two ships, *Aeolus,* was barely the size of Columbus' flagship, the *Santa Maria!* Accommodations may have been a bit less crowded than in Columbus' time, since *Aeolus* carried a crew of only twenty-four, a little over half the crew of the flagship of the great discoverer. What progress had occurred in the three and one half centuries since Columbus' first voyage was partly in the navigational instruments used, partly in the foods and drinking water on board. There were excellent canned foods available, reliable means of preparing hot meals even on stormy days, and an ample supply of drinking water, beer, and stronger spirits. But on stormy days, the ships rolled and pitched just as much as the Spanish vessels of the late fifteenth century. It was early spring in the high latitudes, and great masses of birds were flying northward, to their breeding grounds. Huge swarms of auks and geese, guillemots and gulls, were seen; and one day a whole flock of snow buntings settled on the decks and rigging, resting from their trip, before they resumed their flight.

When *Aeolus* and *Magdalena* arrived at the latitude of northernmost Spitsbergen, they found their way blocked by ice. After maneuvering back and forth while in sight of land, making shore excursions to collect early blooming plants and to hunt for fresh food, the ships anchored in Treurenberg Bay, on the north shore of West Spitsbergen, to await warmer weather and the breakup of the ice that lay to the north and east. Four Norwegian fishing vessels took refuge there, too, only to find that within a day the entrance to the bay was frozen solid, and the expedition, as well as the fishermen, remained there for over four weeks.

Midsummer came, a festival as dear to the hearts of Scandinavians as Christmas, but the land, just shedding its snow cover, did not offer any flowers to decorate the traditional maypole. Instead, the resourceful crew used long strands of green-brown algae, and flags from the ships' locker, to bedeck a pole made from driftwood, and served a festive meal of reindeer steak, together with appropriate liquid refreshments. There were Swedes, Danes, Norwegians, Finns, several Lapps from the fishing vessels; there were songs and speeches, and a great bonfire, while to the north the midnight sun shone over a brilliant field of ice.

When the sun is high in the sky during the short Arctic summer, the days can be surprisingly warm, and though the daily mean temperature, carefully calculated by the staff, was only about 2 degrees Celsius, 35 degrees Fahrenheit in the second half of June, close to the ground in protected spots the temperature rose as high as 19 degrees Celsius, 66 degrees Fahrenheit. The scientists continued their collecting on land and, by careful dredging, in the bay, and established several bases whence, it was hoped, an accurate survey of Spitsbergen could later be carried out. Torell's plan called for a small party of men, proceeding on dog sleds, to make a thrust northward, across the ice. More than thirty years earlier a group of men of the British Navy, commanded by Edward Parry, did just that, and reached latitude 82° 45', a little over 400 miles from the North Pole. If a group started early in April, said Parry in his report, as soon as there was enough daylight to move, it would not have to contend with the difficulties of an uneven ice surface, nor with soft, thawing snow, nor with the southward drift of the ice floes that continually interferes with a northward push. But Torell's group was too late in arriving in northern Spitsbergen, their intended starting point, and the original plan had to be abandoned. In its place, Torell organized a series of trips in the whaleboat carried aboard *Aeolus*. Small but strong, the boat could carry eight men and enough supplies to last for three weeks.

Torell, Nordenskiöld and Petersen, accompanied by four crew members, carried out four trips in the icy, treacherous waters off the northern coasts of Spitsbergen. The men travelled during the night, since there was continuous light, and rested during the warmer hours of the day: sailcloth was spread on the ground, they put up their tent, rolled up in their sleeping bags and slept soundly. The two scientists kept records of all their observations. Torell was more interested in plants and animals, while Nordenskiöld identified rock formations and, in some dozen places, made astronomical observations to determine the correct position of prominent landmarks. On later expeditions, the landmarks determined by Nordenskiöld served as bases for an accurate survey of Spitsbergen. The observations, gathered by Nordenskiöld, were the basis for his map of northern Spitsbergen, published as part of the scientific report of the expedition. This map, dated 1861, provides detailed information on the rock formations found along the coasts and on the islands offshore, and it was the first geological map of any part of the Arctic. It is a landmark in the scientific study of the polar regions and, although its existence is largely forgotten, still stands as a tribute to the skill of its compiler.

Travelling about the lonely waters off northern Spitsbergen, the party of explorers was struck by the amount of flotsam and jetsam found on beaches. Besides large masses of driftwood, they came across cork from fishermen's nets, lost off north Norway, and carried northward by ocean currents. But the most dramatic of their finds was a large bean, nearly an inch and a half in diameter, native only to the West Indies. Similar beans are washed ashore from time to time in north Norway, but this was their first authenticated presence north of latitude 80°, giving dramatic proof of the far reach of the currents that cross the entire Atlantic Ocean, from the West Indies to the very doorstep of the North Pole.

Collecting and classifying plants was of the greatest importance to the members of the expedition, but of equal interest was the animal life of Spitsbergen. Two hundred or more years of whaling had, by the mid-nineteenth century, thinned out the greatest part of what must have been immense herds of those huge beasts. But the islands still teemed with walrus and with a large number of polar bears.

Nordenskiöld described an encounter with walruses, that took place when a sudden fog bank enveloped sea, ice, and land in its impenetrable blanket. The small whaleboat, moving noiselessly in the fog, came within a few yards of a large ice floe, where a herd of thirty to forty walruses was resting, completely unaware of their visitors. One of the sailors suddenly shouted, and all the animals slid into the sea with a mighty roar, disappearing in the water. Within a matter of seconds, they surfaced again on the far side of the floe, treading water so that they could see what was going on, their huge bodies partially above the water, with their large heads, with long mustachios and gleaming tusks, gazing apparently without fear at their strange visitors.

The polar bear was very much part of the animal world of Spitsbergen in the mid-nineteenth century, and was frequently observed on land and on the sea ice. On one occasion, Nordenskiöld had an unexpected encounter with one of these large animals. It happened on one of the offshore islands of northern Spitsbergen: Nordenskiöld started out to climb a high peak, to make a sketch map of the island and its surroundings. Not very much interested in hunting, he landed on the island armed only with his sextant, a simple surveying instrument, and his sketch pad. He was within a short distance from the peak, when he suddenly realized that someone had arrived there before him: a large polar bear was standing on the rocks looking out over the sea for its prey. As he later told the story: 'The bear had caught sight of me, and I did not dare to run back to the boat. Instead, I went straight on toward him, believing that he would get scared and run away, since I had always seen polar bears behave that way when they met human beings. But I miscalculated his actions: the bear started to circle around me, and soon we were so close to each other that I could have hit him with a stick. He finally stopped on a large rock, standing a bit above me, hissing and stomping, while I stood below, shouted and yelled with all my might and threw large stones at him, without the slightest effect. Finally a stone hit his paw, resting on the rock; the pain, or perhaps the fact that his curiosity was satisfied, made the bear retreat. I followed him a short distance, until he ducked behind a rock, then ran as fast as I could back to the boat.' As Nordenskiöld was telling his companions about the encounter, the polar bear reappeared on top of another rock, as if he had been watching the intruders. Two of the sailors gave chase, but the bear disappeared, and was not seen again.

By late August, the scientific staff had gathered a rich harvest of plants, animals, and rock samples, when suddenly the sea ice disappeared, and the way to the north seemed open. The two young leaders, Torell and Nordenskiöld, were all set to strike out northward, and push as far as weather and ice would allow them, but it was late in the season and sudden storms could endanger ships and men. The counsel of the more experienced seamen prevailed, and *Aeolus* and *Magdalena* set sail for Norway.

The results of the 1861 expedition to Spitsbergen were satisfactory, yet the two principal aims, the push north toward the Pole, and the accurate mapping of the islands, remained unfulfilled. It was quite obvious to Nordenskiöld that further work was called for, on another occasion.

The two ships returned to Tromsö in late September. Most of the scientific staff took the coastal steamer thence, to return home, but Nordenskiöld struck out inland. There was work to do in northern Norway and northernmost Sweden for a mineralogist who had never visited those remote regions. With his knapsack on his back, Adolf Nordenskiöld was off on a four hundred mile hike. Following the trails made by the Lapps as they drive their herds from the Norwegian to the Swedish side of the mountains, sleeping in Lapp huts along the way, he spent the next three weeks getting acquainted with the remotest part of Sweden. Tired and happy, with a knapsack full of rock samples, he arrived in Haparanda, at the head of the great gulf of Bothnia, the northernmost part of the Baltic. There he caught the stage coach, and returned to Stockholm.

V. LOVE, COURTSHIP AND MARRIAGE - 1863

When Adolf Nordenskiöld returned to Stockholm in October, 1861, there was a letter on his desk from the Secretary of the Swedish Academy of Sciences. On September 1, whilst he and his colleagues were still engaged in Arctic research in Spitsbergen, the Academy had elected him to membership.

This was a signal honor for a man still under thirty years of age, to become a member of one of the oldest scientific societies. He must have felt a touch of pride, remembering that two of his ancestors were among the first members of the Swedish Academy, more than a hundred years earlier.

For the next forty years, until the day he died, Adolf Nordenskiöld considered the Swedish Academy of Sciences his home. This was true even in a literal sense, for he lived during more than thirty years in the building where the Academy had its offices, on Stockholm's 'Queen Street', Drottninggatan. He had only to cross the great interior courtyard to get from his flat to his laboratory and to the collection of minerals that absorbed much of his time.

Election to membership in the Academy of Sciences was soon followed by another form of recognition. The Academy had a special fund to support popular lectures on the sciences, and Adolf Nordenskiöld was selected to be Tham Lecturer for the year 1861-62. It was not entirely to his liking to speak before the general public; he much preferred to discuss the results of his travels and researches with colleagues, in a highly technical manner. But he realized that public speaking, too, was a necessary part of a scientists work: to distill his experience into a short presentation, to catch the imagination of a nonscientific audience, and thus gain support for further ventures.

On December 11, 1861, he wrote his father: 'Last Saturday I delivered my first lecture. I cannot say that it went off as I would have wished, but I hope things will improve as I go along. One has to creep before one can walk. I have a lot of work to do, yet I accepted the invitation to speak in order to get some practice. I must get used to appearing before a large audience.'

The winter of 1861-62 brought important changes in his native Finland, too. Nordenskiöld's arch-enemy, Governor-General Berg, was recalled from his post; and a distinguished Russian, General Platon Rokassovskii, was appointed in his place. When Rokassovskii announced that he was calling Finland's parliament to meet in Helsingfors – for the first time in over half a century – it became evident that a more liberal point of view was to prevail in Finnish affairs.

Nordenskiöld's father, never quite reconciled to his son's exile in Sweden, immediately requested an audience with the new Governor-General, and asked him to permit his son to visit Finland. On February 8, 1862, the permission was granted, and during the summer Adolf Nordenskiöld and his father met once again, at the family estate, Frugård.

Frugård was a quiet place now; Adolf Nordenskiöld's mother had died; and the children were all grown up. But his father, in spite of his seventy years, was as eager as ever to spend the summer hunting minerals in his son's company. It was a successful summer, too, for father and son discovered a new form of the valuable metal tantalite. As an homage to Finland, Adolf Nordenskiöld named it tapiolite, after the old Finnish god of the forests, Tapio.

Back in Finland for the first time after nearly four years, Adolf took advantage of his visit and called on his old friend from university days, Carl Mannerheim, at his country estate.

The Mannerheims were one of Finland's most distinguished families: Count Gustav Mannerheim, the father of Nordenskiöld's friend and classmate, had been governor of one of the Finnish provinces under Russian rule and, later, presiding judge of the court of appeal of east Finland. Like the Nordenskiölds, the Mannerheims chose to remain in Finland after 1809, to serve the new Russian rulers, and continue to provide leadership to the country.

Villnäs, the Mannerheim country home, was the most elegant estate in all Finland. Situated near the southwest coast, Villnäs had the quiet, unostentatious style of the late 18th century. Every item of furniture had been chosen with care, and the elegance of the interior was complemented by the lovely garden and orchards surrounding the mansion. Life in Villnäs was formal; it was a place where, in the words of a contemporary diarist, one had to be careful of his speech to be certain that everything said was in good taste. There were servants to attend to the needs of guests, for Carl Mannerheim and his three sisters, Sophie, Anna and Vilhelmina were popular among their contemporaries and many a friend was invited to spend some days at Villnäs.

But there was appreciation for less worldly things, too, in the Mannerheim family. Count Gustav was an amateur entomologist of distinction,

who spent his summers roaming all over Finland, and accumulated a collection of more than one hundred thousand insects. His children knew well the devotion of a dedicated scientist to his studies.
Carl Mannerheim and Adolf Nordenskiöld became fast friends while at the University of Helsingfors. Together they took part in student festivities, but while Nordenskiöld was singled out for severe punishment for his political views, Mannerheim managed to get by with nothing more serious than the loss of a semester's time. In 1858, when Finnish students decided to celebrate the fiftieth anniversary of Finland's last battle against Russia, it was Carl Mannerheim who recited the lines of the poet Runeberg, an homage to Finland that is still remembered:

Here held a race Suomi's land,
And holds it yet; 'neath sorrow's hand
It grew to fate more pliant;
No sacrifice too great is known,
Its mood and calm are fixed as stone,
Its faith is death-defiant;
This is the race we call our own.

Visiting at Villnäs, Nordenskiöld met Anna Mannerheim, who was then twenty-two. She was a dark-eyed beauty, and very much a cosmopolitan. As a teen-age girl, she spent several years in a private school in Switzerland, where she acquired a near-perfect command of French and, through close friendship with several American schoolmates, a thorough knowledge of English as well. She had all of the grace and self-assurance that her family provided; she knew something about single-minded devotion to science from her father. Small wonder that Adolf Nordenskiöld, who remembered her only as a teen-ager from their meeting five years earlier, fell head over heels in love.
But the time was not yet when he could declare his feelings and ask Anna Mannerheim to marry him. He had to return to his post in Stockholm, to his work, and to his new status as a member of the Swedish parliament. In the spring of 1860 he became a Swedish citizen, thus returning to the country of his ancestors, who had been ennobled a century earlier by the king of Sweden. As their descendant, and as a Swedish subject, he claimed his right to sit in the House of Nobility of the *Riksdag*, the Swedish parliament. His claim was accepted, and Nordenskiöld took his seat in the *Riksdag* during the fall of 1862.

It was an exciting time to assist at the parliamentary debates, for great changes in the political life of Sweden were in the offing. De Geer, the Minister of Justice, introduced a proposal for electoral reform that would abolish the old medieval assembly, composed of the four estates of nobility, clergy, burghers and farmers, and replace it with a parliament of two chambers, elected by a much greater number of citizens than was hitherto the case. Nordenskiöld did not take part in the discussions, but listened carefully; the proposal for electoral reform, aimed at abolishing old privileges, was very much to his liking, in accord with his liberal views.

It was during the *Riksdag* sessions that one of Nordenskiöld's close friends, Harald Wieselgren, approached him with an idea. There was obvious need for a place in Stockholm where young men of liberal views could meet. Wieselgren proposed a society, to be called 'Idun', where writers, scientists, artists could get together and discuss current affairs. Nordenskiöld was enthusiastic about the idea, became one of the founders of 'Idun', and seldom missed its meetings, held in the Hotel 'Gillet' near the center of Stockholm.

But the busy life of the capital, his work at the Museum, his attendance at the sessions of the *Riksdag*, could not take Adolf Nordenskiöld's mind off the memory of the girl he had met during the golden summer days, in Finland. Soon he found an ideal excuse to absent himself from Stockholm: one of his colleagues at the Museum asked him to undertake a study of sea ice in the Baltic, in the area of the Åland Islands. It was a short distance from the Ålands to the Mannerheim estate, and to make things easier, Carl Mannerheim invited his school friend to be present at his marriage to Hélène von Julin, on December 31, 1862.

Nordenskiöld spent Christmas with his father and his brothers and sisters at Frugård, and left after the holiday to attend the wedding of his friend, in southwest Finland. Carl Mannerheim's marriage was the social event of the year. Several years earlier, when his father died, Carl became head of the family and inherited the title of Count. His bride's people, the Julins, were also well connected, and the cream of Finnish society attended the wedding festivities. Professor Nordenskiöld was, in the eyes of all, the most eligible bachelor at the wedding. In a photograph taken at the time, he looks handsome and distinguished, his hair greying at the temples, his clear blue eyes fixed on the camera. His personal courage, standing up against the powerful Governor-General, earned him admiration all over Finland; his Arctic adventures and the important post he held in Sweden only added to his stature.

To his friends and contemporaries, the obvious thing was that the Professor was in love. 'We all knew that he was in love,' wrote one of the wedding guests afterwards, 'but it was hard to decide who was the object of his affections.' Before long, the secret was out. Family tradition has it that Adolf Nordenskiöld proposed to Anna Mannerheim during a sleigh ride on the frozen Baltic; in his own words, he came to Villnäs hesitating, and left jubilant. On January 12 his suit was accepted; he wrote his father the next day: 'Yesterday I became engaged to Anna Mannerheim. You could never, in all the world, find a more noble, charming and lovable daughter-in-law, and I hope your blessings will be with us when we enter our new life together.'

In mid-January, 1863, Nordenskiöld left Finland, but spent a week en route in the Åland Islands, a short distance from his fiancée's home. Mail between Sweden and Finland moved at a haphazard rate during the winter: whenever weather and ice permitted, the Åland islanders carried the mail sacks in small boats to the Finnish coast. Nordenskiöld stayed in the village of Kumlinge in the islands, where mail was transferred from boats that plied to Sweden to others relaying it to Finland. It was in the little inn of Kumlinge that he wrote the first of many hundreds of letters to Anna:

'A month ago I spent the night in this very place. How much has changed in that month. Then I hurried on, in spite of wind and weather, sustained by the hope that I shall see you once more; now my steps are heavy as they lead me further and further away from the one who means more to me than life itself. Then I was anxious and timid about the way a young and beautiful girl would receive me; now I am sustained by the hope, nay, by the certainty that when we meet again after many a long month, there will be love and happiness in your eyes, too. It is this certainty that will be my only delight during the hard times while we are apart. Every line you send me will strengthen that hope, and give me more joy than the greatest of pleasures Stockholm has to offer.'

Through spring and early summer, Adolf Nordenskiöld was a busy man. Realizing that his bachelor apartment would hardly be acceptable as proper quarters for a newly married couple, he managed to prevail upon the officers of the Academy of Sciences to let him take over part of the main floor of its building as his living quarters.

The building that housed the Swedish Academy of Sciences and the National Museum of Natural History in the 1860's still stands on

Drottninggatan, a narrow and busy thoroughfare of Stockholm. Nordenskiöld's apartment was on the east side of the structure, its window looked out over a peaceful and pleasant churchyard. During the spring, he wrote his fiancée, the Academy had had the entire flat painted, and had put in an elegant tiled stove in the living room. When Anna and her mother came to Stockholm, in May, she picked out the wallpaper and gave her approval to the whole place. And, since the flat might not be ready by the time of their wedding, Adolf's aunt put her own apartment, complete with cook and chambermaid, at their disposal, while she took off for an extended holiday in Italy. Furnishings came both from Villnäs and from Frugård, and the groom-to-be surveyed their future apartment with satisfaction.

But Adolf Nordenskiöld was all too conscious of the great difference between the spacious and elegant world of Villnäs and the relatively cramped apartment in Stockholm. 'I must ask you to share a modest existence,' he wrote Anna in June. 'I have neither gold, nor goods, nor grounds to offer you.' Her answer was as reassuring at it was affectionate: 'You shall have a wife,' she answered, writing in English, 'whose smile would vanish forever if she could not spend her life by your side.' The Professor was far too much in love to even consider a prolonged absence from his wife-to-be. He stated in his autobiography, 'I had dismissed any further Arctic travels from my mind, as a matter of course.' When Otto Torell wrote, asking him to consider another trip to Spitsbergen, he told his fiancée about it and made clear his intentions concerning any future exploratory journeys: 'At Villnäs, we joked about another trip to Spitsbergen. Unexpectedly, I received a letter from Torell, my brave travelling companion. It was about a new journey, to include a winter's stay, and another attempt to reach the North Pole, all according to our old agreement. I already answered him, with a definite no. I can no longer be separated from my Anna, nor will I cause you any worry, my beloved.'

Adolf Nordenskiöld and Anna Mannerheim were married at Villnäs on July 1, 1863. The young couple left for Sweden right away, and spent their honeymoon in a sleepy and charming town on the west coast, Marstrand. In September, 1863, they took up their residence in the house of the Academy, in Stockholm.

VI. NORDENSKIÖLD'S FIRST ARCTIC COMMAND – 1864

Adolf and Anna Nordenskiöld settled down quickly to life in Stockholm. She was busy furnishing their apartment, making new friends in the capital, writing lengthy letters to her mother and sister in Finland. Adolf Nordenskiöld added a new position to the one he already held in the Museum of Natural History: he became a lecturer at the Swedish Military College. He was happy, satisfied with this work and he wrote later, in his autobiography, that it was quite natural for him to have dismissed all further Arctic travel from his mind. His new responsibilities clearly demanded his presence at home.

Within a few months a new set of circumstances arose and all of Nordenskiöld's resolutions to stay at home and become an armchair scientist were scattered to the winds. A new expedition to Spitsbergen was in the making, and he was offered the position of scientist-in-charge. It was a hard offer to resist, the first opportunity to run his own show. The size and shape of the earth had long intrigued scientists, and in the mid-eighteenth century surveys were carried out near the Equator, in South America, and near the Arctic Circle, in Sweden, to determine these important characteristics of our planet. A century later much more refined instruments had become available and there was a strong interest to re-run the surveys, including the measurement of an arc of the meridian as close to the North Pole as possible. Since an accurate survey could not be made on the Polar Sea, Spitsbergen, located at a high latitude and easily accessible during the summer, was chosen for the purpose. One of the main tasks of Torell's 1861 expedition to the islands was to lay out the bases for such a survey.

But conditions of sea ice were unfavorable during the 1861 season, and while the stations for the northern end of the survey, in North Spitsbergen, were selected, it proved impossible to carry out the work in the southern part of the archipelago. The Swedish Academy of Sciences, anxious to see the preliminary work for the survey completed, applied for a modest government grant that would allow a small party to go to Spitsbergen and do the work. The man selected to head the expedition was a young geodesist who had started the work in 1861, Karl Chydenius. But he became ill during the winter of 1863-64, and died in March 1864. Nordenskiöld was asked to take his place and lead the expedition.

The charge given Nordenskiöld and an astronomer from Lund, Dunér, was to establish a series of bases in south Spitsbergen for the measurement of a degree of latitude. However, since a ship had to be chartered to carry the two men to Spitsbergen, there was an opportunity to do some zoological and botanical research as well; and the generosity of the Minister of the Navy, Count von Platen, made it possible for a Finnish zoologist, Malmgren, to join the expedition.

Both Dunér and Malmgren had had previous experience in the Arctic: they had both taken part in Torell and Nordenskiöld's 1861 expedition to Spitsbergen. Since the objective of their journey was limited to completing the preliminary survey of the Spitsbergen archipelago, there was no reason for an early departure, and the three men agreed to meet in Tromsö at the end of May.

Anna Nordenskiöld was expecting her first child early during the summer, and decided to await her confinement at her mother's, in Finland. Adolf traveled by railroad to Oslo, and continued his journey to north Norway by coastal steamer. It took ten days to reach Tromsö, and the tedium of the trip was relieved only by the presence of a professional photographer aboard ship, who introduced Adolf to the mysteries of his newly acquired camera. Taking pictures was an involved business in the 1860's: the photographer carried not only a large camera, tripod, glass plates, but he had to have chemicals for developing, paper for printing, and a portable darkroom to do the work. None of the photographs taken by Nordenskiöld during his 1864 expedition survive, but engravings made from his pictures show that he had an eye for light and shadow, and a sense of the dramatic.

This was the first time Adolf Nordenskiöld was in charge of an expedition, and though his funds were more modest than had been the case in 1858 and 1861, he did well in chartering a vessel and hiring a crew. That this could be done was due to the help and cooperation of the merchants and shipowners of Tromsö, who had met Nordenskiöld on his two earlier voyages and made a special effort on his behalf.

The ship chartered for the 1864 expedition to Spitsbergen, the *Axel Thordsen*, was neither a modern vessel nor a large one. Built in 1810 as a small gunboat serving the coastal defenses of north Norway, she took part in actions against English attempts to land near Tromsö during the Napoleonic wars. In the ensuing years she saw service as a fishing vessel, and because of her age, could be chartered for a modest sum. The *Axel Thordsen* was about sixty feet long, sturdily built of heavy oak planks, to withstand the buffeting waves of the north Atlantic. There was a small stateroom at the aft end of the ship, that was divided into two sections with a tiny crawl space connecting them. In the rear section, that was not quite high enough to allow a man to stand upright, were the berths for the three scientists, low and narrow, but kept warm through thick reindeerskins that served as mattresses and blankets. In the fore section the only light came from a swinging oil lamp; there, supplies were kept and the zoologist Malmgren had his instruments, boxes, and bottles for specimens to be collected on the journey.

The *Axel Thordsen* carried four rowboats that were to be used for landing parties in areas inaccessible to the ship. The boats had been secured on deck, as had the boxes that held enough supplies for five months. A ship going to Spitsbergen should have been equipped to stand an Arctic winter, had she become icebound, but Nordenskiöld's funds were limited, and he could not lay in a year's supplies. Furthermore, the deck and tiny cargo space of his ship could not have held any more boxes or barrels, at any rate.

As was the case on every one of Nordenskiöld's Arctic voyages, several of the crew members, including Captain Hellstad, had sailed with him on at least one earlier occasion. The men liked Nordenskiöld, liked the way he was always ready to listen to their stories, the way he would question them about their experiences on northern seas. There was a good spirit aboard the *Axel Thordsen* as she cast off her moorings on June 7, 1864, about to be towed north across Tromsö Strait, toward the open sea.

It was while waiting for a favorable wind at the northern entrance of Tromsö Sound that a postal streamer, the *Nordkapp*, caught up with the little schooner. There was a sudden flurry of flags on the steamer's mast, frantically signalling for the expedition's leader to come aboard. A telegram was received in Tromsö a few hours after his departure, and the *Nordkapp's* captain thought it important enough to insist on delivering it personally. The telegram came from Finland, informing Nordenskiöld that all went well, and it was signed: 'Anna and a lively little daughter.'

After several days, the small ship sailed into the Norwegian Sea and made its first landfall at Bear Island.

Bear Island is a small, rocky piece of land, half way between Tromsö and the southern tip of the Spitsbergen archipelago. There is a Norwegian radio station on the island now, but a century ago it was barely known, and on his two previous expeditions Nordenskiöld had tried, unsuccessfully, to land there and learn something about the place. Bear Island stands like a rocky platform, with sheer cliffs 100 to 200 feet high, and even small boats find it difficult to land in the unprotected coves hollowed out by the incessant pounding of waves against its rocky ramparts. An added difficulty is created by heavy mists that surround the island through much of the summer: the meeting and mixing of warm and cold waters in the vicinity of Bear Island results in almost constant fog. As a breeding place of birds, though, Bear Island has few equals, and the chatter of birds on their nests, dipping in the offshore waters, flying back and forth, is so loud that at times it drowns out the steady noise of the breakers. The waters offshore are unusually rich in plankton, the microscopic plants and animals that fish and whales feed on, and to this day Bear Island remains a favorite with Russian and Norwegian fishermen.

Nordenskiöld and his two companions managed to land on Bear Island in June 1864. It is a desolate place, with but little vegetation, consisting of tiny clumps of grass and wildflowers that manage to gain a foothold in cracks among the rocks, protected by an overhanging boulder or rock ledge. The three scientists took some photographs that Nordenskiöld developed on the spot, using a half-ruined hut, built by stranded Russian fishermen, for a darkroom; they made a map of the island that for more than thirty years served as the base for marine charts; and they fastened a metal marker in a rock, four feet above the high tide, as a base for later measurements of the rising or sinking of the shoreline.

Leaving Bear Island after a two-day stay, the small schooner set its course for the southern tip of Spitsbergen, but ice surrounded the entire southern and eastern parts of the archipelago. There was nothing to do except wait, and the three scientists decided to fill the time with visits to the great fjords on the west side of the main island.

The *Axel Thordsen* anchored in a small cove inside Ice Fjord, one of the deep bays in western Spitsbergen, and the scientists undertook a number of excursions on land. Malmgrén collected zoological and botanical specimens, while Nordenskiöld and Dunér devoted their attention to geology and paleontology. They were especially pleased to find numerous well-preserved fossils, shells as well as parts of the skeletons of animals that were identified as belonging to the period of the great saurians.

After one of their wanderings, the scientists returning to their vessel found a British ship, the yacht *Sultana*, anchored nearby. The yacht's owner, Mr. Birkbeck, a wealthy Londoner, invited them to dine aboard, and it was quite an experience, after living in the close and crowded quarters of their small schooner, to enjoy the spacious hospitality of their neighbor. In Nordenskiöld's words, 'they had the opportunity to admire the elegance and comfort, uncommon in these latitudes, with which the *Sultana* was provided, and at the same time they were astonished at the idea of sailing in this beautiful but fragile shell through seas strewn with drift ice, without serviceable boats and other proper equipment. A collision with the smallest ice floe would have been sufficient to drive a hole in her side.'

Mr. Birkbeck and his party were interested in the opportunities for hunting and fishing offered by the remote islands of Spitsbergen. One of the guests aboard had other, scientific interests as well – the zoologist Newton from Cambridge University. When a seal was shot by the party, Newton decided to bring it over to the Swedes, to add to their collection of specimens. The crew of the *Axel Thordsen* broke out the ship's ladder to spare the visitor the trouble of climbing aboard, but it was more a nuisance than a help, and the English 'milord', as the crew referred to him, slipped and fell into the icy water. He was promptly rescued and, true to the image of the imperturbable Englishman, came aboard soaked but with his pipe still firmly clenched in his teeth. Clearly this was an unusual situation, and the visitor was offered a glass of strong spirits that set his mind at ease and allowed him to return to his quarters in an excellent mood.

By early August the offshore ice in south Spitsbergen usually melted, and the *Axel Thordsen* set sail for the Great Fjord, the deep bay on the southeast side of Spitsbergen. On the way southward they encountered a Tromsö vessel they recognized as having seen before their own departure, and though they did not expect any mail from home, they were anxious to speak to the ship, and get some news from the 'outside world'.

The men aboard the *Axel Thordsen* wanted to find out how the American Civil War was going and, a matter of even greater interest, what news there was about the war between Denmark and Prussia. Swedish neutrality was not yet firmly established, and the men wanted to find out whether Sweden had chosen to come to Denmark's aid in her unequal struggle against the military giant, Prussia.

After fighting off ice floes, the small schooner finally caught up with the Tromsö vessel, sent a boat alongside, and invited her captain to join the Swedes for a chat. There was a rule in effect in those days, forbidding the fishing vessels bound for the dangerous waters off Spitsbergen to carry any alcohol aboard, partly in response to the strong temperance movement in Norway, partly to prevent accidents arising from the liberal enjoyment of spirits. The Tromsö ship may have been in a hurry to get to its destination, but the offer of a drink induced her captain to accept the invitation. He did not have much news of the world at large to offer, but he told his hosts of Danish defeats, and of the continuing neutrality of Sweden in the conflict.

Nordenskiöld had already sent a short message to his wife with the men aboard the English yacht *Sultana*, several weeks earlier. But the yacht's return to England was subject to wind, weather, and the presence of game in Spitsbergen. The Tromsö fisherman was on his way home, with a good catch in the hold. Adolf Nordenskiöld grabbed his pen and, 'while the skipper of the Tromsö boat was fully occupied with his glass of toddy', dashed off a brief report, reassuring his wife that all was well, and telling her his plans for the remainder of August, and his hope of returning early in September to Norway.

After this short interlude, the schooner continued on its southward course, rounded the southern tip of Spitsbergen, entered the Great Fjord, and anchored near White Mountain, a landmark of the area that was chosen as one of the bases of the survey. Carrying their instruments, the party climbed with great difficulty over the rough gravel and half-frozen deep snow on the flanks of the mountain. But the view from the top was worth the effort. To the northeast, more than a hundred miles away, they could make out a sizable island dominated by twin peaks, visible across a vast expanse of impenetrable sea ice. To the north, the mountains and glaciers of Northeast Spitsbergen stood out in the clear, cold sunlight, separated from the observers by the waters of Hinloopen Strait, the divide between the two main parts of the archipelago of Spitsbergen.

Nordenskiöld and Dunér went to work with the theodolite, measuring angles and noting the results; but it was not an easy task. On the peaks they had climbed earlier, the snow had already melted and the instrument could be placed on a firm footing, using a stone or a boulder for its base. But White Mountain was still snowbound, and the observers had to build a small snowy pyramid, flatten its top, and place the instrument there in a level position. One of the observers lay flat in the snow, measuring angles on the horizon, while the other wrote down the figures in his notebook. It was hard work, made even more difficult by the icy wind that blew constantly; and after completing their work, Nordenskiöld, Dunér and Captain Hellstad were glad to pack up the instruments and return to their camp at the foot of the mountain, to enjoy a hot meal.

During their absence, the rest of the crew went out to hunt for reindeer, and the two parties reached their tents at the same time. But they did not count on an uninvited visitor: a polar bear had come upon the camp, and gave it a thorough going-over. Having carefully inspected two woollen jackets and a sleeping bag, and discarding them as unfit to eat, the bear found a whole side of roasted reindeer meat. He devoured it, not even leaving a bone, and finished off a pot of reindeer fat, carefully saved by the cook for fuel. With his appetite partially satisfied, the bear continued his investigations, tore the tent in two, left a piece of uncooked reindeer meat untouched, considering it obviously unfit to eat, opened a bag of biscuits and scattered it all over the place, and then took to his heels when he heard the approaching humans.

It took over an hour to bring some order to the chaos the bear left behind, and the men decided to set a trap for it. The solution agreed upon was to tie a string around a nicely prepared piece of meat, and the other end of the string around the ankle of the ship's cook, whose dignity was so grievously insulted by the intruder. But the cook, possibly out of fear of being carried off by the polar bear, refused; and after some talk around the campfire, everyone crawled into his sleeping bag and fell asleep.

Soon another noise was heard, a strange kind of clatter. Everyone scrambled out of the tent, only to see a huge bear scamper away, moving so fast that he was beyond rifle range before anyone could fire a shot. It was a smart enough bear, though: he finished off all the meat prepared for breakfast and for lunch for the next day, and was about to drink reindeer broth, set out to cool in metal cups, when he upset one of the cups and woke up the whole party.

The three scientists were deeply disappointed: they had already discussed the matter of disposing of the bear's skin, to be made into rugs, and looked forward to a meal of polar bear meat. But none of the Norwegian sailors would hear of eating the meat of a polar bear: they considered it dangerously poisonous, and the younger men believed that, eating it, they would turn prematurely gray. In the years since Nordenskiöld's expedition the superstitious sailors' refusal to eat polar bear meat was justified by science: it is now known that they are often infected with trichinosis, a serious disease that occurs in pigs, and presents real dangers to human beings. On at least one occasion, during the Second World War, an entire German naval crew, sent to the Arctic to establish a secret weather station, died, having contracted trichinosis in this manner.

Having completed their work, and believing that ice conditions north of

Spitsbergen were favorable, the scientists aboard the *Axel Thordsen* decided to try their luck and attempt a cruise toward the far north. But sailing along the west coast of Spitsbergen they came upon a lifeboat, loaded to the gunwhales with shipwrecked Norwegian fishermen. The men were picked up, and reported that they were only the vanguard of a much larger group, the crews of three ships crushed by ice some weeks earlier north of Spitsbergen.

Some of the shipwrecked sailors from the remaining six lifeboats were rescued by Norwegian fishing vessels, but there were still twenty-seven extra hands aboard the small schooner *Axel Thordsen*. There was barely any room to move about on board; food was running out; and there was no choice left to Nordenskiöld but to return as fast as the sails would carry them to Norway.

It was a strange journey back home, on a ship crowded far beyond its capacity with men who had had to leave their own vessels behind, with all they had caught during the season, men who had nothing but a long, hard winter to look forward to. Many of the rescued men were Lapps, who had joined the crews to earn a better living than their own bleak world of the mountains of North Norway would afford. They still wore their characteristic costumes, blue, smock-shaped jackets with striking embroidered bands, square pointed caps, baggy trousers tucked in skin boots. They could be easily set apart from Norwegians and Swedes by their speech, by their short stature and darker skin. They kept to their assigned space on deck throughout the journey, never complaining about the loss of their earnings, grateful for their rescue from the prospect of the cold and merciless winter in Spitsbergen.

The journey back to Norway took longer than the outbound trip. First, the *Axel Thordsen* ran into a storm, later, as it approached the islands off the Norwegian coast, into dense fog. The wind had died down completely, and the ship was drifting, noiselessly, seemingly without aim. There is something frightening about the fogs in the North Atlantic: one moment the sky is blue, the sun is reflected on slowly rolling seas, the birds skim along the water close to the ship. Within a matter of minutes, the fog rolls in, and the outside world disappears, leaving the ship in a thick envelope of swirling mist. The slapping of water against the timbers becomes the only sound in a gray, trackless wilderness. Even today, when ships are equipped with all manner of electronic navigation gear, they still have to slow down to a crawling pace, while the haunting sound of the foghorn warns others ships. A century ago the practice was to ring

the ship's bell every other minute; the vessel seemed to stand still, its sails slack, the men anxiously scanning the impenetrable fog.
Nordenskiöld, Dunér and Malmgren became so impatient with the fog-bound ship that they decided to strike out by rowboat for Tomsö. In this manner they covered the last sixty miles of their journey, and were happy to see the wharves, houses and the church steeple of Tromsö emerge from early morning mists. It was September 13, 1864, and Nordenskiöld's first concern was to call at the house of his good friend Ebeltoft, to get news from his family. All was well with Anna and the baby, and with his mind at ease, Nordenskiöld and his companions returned to Stockholm.

VII. THE LAST ATTEMPT TO RETURN TO FINLAND – 1866-67

The winter of 1864-1865 found Adolf Nordenskiöld back in Stockholm, busier than ever. He worked in the Museum, he lectured on chemistry at the Military College; and he spent much of his time writing up the results of the previous summer's expedition to Spitsbergen.

It was about this time that Nordenskiöld first turned his attention to a subject that was, in the years to come, to be his main interest: the history of science. History as written and taught in the 1860's dealt with the deeds of the great and famous; it chronicled battles and conquests, described treaties of peace, and discussed alliances. All in all, history paid very little attention to man's endeavors to know his world, to the lives and works of the pioneers of modern science. Yet it was precisely to this subject that Nordenskiöld adressed himself when he published a short article on the life and achievements of Carl Wilhelm Scheele. Who was Scheele, and how did Nordenskiöld, a man fully occupied with his own scientific work, happen to decide to dig up a few pertinent facts on the life of a forgotten man, who had spent much of his life as a pharmacist in an obscure Swedish town?

Adolf Nordenskiöld owed his interest in the pioneers of science to his father. Gustav Nordenskiöld studied chemistry and mineralogy in Stockholm in the early 1820's, when he met men who remembered the golden age of Swedish science, the second half of the eighteenth century. He told tales about the early Swedish men of science to his son, and as Adolf was growing up, he read in the library at Frugård the works of Linnaeus, who first developed a classification of species, of Cronstedt and Bergman, founders of mineralogy and crystallography. Later, working in Stockholm, Adolf Nordenskiöld remembered his earlier readings, and decided to find out whether any of the original papers or correspondence of these pioneers had survived. Thus it happened that he became interested in Scheele.

Carl Wilhelm Scheele lived during the second half of the eighteenth century; he never had a university education, but acquired the fundamentals of science during his training as a pharmacist. He died at the age of forty-four, in 1786; during his short life he discovered and isolated oxygen, hydrogen, barium, manganese, molybdenum, and wolfram, to name only his more important achievements. It is said of him that his record as a discoverer of new substances is unequalled, in spite of his poverty and his lack of even ordinary laboratory equipment. He spent his most productive years in a small provincial town, Köping, in central Sweden; and, though his work was recognized by his election to the Swedish Academy of Sciences, the results of his experiments took quite a long time to get into print. As a result, his work was quickly overshadowed by that of his Western European contemporaries, Priestley and Lavoisier, and he himself was quite completely forgotten. Nordenskiöld spent some thirty years searching for Scheele's writings, and finally succeeded in rehabilitating him in the eyes of the world of science.

Digging through dusty papers, consulting scientific journals that had lain untouched on library shelves for decades, Nordenskiöld became fascinated with the history of early science. Today, long after his achievements as a mineralogist have faded into insignificance, and his fame as an explorer has waned, his work in the history of science lives on.

During the following summer, in 1865, the Nordenskiöld family returned to Finland. Anna and her baby daughter spent the holidays on the Mannerheim estate. Adolf went to Frugård first, to visit his ailing father. Gustav Nordenskiöld was seventy-three years old, and though he would have liked to have wandered with his son through Finland, looking for unusual minerals, his health was failing, and for the first time Adolf went on alone, returning to the haunts of his youth.

In September, back in Stockholm, Adolf Nordenskiöld had a brand new concern: he was trying his luck as an inventor. Observing that a safe, even though burglar-proof, offered no protection in case of fire, he designed a safe with double walls, creating a vacuum between the walls. A tube, connected to a water pipe, led to the space between the walls; in case of fire, the plug of this pipe, made of a special alloy, would melt at the temperature of one hundred degrees centigrade; and the inner wall would be protected by a water jacket.The principle was very close to that employed by modern sprinkler systems, and Nordenskiöld was convinced that his fire-proof safe would be a financial success.

He did not have the capital to manufacture his invention, and turned to one of the wealthy businessmen of Stockholm, Johan Vilhelm Smitt. Smitt, some ten years Nordenskiöld's senior, had left Sweden for Argentina as a penniless youth, made a fortune there, and returning home, increased his fortune several times by investing in real estate, and becoming a partner of Alfred Nobel, the inventor of dynamite. Smitt was an amateur botanist, too; he had published a book on Scandinavian mushrooms a few years earlier; and the two men met at a scientific gathering.

Smitt liked the idea of a fire-proof safe, and decided to invest some money in it. Realizing that the Swedish market was far too small to offer real opportunities for such an invention, he invited Nordenskiöld to join him on a journey to London, there to patent the product. The two men travelled to London and obtained a British patent. It was Adolf Nordenskiöld's first visit to the British capital, and while he would have liked to have met with fellow scientists and attend scientific meetings, all of his time was taken up with business negotiations. He returned home full of optimism. Writing his father about the trip, and about the patent, he was convinced that it would yield a handsome profit, and develop into a world-wide business.

There is little of the subsequent fate of the fire-proof safe to be found in Nordenskiöld's papers. The company manufacturing it was organized in Stockholm, but the idea never caught on, and Nordenskiöld's only real gain from it was his friendship with Smitt, that was to last the rest of his life. On this, as on later occasions, Nordenskiöld's optimism proved to be far stronger than his business sense.

As the winter was closing in on Stockholm, Adolf Nordenskiöld's thoughts turned to Finland once more. Soon snow would cover the rolling plains between Helsingfors and the old estate at Frugård; the Gulf of Finland would be icebound; and he could see himself walking home from his laboratory through the dark, snowy streets of the Finnish capital. It was in this mood that he wrote his father in late November, 1865.

'Although I have been living here for nearly ten years, I consider myself a Finn, and so does my wife. We are often seized with a strong longing for home. Because of this, I have decided to return as soon as I get an opportunity to do so, and I am going to ask my brother Otto to find out about this from people at the University, but without mentioning any particular desire on my part.' He went on to say that he would accept either a University appointment or a post in the civil service, such as director of the Geological Survey; he felt that he could leave Sweden without being criticized, that his friends and associates would understand that his desire to return to Finland was stronger than his ties with Sweden.

Early the next year, Gustav Nordenskiöld died, and was mourned by his son deeply, for their relationship remained strong and close, in spite of their physical separation. But the desire of Adolf Nordenskiöld to return to Finland was not the least affected by his father's death. The time seemed right, and circumstances appeared favorable. The professorship of geology and mineralogy, for which Nordenskiöld was seriously considered before he ran afoul of the authorities and emigrated to Sweden in 1857, was still vacant. Russia's attitude toward Finland had softened: the Finnish parliament met several times in the 1860's; censorship was relaxed; and a general belief that relations with Russia were on the mend had pervaded Finland.

The university authorities considered the problem of filling the chair of geology and mineralogy, and Adolf Nordenskiöld was immediately mentioned as the outstanding candidate. Count Armfelt, who had been Vice-Chancellor of Helsingfors University, had become Secretary of State for Finland, in the imperial administration in Saint Petersburg. His successor as Vice-Chancellor, Indrenius, wrote him on March 20, 1867 that the chair of geology was still vacant and that Nordenskiöld was still very much interested in applying for the position. Count Armfelt's reply roused hopes in Nordenskiöld's friends that his appointment was very likely to be approved in Saint Petersburg, and they told him the good news.

Aware that he might well be given a chance to return to Finland and occupy the University chair he had desired all along, Adolf Nordenskiöld decided to lay his cards on the table and make clear his position, both in terms of his aims and ambitions regarding his future University career and his attitude toward Finland's Russian rulers. In a letter, dated April 18 and addressed to his friend August Ahlquist, professor of linguistics at Helsingfors University, he wrote that he was anxious to return to Finland because he felt that his presence there would contribute to the growth and flowering of scientific activity. He then proceeded to lay out a program of work for the next decade or so, that would take Finnish scientists not only to the far corners of the Russian Empire, but over the rest of the world as well.

If the government of Finland was willing to spend the sum of fifty thousand marks a year on scientific research, wrote Nordenskiöld, the equivalent of the cost of supporting one hundred soldiers, Finnish scientists could within a few years take their place in the forefront of scientific exploration and research. 'With such an annual sum supporting our work, were it properly administered, we would be able to send expeditions for the purposes of natural history, geology, geography, philology, and ethnography to all parts of the globe, and no other nation would be able to match it. In a few decades we could accumulate unique collections in natural history and ethnography at the University of Helsingfors.'

While mentioning the need to continue geodetic work, both in the Arctic and near the Equator, Nordenskiöld was especially interested in organizing expeditions to the interior of Russian Asia. 'Savage tribes are now rapidly disappearing as civilization is advancing. This makes it necessary to collect as soon as possible what is left of their languages and their customs, otherwise all knowledge of these peoples, and more importantly, of the early stages of the development of our civilizations, will disappear without a trace.'

Anticipating his friend's scepticism, Nordenskiöld added: 'You shake your head, looking at all these Utopian schemes. Often, when contemplating these goals, I do, too, but then the idea of the hundred soldiers revives my hopes. Why shouldn't we be able to make our country contribute the money equivalent to the cost of such a small force to scientific research? And if we get the money, we certainly can get the men to carry on these investigations. There is no people better fit for this work than the Finns. I tested them in Spitsbergen myself.'

Encouraged by favorable reactions from Finland, Nordenskiöld decided to take the necessary formal steps and apply for the chair of geology at Helsingfors. On June 1, he wrote to his old teacher and close friend, Professor Arppe, in Helsingfors.

'I have planned to write you for a long time, to ask for your support of my application for the professorship in Helsingfors. As the time for a decision approaches, I am full of longing for home . . . Were I to come back to my fatherland, I would work ten times as hard, and therefore I want to come home, even if it must mean a financial sacrifice.'

Realizing that his past record of being an outspoken opponent of Russian oppression would be taken into account, he wanted to assure Professor Arppe on this point. 'You asked my friend Malmgren whether I was still a *rabblerouser*. In some ways this may still be the case, but now I understand that, were I to become a Finnish subject once more, *I would have to accept Finland's present laws and international conditions as a base of my work in the future, and I do this without reservations.* I have made this quite clear to the Russian minister here in Stockholm, and he wrote to the Governor-General in Finland, reporting to him my declaration of loyalty.' In a more formal letter, addressed ten days later to Professor Arppe, Nordenskiöld repeated his pledge.

Arppe was as anxious as ever to see his best student follow in his footsteps and become a member of the Helsingfors faculty. He wrote the Secretary of State for Finland, reported Nordenskiöld's pledge of loyalty to Finnish laws, and added, 'Surely ten years' exile – during which time he brought honor to his fatherland – is sufficient to make amends for a rash moment.' The Secretary, in his answer, agreed that Nordenskiöld was indeed the outstanding candidate for the chair of geology in Helsingfors; and he, too, believed that during the ten years Nordenskiöld spent in exile he must have calmed down a great deal. However, he cautioned Professor Arppe that all was not yet in order, and that certain authorities within Finland might well object to Nordenskiöld's return. He ended by warning Arppe that, even though the University faculty voted unanimously for Nordenskiöld's appointment, their recommendations might be turned down, especially since an edict by the Emperor could be used to prevent him from taking up Finnish citizenship, having given it up at an earlier time.

While letters were going back and forth between Helsingfors and the Russian capital of St. Petersburg, Adolf Nordenskiöld was convinced that the wheels of administration were turning in the right direction, and that his appointment to the Finnish University was merely a question of time. In June, 1867, the Swedish government requested him to join the distinguished physicist Anders Ångström, on a trip to Paris. Sweden was about to go on the metric system, abandoning old local weights and measures, and the two scholars' task was to take the standard meter and kilogram kept in the Swedish capital to Paris, and compare it with the originals, made in 1791.

It was an exciting time to be in Paris, the summer of 1867. There was a World's Fair, taking place in the western part of the city, where the Eiffel Tower now stands. Napoleon III sat on the imperial throne; Offenbach's operettas were the rage; and people of means from all over Europe hurried to Paris to see and to be seen.

The two Swedish scientists arrived in Paris in August, to find that their colleagues, like many Parisians, were on vacation, and that they were in for a long wait. It was a pleasant wait, though, filled with excursions to the World's Fair, visits to the theater, lunches and dinners with old friends from home and with new acquaintances from among French scientists. Yet all this time Finland was on Nordenskiöld's mind.

Anna Nordenskiöld spent the summer in Finland, with her mother, and Adolf wrote her: 'Were I to be appointed to the chair in Helsingfors, I plan to come to Finland as soon as I return from here to Stockholm.' Later, he wrote that he was certain that his appointment would be made in mid-October. He added: 'I am so determined to move to Finland that even if they offered me a beautiful villa in the best suburb of Paris, and enough money to lead a life without worries, I would still prefer a country place in Finland!'

Little did he suspect that, several months earlier, the Finnish authorities had already decided to veto his appointment. Count Adlerberg, Governor-General of Finland, wrote to the Secretary of State for Finland in St. Petersburg on June 4, 1867: 'The Chief of Police told me that he had reported to the Minister of Interior in St. Petersburg on the danger of allowing Nordenskiöld to return to Finland. You know how I feel about this matter: rather than allowing individuals of this type to return, we ought to be grateful to be rid of them. Professor Arppe, the Rector of the University, says that he will be responsible for Nordenskiöld's conduct, but the Vice-Chancellor refuses to accept this statement. Frankly, it would be best if Nordenskiöld's appointment would be rejected by the highest authority in St. Petersburg, rather than by me, since I would then be accused of opposing the present liberal trend in the administration.'

The Governor-General pointed out that three scientists had applied for the appointment, that two had been eliminated by the University faculty, and that Nordenskiöld was the unanimous choice. He considered this a deliberate insult to the authorities and added: 'If we allowed Nordenskiöld to return and to take this appointment, even if he were to behave himself in the future in the best possible manner, the very fact of his return might result in a popular demonstration that would harm the government.'

Opposed by the police, Adolf Nordenskiöld did not have a chance. Rather than admit that it was the word of the police that overrode the views of the University, the Vice-Chancellor advised the University on November 21, 1867, that since Nordenskiöld moved to Sweden and entered in the service of the Swedish government, and therefore ceased to enjoy the rights of Finnish citizenship, he could not be readmitted to that citizenship, and, hence, was ineligible for the appointment.

Nordenskiöld returned from Paris, having accomplished his mission, at the end of September. Two months later, he received word from Finland that his appointment was turned down, and saw his last hope of returning to his homeland shattered. There is no written evidence of his disappointment, of his bitterness. But it cannot have lasted long, for within a matter of weeks he turned his thoughts to the future. Sweden was to be his home, henceforth his base for work, for explorations. There was work to be done in the Arctic, and it was to another Arctic voyage that Adolf Nordenskiöld devoted all his energy during the winter of 1867-1868.

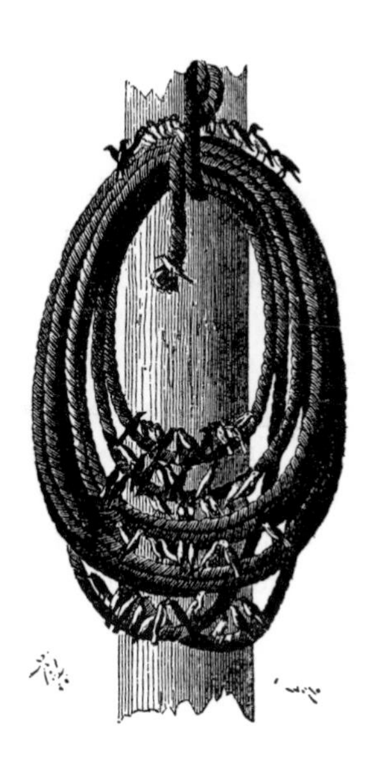

VIII. SOFIA'S JOURNEY: AN ARCTIC RECORD – 1868

The task of finding support for another expedition to the Arctic must have seemed difficult even to a man of Nordenskiöld's enthusiasm and optimism. When the Swedish parliament provided a modest sum for the support of his 1864 expedition to Spitsbergen, it became quite clear that no further support could be expected from that source. The leaders of government and of the scientific community of Stockholm were unanimous in their opinion that Sweden simply could not afford to finance any more Arctic adventures, even though the support given to Nordenskiöld and to Torell in 1858 and 1861 was so skimpy as to oblige the scientific staff to pay their own expenses. Clearly, the government could not be counted on. Nordenskiöld had to turn elsewhere if he wanted to continue his work in the Arctic.

Help came from an unexpected quarter, from the business community. The ten years that had passed since Nordenskiöld first settled in Stockholm, had been years of change. During that decade the first steps were taken that transformed Sweden from a backward, slow-moving, old-fashioned country of peasants, small businessmen, and conservative civil servants into one of the most advanced industrial societies of our world. These changes took place in the realms of politics and business. Adolf Nordenskiöld took part in the process of political change, and benefited immensely from the growth of the Swedish business community.

The great change in Swedish politics was the replacement of the old *Riksdag*, the parliament composed of the four estates of nobles, clergy, burghers and farmers, by a modern parliament composed of an upper and lower chamber. The House of Nobility, after years of arguing the question of parliamentary reform, voted itself out of existence in 1865, thus paving the way for elections to the new legislative bodies. Nordenskiöld, who had served in the House of Nobility during its last few years of existence, voted for parliamentary reform, for a legislature elected by direct suffrage: this was in accord with his own ideas of a liberal society.

As far as Sweden's economy was concerned, neutrality, maintained ever since the Napoleonic Wars, made a big difference. Whereas Sweden throughout much of the seventeenth and eighteenth centuries devoted the greater part of its resources and manpower to wars, neutrality, gradually accepted by all Swedes as one of the guiding principles of the country's foreign policy, reduced military expenses to a much lower level than in earlier periods, and allowed other uses to be made of state funds thus available.

There was an equally significant change in the economic structure of the country. Mining and industry did play an important part in the economy of those regions endowed with metals and minerals. The rest of Sweden remained a land of farmers, most of whom eked out a poor living from the skimpy harvests of their stony acres. Sweden's great forests, and the minerals that lay below the surface in the vast North country, were untouched until the second half of the nineteenth century. In 1850, Swedish industrial output lagged far behind England, Belgium, Germany and France, the advanced industrial countries of Western Europe.

But modern industry was making headway in Sweden. Railroads started in the mid-1850's, iron and steel, wood products and textiles, machines and ships were beginning to be produced in Swedish plants. Some of this business activity took place in Stockholm, but the true headquarters of the Swedish business community was Göteborg. There, in the southwest of Sweden, was the country's only ice-free port, giving direct access to the Atlantic Ocean, opening Sweden's doors to world trade. There, new enterprises were launched, shipyards, factories, breweries, banks. Göteborg was the home of Sweden's first business tycoons.

It was to the prosperous businessmen of Göteborg that Adolf Nordenskiöld adressed his plea, asking for support of an expedition to the Arctic. He did not even have to make a direct appeal, for he had the good will and support of the representative of Sweden's government in Göteborg county, Governor Count Albert Ehrensvärd. To enlist Ehrensvärd's support and, through his help, the financial sponsorship of the Göteborg business leaders, Nordenskiöld appealed to their sense of pride in Scandinavian seamanship. He pointed out that England, France and Germany were all ready to field an expedition to the Arctic. Could Sweden afford to be left out of the race?

'We, and only we, can organize a scientific expedition where everyone, from the commander to the cabin boy, is so familiar with the weather and the ice of the Arctic seas that he can face their difficulties and dangers with complete confidence.' So wrote Nordenskiöld in a memorandum adressed to Count Ehrensvärd, to be circulated among Göteborg businessmen. Within a matter of a few days, Nordenskiöld's modest request was oversubscribed by half again as large a sum. He had only asked for enough money to hire a fishing vessel in Tromsö, the sum made available allowed him to make his dream come true, to face the Arctic in a steamship.

In his autobiography, Nordenskiöld wrote that the business leaders of Göteborg responded at once to his appeal. The largest amount contributed towards the costs of the 1868 expedition was from Oscar Dickson, head of the Göteborg firm of James Dickson and Company. In July, 1868, before Nordenskiöld sailed for Spitsbergen, he dined in Göteborg with Count Ehrensvärd and the merchant magnates who had so generously given their support to the expedition. Oscar Dickson and Adolf Nordenskiöld met for the first time that day, and the lives of both men were changed because of their association with each other. Dickson became Nordenskiöld's principal supporter for the next fifteen years, and some of the glory earned by Nordenskiöld was reflected on his sponsor.

Oscar Dickson was an unusual type of businessman. His father James came to Sweden from his native Scotland, in the early years of the 19th century, and built a sizable fortune in shipping and wholesale trade. Oscar, born in 1823, entered the family business when he was eighteen years old, and in six years was promoted to the post of general manager of the Dickson enterprises in northern Sweden. The Dickson family were the first to invest in the opening of northern Sweden, especially of its immense and largely untouched stands of timber. Starting in the early 1850's they bought up large tracts of forest, built saw mills on the Baltic, and became the greatest single industrial concern of Sweden's northland. Under the management of Oscar Dickson, the family business prospered and in those days of low taxes a huge fortune accumulated in his hands. But Oscar Dickson never concerned himself solely with the day by day running of the many enterprises under his command. He had other ambitions, and preferred to see himself in the role of a true captain of industry, a statesman on intimate terms with royalty, a benefactor of the arts and sciences. Some years before he and Nordenskiöld had met, Dickson had married Countess von Rosen, daughter of a distinguished nobleman, and thus gained entry into the world of aristocracy. Hearing of the plans of a Swedish scientist who wished to explore the Arctic, Dickson seized on the occasion to make a major contribution to science. It fitted his concept of a modern-day Maecenas, a true philanthropist supporting a deserving cause.

Nordenskiöld, having obtained funds to finance a northern expedition, wasted little time to round up further support. Count von Platen, Minister of the Swedish Navy, looked upon a scientific expedition to northern seas an an excellent means to offer unusual seagoing experiences to the officers and enlisted men under his command. When Nordenskiöld submitted a request to the Navy Department, strongly supported by the Academy of Sciences, asking that a government-owned steamer be made available for the expedition, both the Minister of the Navy and the Chief of Naval Operations gave their full support. Within ten days, Nordenskiöld was notified that a postal steamer, originally built for service between south Sweden and Germany in Baltic waters, was placed at the expedition's disposal.

Sofia, the postal steamer made available by the government, was built four years earlier by a Swedish shipyard. Rigged as a brigantine, with an engine of nearly 270 horsepower, it was the most powerful vessel Nordenskiöld had been able to use in his Arctic explorations. But the Navy's help did not stop at putting a ship at his service. Baron Fredrik Wilhelm von Otter, one of the Navy's most promising younger officers, was given command of the ship. Von Otter, who reached the rank of full captain at the unusually early age of thirty-five, turned out to be an exceptionally capable man, whose action saved ship and crew at a critical moment during the voyage. His second-in-command was a young Navy lieutenant, Louis Palander, who was to be associated with Nordenskiöld on a later voyage, that of the *Vega.* The crew of 14 seamen consisted of volunteers from the Navy.

Besides Nordenskiöld, there were seven scientists aboard *Sofia,* zoologists, botanists, physicists, and a ship's doctor. This was the first time Adolf Nordenskiöld did not have to save and skimp, the sum put at his disposal allowed for all expenses connected with the voyage. As for the purpose of the trip, while all scientists aboard hoped to add to the already existing collections of fossil and living plants, of marine life, of rocks, kept in Stockholm, what they really hoped was to sail further north than any ship had been able to do before them.

The nature of the area surrounding the North Pole was still a mystery in the 1860's. Although the majority of scientists believed that Spitsbergen and Greenland represented the northernmost land masses in the Arctic Ocean, no one had sailed far enough north to prove or disprove the theory. On two previous occasions Nordenskiöld had attempted to do so. He and Torell were repelled by unfavorable weather and ice conditions in 1861, and in 1864 his encounter with the shipwrecked Norwegian sailors made him give up his attempt to sail northward, in order to bring the men he had rescued back to Norway. 1868 looked like the year to try for the big prize, to take a long look at the heart of the Arctic Ocean. He had an iron ship, powered by a steam engine and not dependent on wind; if he waited until the pack ice melted sufficiently, in late summer, to allow a push northward, he might reach a higher latitude than any man before him.

Nordenskiöld believed that, during the month of September, the waters north of Spitsbergen were likely to be icefree to a large extent. His reasoning was based on the observation that during the polar summer a sizable part of the ice was likely to melt, that another part of the ice was broken up by continuing action of waves, and that the Arctic current, southward bound between Spitsbergen and Greenland, was carrying much of the remaining polar pack ice with it. What he did not realize at the time, since no one had then penetrated the eastern reaches of the Arctic Ocean, was that other currents from the waters north of Siberia flowed westward towards Spitsbergen, carrying large amounts of ice, that replaced, as it were, whatever ice was lost due to melting, wave action, or southbound currents. Unaware of this, Nordenskiöld prepared for a northward push as far as the ice would allow.

The Academy of Sciences in Stockholm provided the necessary instruments; enough food was put aboard to allow for spending the winter in the north if the ship were to be frozen in, and when the last item of importance, concentrated lemon juice, arrived from England, *Sofia* sailed from Göteborg on July 7, 1868. A fortnight earlier, Anna's second child, a boy, had been born, and Adolf Nordenskiöld's last letter to her before leaving for the Arctic dealt with the choice of the boy's godfathers.

After touching Spitsbergen's coast in several places, *Sofia* attempted to sail westward, to reach Greenland. Ice stopped the attempt, and the ship returned to the northern shores of Spitsbergen. There, a small Norwegian vessel brought a load of coal for the burners, four of the scientists left the group, returning to Norway, and *Sofia* turned northeast, to try its luck.

There were ships aplenty in those northern waters. No less than twenty-five fishing and sealing ships from Norway cruised in the Arctic north of Spitsbergen, there was a small English team looking over the scene, and a German expedition, having tried earlier to reach Greenland from Spitsbergen, got as far north as latitude 81 degrees and 4 minutes, before turning back. The time was ripe to make the final push.

Well bunkered with coal, *Sofia* turned north from Spitsbergen on September 16, and two days later, on September 18, Captain von Otter, having taken sights twice, had the Swedish flag hauled to the top of the mast, and fired a salvo from the small gun aboard. They reached the latitude of 81 degrees and 42 minutes north, further than any ship had ever been before.

In his report, Captain von Otter described the occasion: 'I consider the honor of the flag to have been maintained, since we reached a point where I took a noonday reading of the sun from the deck of a ship at a place four hundred nautical miles from the Pole, something no one has done before . . . We could not have reached this latitude without breaking ice floes in many places where a sailing vessel could never have gotten through. When we stopped, there was no open channel in sight, nor was there any sign of water reflected on the sky. And when *Sofia* had reached her place of honor, at 81 degrees and 42 minutes, I dare say a man with a boat hook could have walked on ice floes six miles in any direction.'

Two of the scholars who took part in the expedition, published a brief description of the journey the following year, 1869. In it, they pointed out that to reach the North Pole man will have to make the final push on foot, across the frozen surface of the polar seas, or else a flying machine will have to be invented to accomplish the task. More than half a century was to pass before the American flyer, Richard E. Byrd, became the first man to fly over the North Pole. He, too, chose Spitsbergen as his starting point, and took off for his pioneer flight from Kingsbay, on the west coast of the archipelago.

Sofia did penetrate the icepack farther than any ship before, but Nordenskiöld was not yet satisfied. Winter was beginning to show its strength, days were getting shorter, it was cold on the little ship's deck, cold even in the crowded cabins below. But there were enough supplies for the twenty people aboard to take the risk of being frozen in for the season. During the first week of October, *Sofia* sailed once more north from Spitsbergen, attempting to surpass its earlier record.

Luck was not with them this time. On the morning of October 4, a storm churned up the seas and as the steamer was rolling in a sea filled with blocks of ice, a large icefloe hit the starboard side, and stove a sizeable hole below the waterline, in the aft hold where coal was kept. Captain von Otter had the hole temporarily closed, to avoid taking on more water, and *Sofia's* course was set for the nearest point on Spitsbergen's north shore.

Dr. Nyström, the ship's physician, gave a much more detailed account of the event. 'The storm was raging, shaking tackle and rigging, and *Sofia*, like a hunted stag with a deadly wound in its side, was hurrying, with all sails set and engines pounding, for the nearest haven. There was no time to waste, it was a question of survival. More steam! More sails! came the orders from the bridge. A giant wave approaches, breaks over the bow, and throws its mass of water against the sails, making the ship heel over, until the water runs off over the topsail, while the rest of the water sweeps over the afterdeck. All this time the ship is leaning over to the side where the leak is, and water is pushed in with greater pressure. We are about one hundred miles from the nearest harbor. Water is rising below deck, and beginning to penetrate into the boilers. We cut a hole in the deck, trying to get a pump working, without success.'

In the end, it was a bucket brigade that saved *Sofia*. A pencil sketch, made by one of the men aboard and still in the von Otter family's possession, shows all hands busily dipping their buckets in the water covering much of the aft hold, passing it on up to the deck.. 'Hold on, fellows!' – shouted von Otter – 'a few more hours and we shall reach a harbor.' It took eleven hours, for scientists, officers, enlisted men, standing in ice-cold water up to their knees, to keep the ship afloat, until they reached safety at Smeerenberg Bay, in northern Spitsbergen. After a warm meal, and some sleep, the ship got under way again, and made it to Kingsbay, on the west coast. There it was beached, and the ship's carpenter repaired the gaping hole in her side.

The season was late, for *Sofia* did not leave Kingsbay in western Spitsbergen until October 12, but Nordenskiöld was anxious to make one more attempt to penetrate northeastward, to learn more about fall conditions of the seas around Spitsbergen. But the pack ice was closing in, deck and rigging were shrouded in ice, and there was nothing left but to turn southward, to Norway. On October 20 the little steamer was welcomed with open arms in Tromsö, supplies and coal were taken aboard, and on November 15 *Sofia* made her triumphal entry into Göteborg harbor.

The 1868 Arctic expedition made Adolf Nordenskiöld world famous for the first time. His earlier work in mineralogy had been well received, the collections he and his fellow scientists had brought back from the expeditions of 1858, 1861 and 1864 were truly valuable as the basis for detailed studies of the world of the Arctic. But it was the bravery of the small band of Scandinavians, aboard a cockleshell of a steamer, flinging themselves against the full fury of the Arctic to achieve an impressive record of penetrating further north than any man before, that caught the world's imagination.

Nordenskiöld's achievements were recognized throughout the world of science. The Royal Geographical Society of England, foremost advocate of polar research, awarded him its Founder's Medal. The citation, read by the famed explorer Sir Roderick Murchison, summed up Nordenskiöld's achievements:

'The Founder's Medal has this year been awarded to Professor Nordenskiöld, of Stockholm, for having performed a leading part in designing and carrying out the late Swedish expeditions to Spitsbergen, by which not only has our knowledge of the geography of that part of the world been much improved and illustrated by an excellent new map of those islands, but whereby great additions have been made to our acquaintance with the zoology, botany, geology and meteorology of the Arctic Region.'

King Carl XV of Sweden made it known that he wished to bestow open Adolf Nordenskiöld the order of the North Star. But the offer was politely declined: Nordenskiöld said that his belief in a free society of equals prevented him from accepting any decorations from his sovereign. Yet the following year he did accept a decoration from the King of Italy, believing that this was a recognition of his work by a foreign country, rather than a royal gesture from the throne.

In his autobiography, Nordenskiöld paid full tribute to the superb seamanship of Captain von Otter to whom, he said, all aboard owed their lives. He added that *Sofia*, built for commerce in the Baltic, was certainly not strong enough to withstand a storm in polar seas, sailing in the dark, surrounded by ice floes. To tackle those dangers, he wrote, and to make another, perhaps more succesful attempt to approach the North Pole, a stronger vessel would be needed, built to withstand the pressure of the ice pack, and well provisioned with food and coal. Obviously, he was planning his next polar expedition.

This time, Adolf Nordenskiöld could and did plan ahead, secure in the knowledge that financial support would be available for his efforts. Less than a year after his return from the recordbreaking journey aboard *Sofia*, he received word from the most generous contributor to the 1868 expedition, Oscar Dickson. Dickson offered to bear part of the cost of a new expedition to Spitsbergen, one that was to spend the winter there, and attempt to reach the Pole the following spring, using sleds across the polar icecap.

IX. THE FIRST TRIP TO GREENLAND – 1870

Oscar Dickson's offer to contribute to the expenses of a new Arctic expedition was exciting news to Nordenskiöld. But it was characteristic of him to have put even such an important matter aside, to engage wholeheartedly in a totally different pursuit, campaigning in a parliamentary election.

There never was any doubt of Adolf Nordenskiöld's complete devotion to his scientific interests. Yet at the same time, he managed to become involved with many other matters, and plunged into pursuits other than scientific, though he always returned after a few weeks or months to his laboratory and to his study.

1869 was a momentous year in Swedish history: for the second time, members of parliament were to be elected by direct suffrage, under the terms of the reform laws passed four years earlier. Nordenskiöld decided to take full part in the electoral campaign, he spoke on behalf of liberal candidates throughout the city, and was quickly identified as a 'fighting liberal'. This, and the fact that the success of his 1868 polar expedition made him one of the best-known men in Stockholm, led to his nomination on the liberal slate. Much to his own surprise, he was elected, and served the first of his several terms in the lower house of the Swedish *Riksdag*.

Being a liberal meant that he was regarded as a potentially dangerous radical by the more sedate members of the Swedish upper class. As he puts it in his autobiography, the 'neo-liberal society' he belonged to was a sleepy, rather inactive group, more devoted to discussions than to action. Universal suffrage, the right for labor to organize, minimum working hours, these demands were barely visible on the distant political horizon. When it came to action in parliament, very little was actually accomplished. In Nordenskiöld's words, when, confronted with the list of their supposed misdeeds, the liberals could rightfully say: 'Hell's bells, did we do *all* that?'

Being a Member of Parliament was an honor to Adolf Nordenskiöld, an expression of the faith of his fellow citizens in his integrity. But, though he was re-elected several times to the *Riksdag*, he remained a 'backbencher', preoccupied mostly with legislation that was directly concerned with higher education and with the state's role in scientific matters. He continued to work in his laboratory, riding herd on the collections in the Museum, teaching chemistry at the Military Academy, and lecturing in geology and mineralogy at the School of Engineering. Yet with all this,

his heart was in polar research. The success of his expedition in 1868 and recognition by fellow-scientists was encouragement enough. What was even more important, he realized that, for the first time, he no longer needed to worry about financial support. He had found a true *Maecenas*, the man he described as grandiose and generous, Oscar Dickson.

In the fall of 1869, when the electoral campaign was over, Adolf Nordenskiöld sat down in his laboratory and sketched out a plan for a new assault on the North Pole. Encouraged by Dickson's continuing interest, he sent the plan to him, and asked for a forthright appraisal. On December 8, 1869, Dickson responded.

Dickson was enthusiastic about the possibility of a new polar expedition. 'As I understand it, this new expedition will cost more than any of the earlier ones, and therefore it will be necessary to make every possible effort to have the costs underwritten. But these efforts will need to be supported by a detailed plan, including an approximate budget. I am convinced of one thing, though, and can certainly convince others of it, that with the generous sources of support available here we have a greater chance of success than any other nation. Now or never is the time to attempt to reach the Pole!'

A few days later, Dickson took a searching look at Nordenskiöld's proposal and his tentative budget. The plan for the new expedition was to establish a land base on one of the islands off North Spitsbergen, spend the winter there making scientific observations, and as soon as weather permitted, making a dash northward, across the polar ice, with the North Pole as the ultimate objective.

Nordenskiöld set up a tentative budget of 70,000 Swedish riksdaler. Dickson offered to subscribe nearly one-third of the total costs, 20,000 riksdaler, and to help enlist the support of others. However, he made his contribution dependent on a matching contribution from the Treasury. Taking the government's support of the 1868 expedition as a precedent, when a state-owned steamship was put at Nordenskiöld's disposal, together with officers and men, Oscar Dickson suggested that the Treasury and Navy Departments repeat this gesture, and provide the expedition with a ship, its crew, and necessary supplies.

To make a dash across the polar icecap required sleds, and animals to draw the sleds. The expedition could not depend on hunting as a means of getting food; instead, they would have to use draught animals that could be killed, and their flesh used for food, if the need arose. The draught animal generally used in Northern Europe was the reindeer, while in Greenland dogs were employed to drag sleds. Thus, the first question confronting Nordenskiöld was that of the choice between reindeer or dogs.

Since the choice was of the greatest importance to the expedition, Dickson offered the services of his own employees, stationed throughout northern Sweden, to inquire about the reindeer's carrying capacity, his endurance, his needs of fodder, and even the amount of meat a reindeer would yield when slaughtered. Questionnaires were sent out to a number of people in Lapland, where most of Sweden's reindeer live, and the returns were most encouraging.

Reindeer when dragging sleds are usually harnessed in single file, and can cover anywhere from thirteen to thirty miles in a day. They depend on moss as a fodder, supplemented by coarse grain; they need freedom to browse when not working, since keeping them in an enclosure may induce sickness; they can swim across water; and last but not least, a full-grown reindeer may yield over one hundred pounds of meat when butchered.

The prospects of using reindeer were bright indeed, but to find out about Eskimo dogs it was necessary to go to Greenland. Dickson offered to pay the expenses of a trip to Greenland by Nordenskiöld, and for good measure added to it a sum sufficient for the travel of at least three other scientists. Important as it was to investigate the question of using dogs, Nordenskiöld was not the man to let the opportunity to visit a part of the polar world unknown to him slip by without carrying out some scientific work.

Greenland was a Danish possession, its trade being administered by a state-owned company that bought up Greenland's few products, mostly whale meat and eider down, and in turn supplied guns and ammunition, tea, coffee, sugar and other staples to the Eskimo and to the Danish administrators residing on the island. Small Danish sailing ships, taking several weeks for the journey, provided the only available means of transportation to Greenland. The Danish government, when approached by Nordenskiöld, promptly assured him that transportation was going to be available for himself and for his colleagues.

The principal purpose of the journey was to interview people in Greenland on the subject of the fitness of dogs for a journey towards the Pole. In addition, Nordenskiöld planned to have one of his colleagues, the botanist Berggren, do some work on the vegetation of the Greenland coast, while the two others, geologists Öberg and Nordström, were to assist in determining exact locations for a number of places the group was to visit, to collect fossil plants and animals, and to gather samples of the fauna and flora of the waters surrounding Greenland. The Swedish Navy loaned the necessary equipment to take samples from the sea, and the Swedish Academy of Sciences provided chronometers and astronomical instruments.

In the midst of his preparations for the trip, Nordenskiöld received yet another honor for the achievements of his work in the Arctic. Early in 1870, Alexandre de la Roquette founded a special gold medal, to be awarded by the Paris Geographical Society to those who made the most significant contributions to the knowledge of the Arctic. On April 21, the Society selected Nordenskiöld as the first recipient of the Roquette Medal, for his explorations in Spitsbergen and in the Arctic Ocean.

On May 15, 1870, Nordenskiöld and his three companions sailed from Copenhagen aboard the Danish brig 'Whale' for Greenland. It was a long and troublesome trip, the ship had to hove to for a fortnight off Greenland's southern tip to ride out a severe storm. They finally landed at Godhavn, on the west coast, on July 2.

Conversations with the resident Danish officials soon convinced Nordenskiöld that using Eskimo dogs on his projected polar journey was virtually impossible. No single settlement in Greenland could sell him enough dogs, and if he purchased them from several places, there was the dangerous possibility that one or more of the animals might be infected with distemper. An outbreak of the disease had recently taken place in Greenland, there was no cure for it, and if only one animal was a carrier, all others could be infected and the entire pack would be wiped out. The official purpose of the journey was thus accomplished, and the scientists could devote the rest of the summer to their studies.

Nordenskiöld's main interest was to explore as much of the interior of Greenland as was possible for a small party. It was a strange fact that, even though Europeans had lived on the island's coast for centuries, no one had ever attempted to penetrate inland. The vast glaciers, visible from the coast, looked forbidding enough, but there was also the attitude of the Eskimo who regarded the inland region with a kind of fear, as the abode of evil spirits. A Danish merchant had attempted to explore the inland area, in 1751, but had turned back within less than ten miles of the coastline: neither he nor his party were properly equipped, and the nights were so cold that, without the protection of tents or sleeping bags, they risked dying from exposure. Three years before Nordenskiöld's arrival, the well-known British mountain climber, Edward Whymper, had started out with sleds drawn by dogs towards the interior, but had turned back within a few miles of the coast, because the dogs could not negotiate the difficult terrain.

When Nordenskiöld consulted senior Danish officials in Copenhagen, men who spent many years in Greenland, it was their unanimous opinion that a journey to the inland ice region was impossible. To refuse to believe men with extensive experience and thus to risk possible disaster was not Nordenskiöld's way. But neither was he prepared to take these opinions at their full face value: he compromised by asking the two geologists in the party to concentrate on geological studies along the coast, while he and the botanist attempted what he called 'a little excursion on the ice.'

The Danish officials helped the party hire whale-boats, and men to row, and on July 19, having selected what seemed a favorable spot where climbing over the sheer wall of ice was possible, Nordenskiöld, Berggren, and two Eskimo started on the journey inland.

The four men carried their food and their sleeping bags on a sled, but the labor of proceeding over the rough surface of ice, climbing over ridges and then sliding down on the far side, made them decide to leave the sled behind and to carry food and equipment on their backs. After crossing an area of deep clefts and crevasses, they came out on a plateau, 250 meters, 800 feet above sea level. The surface of the ice resembled that of a stormy sea that suddenly was frozen stiff, with short yet steep ridges and shallow depressions, occupied by small ponds that had to be avoided, making for very slow progress.

The weather was clear, temperatures in the shade near freezing while in the sun the thermometer would register between 24 and 27 degrees Celsius, 75 to 80 degrees Fahrenheit. But nights were cold, the temperature always dropped to or below freezing, and since the party had no tents and only two sleeping bags for four people, they got but little sleep. What rest they enjoyed was mostly at mid-day, in full sunlight, while the two scientists took observations of elevation and latitude, to measure the distance they had covered from their starting point on the coast.

Before starting out Nordenskiöld pointed out, in mock seriousness, that the Greenland icecap was a most inappropriate place for a botanist, since it was known to be devoid of any vegetation. But the botanist's keen eye soon discovered on the ice, and in a layer of grey dust that occurred nearly everywhere on the surface, a brownish alga. This microscopic form of plant life plays an important part in the life cycle of the icecap, for through its absorption of solar radiation it exudes warmth and creates deep holes in the ice, thereby hastening its melting. Thus the presence of lakes, ponds, valleys and waterfalls in the icecap can be explained in part.

After two days, the two Eskimo decided that they had gone far enough, and returned to the coast. By that time the small party had reached a point 1400 feet above sea level, and Nordenskiöld decided to push further inland. He and Berggren spent the night at the place where the Eskimo had left them and started out in the morning. The majesty and loneliness of the icecap were truly impressive: except for a couple of crows they saw on the morning of the third day, there was no trace of any living thing. Yet it was not a silent world: by bending close to the ice surface, they could hear a humming noise, the sound of water running underneath the ice. Occasionally there was a loud, single report like the shot of a cannon, as a new crevasse opened in the ice.

After continuing inland for another day and a half, the two scientists were running out of food and decided to turn back, having reached a distance of some thirty miles from their starting point, at an altitude of 2200 feet. Soon thereafter, they came to a large, deep, and broad stream of water, flowing rapidly between clear banks of blue ice. The stream was far too wide to ford, but since they did not meet any water course of this size on their inland journey, the two men decided that it had to become an underground river further on. Following the current downstream, they heard a distant roar, and found the place where the entire mass of water tumbled down a perpendicular slope into depths below, allowing them to cross and proceed on their way.

A short distance further, they saw a column of vapour rising from the ice, and assumed it to be yet another great waterfall. They did find another stream, whose waters fell down deep below the ice, yet there was no splash that rebounded from the depth, to account for the column of vapour that was visible from the distance. Instead an intermittent jet of water, mixed with air, arose from a small hole in the ice, within a few feet of the waterfall, creating what appeared to be very like a geyser. Only here it was water and ice that was responsible for the phenomenon, rather than the action of volcanoes, as in Iceland.

Nordenskiöld and Berggren's 'little excursion on the ice' resulted in interesting observations on the weather conditions found there, as well as the collection of samples of the tiny algae and the fine dust covering parts of the icecap. During their absence, their colleagues had been busy gathering specimens of marine life, and fossil plants from the cliffs and tiny plains along the coast. There was one other matter that claimed Nordenskiöld's attention: he was anxious to collect meteorites that, so he assumed, would be found in the central section of Greenland's west coast.

Offering a reward to any Eskimo who would bring such specimens to his attention, he was delighted to get word that large meteorites could be found on the west coast of Disko Island, a short distance from the expedition's base. Upon his arrival, he found a group of huge stones, the largest of them weighing twenty-five tons. Excited as he was about his find, Nordenskiöld was unable either to move these enormous stones, or to transport them back to Europe. The following year, after long negotiations with the Danish government, two Swedish warships were sent to Greenland, under Captain von Otter's command, to bring the stones back. The largest is still on display in front of the National Museum of Natural History; its arrival in Stockholm harbor, and its subsequent journey across the capital aboard a specially constructed carriage, was a minor sensation.

With his customary tact, and his strong feeling for Scandinavian unity, Nordenskiöld arranged to have the two lesser stones delivered to other Nordic capitals. One is in Copenhagen, the other, in Helsingfors, on display to this day.

There were no telegraph lines between Greenland and Europe in 1870, communications depended on the slow sailing vessels that linked Greenland to Denmark. In early September, Nordenskiöld and his colleagues had just finished dinner and were enjoying coffee and cigars in the home of a Danish official, when an Eskimo came into view in the water below, paddling his kayak in obvious hurry. He brought a telegram forwarded to the Swedish expedition: six weeks earlier, France and Prussia had gone to war.

Though Sweden was officially neutral, the party had but one thought, to return home and find out what was happening in Europe. Nordenskiöld left immediately for the nearest harbor by rowboat and after waiting for a fortnight for favorable wind, sailed aboard a Danish vessel for Europe. He landed at Helsingör on the second of November, to find that the fighting in France was virtually over. On the very day the Eskimo kayak rider had brought him word of the hostilities, the bulk of the French forces had surrendered at Sedan, Napoleon III had abdicated, and France had become a Republic. Heavy of heart over France's defeat, yet happy to see that Sweden once more was spared from going to war, Nordenskiöld returned home.

The scientific results of the work of the small party of scholars who had spent the summer of 1870 in Greenland were out of all proportion to the modest size of the staff and the expenses involved. The specimens of fossil flora gathered by the expedition were analyzed and described by the Swiss paleontologist, Heer. The marine specimens collected by the group were used to introduce an entirely new approach to marine biology in those far northern waters. Last but not least, Nordenskiöld was thoroughly convinced that Eskimo dogs could not be relied upon as draught animals for an expedition tackling the polar ice, and decided to use reindeer on his projected expedition to reach the North Pole.

X. OBJECTIVE: THE NORTH POLE – 1872

During the long voyage home from Greenland, Adolf Nordenskiöld prepared his report on the work he and his colleagues had accomplished during the summer of 1870. He also sent a résumé of the report to Oscar Dickson, who had provided all the money for the Greenland expedition.

Within a matter of days Dickson replied to the letter, congratulating Nordenskiöld on the impressive scientific results of his journey to Greenland. Dickson went on to assure Nordenskiöld that, though the expenses for the Greenland journey exceeded the budget, he would be glad to cover the deficit until Nordenskiöld could sell some of the specimens he had brought back, converting them into cash. Most importantly, Dickson expressed delight at the confident tone of Nordenskiöld's plans for the expedition to the North Pole, and reassured him of his continuing support.

Much of Adolf Nordenskiöld's time and energy during the year and a half following his return from Greenland was devoted to preparation for the big push to the Pole. By the summer of 1871, financial support from private sources was subscribed to the extent of nearly 50,000 kronor, a substantial sum for the time. A manuscript note in his papers indicates that Oscar Dickson alone offered 20,000 kronor, while two of Dickson's brothers added 5,000 apiece. David Carnegie, owner of Göteborg's leading brewery, subscribed another 5,000 kronor, and a number of Göteborg businessmen and firms made up the rest.

On the strength of this impressive showing of private support, Nordenskiöld addressed the Swedish government on December 15, 1871, requesting its backing for the enterprise. The burden of the request was for a postal steamer, similar to *Sofia,* the ship that made the successful push into the polar ice in 1868, for officers and sailors from the Navy to man the ship, as well as for supplies for a voyage to last at least fifteen months.

'It is my plan' – wrote Nordenskiöld to the government – 'to put up a house on Parry Island, at latitude 80 degrees 40 minutes north, off the north coast of Spitsbergen, a spot I consider the best location in the entire area. The house is planned to be large enough to house twenty or so men, including scientists, officers, and crew. We shall winter there and early in the spring we shall push on northwards, to the Pole if possible, using sleds on the ice.

Our scientific objectives include meteorological and magnetic observations, to be made throughout our stay. Our proposed winter quarters are further north than any before, and weather observations taken at this high latitude will be of vital importance to our knowledge of the climate of Northern Europe. We plan to continue geological and stratigraphic studies that were begun by Torell and myself in 1858, and to carry on an uninterrupted program of studies of animal life on land and in the polar sea all winter long.'

This concise statement of the strategy and aims of the polar expedition shows Adolf Nordenskiöld at his best, a superb organizer, a man with full appreciation of the needs of science, an observer with sufficient breadth of vision to forecast, prophetically, the significance of polar meteorology for the northern lands of Europe. Yet the statement does not neglect what the expedition's backers expected of it, the plan to make a strong, well-supported push towards the Nort Pole.

The government's response was prompt and favorable. Early in 1872, Nordenskiöld was notified that the steamer *Polhem* was put at the expediton's service. *Polhem,* built by a Swedish shipyard, and powered by Swedish-built steam engines, was the first ship with double strength plates, to withstand ice pressure. She saw service in the Baltic for fifteen years, carring mail from the mainland to the Swedish isle of Gotland, and though small – measuring 102 feet in length, 20 feet in width – was reputed to be a good sailor. The Navy also provided a brig, *Gladan,* to carry supplies for the expedition. But as the amount of supplies mounted and it became obvious that two ships could not cope with the task, a small steamer, *Onkel Adam,* was chartered in Göteborg to serve as second supply vessel.

As commanding officer for *Polhem,* the flagship of the expedition, the Navy appointed Louis Palander, who had served under von Otter as second officer on *Sofia,* in 1868. Palander was ten years Nordenskiöld's junior, he came from a Navy family, and had served first as midshipman, later as junior grade officer, aboard Swedish warships in the North Atlantic and in the Mediterranean. In 1870, he resigned from the Navy and took over command of *Polhem,* then a postal vessel, during the exceptionally severe winter of 1870-71, achieving a much-admired record on a difficult run through the ice-filled Baltic, to and from the island of Gotland. The following winter, 1871-72, Palander continued to command *Polhem,* then stationed in Malmö, acting as rescue ship for sailing vessels in distress while en route between the Baltic and the Atlantic.

Palander knew polar waters. He had also become thoroughly familiar with the ship assigned to the expedition by the government and knew her behavior in wintry seas. In 1872, having returned to the service, he was given his first Navy command and a chance to prove his worth.

As it turned out, Adolf Nordenskiöld and Louis Palander complemented each other in a remarkable way. Nordenskiöld's main concern was to carry out the scientific tasks he himself had drawn up for the expedition: collecting specimens and making observations, regardless of the difficulties that might be encountered. But he disliked administrative detail. At home, he always relied on his faithful assistant Lindström, to whom he entrusted the day by day routine of running the mineralogical collections at the Stockholm Museum. To run an expedition, too, he needed help.

Louis Palander was a strict disciplinarian, who ran a 'tight ship'. No matter what circumstances were, on the high seas, or at a winter station frozen in ice, he assigned tasks to every man on every single day. The major decisions, affecting the outcome of the expedition, he always left to Nordenskiöld, but he assumed full responsibility for the fate of the ships and men under his command.

Yet it would be unjust to call Palander merely a capable naval officer, for he was more versatile, and had a wide range of interests. He did not shirk from any task, whether it meant a two-hundred mile hike across ice and snow to explore unknown land, or observing and recording the weather at a winter station. He was a superb photographer whose work served as a basis of most of the illustrations in the published accounts of the journeys he and Nordenskiöld undertook together. To the men under his command, he was 'Chef', the skipper. To Nordenskiöld he proved indispensable.

During the 1872-73 polar expedition, Palander's second officer was a young lieutenant in the Italian navy, Eugenio Parent. Though the Italian Navy had been in existence for barely a decade, it was vitally interested in securing varied experiences for its officers, and Lieutenant Parent came aboard as a result of a special request from the Italian to the Swedish government. The fact that Anna Nordenskiöld's sister had married an Italian diplomat, Francesco Cotta, established a strong bond between the Nordenskiölds and Italy, and without a doubt this had something to do with this unusual assignment.

Polhem also carried the scientific staff of the expedition. Besides Nordenskiöld, this group consisted of two young professors from Uppsala University, F. R. Kjellman, a botanist and A. Wijkander, who served both as a geophysicist and astronomer, and Dr. A. Envall, physician and, by his own choice, photographer. A curator-taxidermist was also part of the scientific staff.

The Navy looked into the matter of food and drink, and assigned a small staff to draw up lists of supplies and clothing. It was decided that, besides the reindeer that were to be taken along as draught animals, four dogs would be aboard, for hunting, and three pigs, to be slaughtered at Christmas to provide fresh meat. The mainstay of the parties pushing towards the pole was pemmican, already used to excellent advantage by British polar explorers.

Pemmican is a Cree Indian word for dried meat, pounded or shredded and made into a paste with fat and flavored with berries. It provides an exceptionally large amount of protein, in small volume, that can be kept indefinitely while dry. Other sources of protein included preserved beef, salt pork, and cheese. Fresh potatoes and vegetables, together with dried fruit, lime juice, coffee, tea, beer, and brandy were to be put aboard, but bread was to be baked daily throughout the winter.

Among the notes addressed to Nordenskiöld by the Navy regarding provisions for the trip, there was a list of rations, drawn up for planning the sled journey over the polar ice. It is a significant document, one of the very first to define on a scientific basis a high-energy diet for a group of men assigned the exhausting task of hacking their way across terrain that could not provide any source of food. Expressed in terms of pounds per man per day, the diet included one lb. of bread, 0.75 lb. of pemmican, 0.17 lb. of preserved potatoes, 0.4 lb. of cooked preserved meat, 0.1 lb. each of coffee and tea, 0.1 lb. of sugar, 2 oz. of lime juice, 1 oz. brandy, 4 oz. of suet, and a ration of tobacco.

While preparations for the expedition were going on, another enterprise connected with Spitsbergen got its start in Sweden. In 1864, while he was carrying out the groundwork for an accurate map of the archipelago, Nordenskiöld discovered a deposit of phosphate in Is Fjord (Ice Fjord), on the west coast of Spitsbergen. In 1870, two Swedish geologists visited the area, and reported that the deposits were indeed of high commercial value, as a base for artificial fertilizer.

Nordenskiöld and Oscar Dickson succeeded in getting a number of Swedish businessmen interested in forming a corporation, The Isfjord Company, for the purpose of sending out two ships and a number of workmen to build a house for engineers and miners, a narrow-gauge railroad from the deposits to the seashore, and a loading dock. The working capital of the company was quite modest, yet Dickson, who underwrote nearly half of it, was satisfied that it would be sufficient for the first, or exploratory phase of the operation.

In order to protect the interests of the shareholders, at the time the company's plan for incorporation was before the Swedish authorities, Nordenskiöld submitted a formal request to the Swedish government. The document, first discussed by the cabinet on February 23, 1871, pointed out that Spitsbergen has always been no man's land, ever since its discovery in the 16th century. Neither the original discoverers, the Dutch, who visited the archipelago on whaling ships, nor the Russians, who fished in the waters around the archipelago in the late 18th and early 19th century, nor the Norwegians who sent several score fishing vessels there every year in the 1860's and 1870's, ever claimed sovereignty over the islands. The Isfjord Company, Nordenskiöld wrote, plans to install a sizable mining enterprise, and wishes to claim title over an area of some 150 square miles in the area of Is Fjord. It would be most desirable, he added, if the entire archipelago of Spitsbergen would come under either Swedish or Norwegian rule. At the time Sweden and Norway formed a personal union, under the King of Sweden.

Norway was Spitsbergen's nearest neighbor, and it seemed logical that the Norwegian government should be the first consulted, to find out whether it was interested in such an annexation. The Norwegian reply was not enthusiastic. The mining company represented Swedish rather than Norwegian interests, and making the islands Norwegian territory would entail policing and other expenses and could possibly lead to conflicts with foreign countries over fishing rights. Yet Norwegian fishing interests were involved and since Norway lay closest to Spitsbergen, reluctantly it was conceded that there would be no objection in making the islands part of Norway.

But there was an international aspect to be dealt with too, and the Swedish government addressed an inquiry to Germany, the Netherlands, Denmark, England, France and Russia. In the note it was pointed out that people living in northernmost Norway, anxious to establish permanent settlements in Spitsbergen, requested their government's support and protection; and that the leader of several Swedish expeditions to Spitsbergen, Professor Nordenskiöld, suggested that such a permanent settlement would be invaluable as a form of support for scientific work.

The Swedish government pointed out that no one had so far claimed sovereignty over Spitsbergen, but that prior to making such a claim on its own behalf and that of Norway, Sweden wished to be certain that none of the nations who were represented by fishermen or hunters or explorers visiting the archipelago, made any objection to such a move.
All of the governments replied in the affirmative, except Russia. In its note, the Russian government pointed out that Russian subjects have been visiting Spitsbergen for a long time, that they had actually established settlements there on several occasions, and that, in their view, the maintenance of the *status quo ante*, of Spitsbergen remaining neutral ground rather than the possession of Norway, would best serve the interests of peace. Free use of the waters off Spitsbergen, and free access to the resources of the archipelago could then continue.
In the light of the Russian reply, Sweden abandoned the project of proclaiming its sovereignty over Spitsbergen. But the Swedish investors of the Isfjord Company were as anxious as before to have some measure of protection of their enterprise and, accordingly, the Swedish government addressed a second note to the nations interested in the Arctic, in the spring of 1872. The note referred to the building of a permanent station, to be used for mining and for scientific purposes, and pointed out that the issue of sovereignty was not involved, only recognition by the several nations of a permanent Swedish settlement in Spitsbergen. The answer this time was affirmative.
Strengthened by international recognition of its special status, the Isfjord Company sent out several ships in the early summer of 1872, a permanent building was put up, well supplied with fuel and food, and a railroad was begun to transport ore to the ships. But the enthusiasm was short-lived. The deposits turned out to be much lower in phosphate than it was first expected, the expenses involved in running an enterprise in the Arctic far higher than foreseen. Within a year, the corporation went out of business, the investors recovering barely one quarter of their money.
The misadventures of the Isfjord Company were a sharp disappointment to Adolf Nordenskiöld. Yet time was to prove him right: fifty years later, an international agreement made Spitsbergen part of Norway, and while phosphate ores in the islands remain untouched, coal is mined there by Norway as well as by the Soviet Union. Nordenskiöld had the right ideas, but the time was not yet ripe to put them to practical use.
When the three ships of the Swedish polar expedition left their home

ports for the Arctic, early in July of 1872, Nordenskiöld was still full of confidence both for the success of the expedition, and for the financial success of the Isfjord mining project. *Gladan* sailed directly to Spitsbergen; *Onkel Adam* loaded forty carefully chosen reindeer, and their fodder, in north Norway; and *Polhem* awaited the arrival of the expedition's leader in Tromsö.

Travelling from Stockholm by land to central Norway, thence by ship to Tromsö, Adolf Nordenskiöld looked forward to this, his fourth Arctic adventure. Fifteen years earlier, he had been one of three young Swedish scientists who paid their own expenses, to become acquainted with Spitsbergen. Now he was in charge of a fleet of three ships, full of supplies to last throughout the winter, all paid for either by public subscription or out of government funds. Scientific instruments were aboard and so were several prefabricated buildings, to serve as winter dwellings and as shelters for instruments. Morale was high, and the chances of scoring a notable success were never better.

Sixty-seven people sailed on the three ships bound for the Arctic. These included the scientific staff, the ship's officers, the seamen, four Lapps from northern Sweden who signed on as herdsmen for the reindeer, a harpooner, and one woman. Her name was Amanda Wennberg, she was the cook on the sole merchantman, the *Onkel Adam;* in Nordenskiöld's words, she was 'an older female, not exactly a shining specimen of her sex.'

The plan was to have the ships meet at the Norway Islands, off northwest Spitsbergen, and sail thence to Parry Island, at the northernmost tip of the archipelago. After unloading all provisions, the forty reindeer, and a large amount of coal for the winter, the two supply ships, *Gladan* and *Onkel Adam,* were to return to Norway. *Polhem* was to winter in the Arctic, with her staff and crew comfortably housed ashore. The attempt to reach the Pole was planned for April, when daylight hours were long: sleds drawn by reindeer were going to be used to transport supplies and lay in depots along the northbound route, across the polar ice.

The experience of more than thirty previous summers, gathered by Norwegian fishing vessels, assured Nordenskiöld that the way to Parry Island would be open in August. In fact, a Tromsö skipper, Elling Carlsen, had sailed his ship, the *Jan Mayen,* clear around the entire archipelago of Spitsbergen during the summer of 1863.

The first sign that all was not well appeared on August 18. A Norwegian steam-driven fishing vessel stopped by the expedition's anchoring place, and the captain reported that he had just escaped from Liefde Bay, barely thirty miles to the east, where he had been caught and imprisoned by ice for several weeks. He added that some eight other ships were still caught in the ice in bays and inlets off the north shore of Spitsbergen, and that the waters to the northheast were frozen solid. In his opinion, there was not much of a chance of the expedition reaching its original goal, Parry Island.

Nordenskiöld did not accept the Norwegian's opinion, and he ordered his ships to sail northeastward, hoping that the ice would have loosened, and that the ships could reach the originally planned anchorage. But the ice was thick and resisted any northward push, and on September 3, realizing that summer was nearly over, he decided to anchor in Mossel Bay, on the northeastern tip of the main island of Spitsbergen. True, the selected winter station was some eighty miles to the south of Parry Island, adding a significant distance to the planned push towards the Pole, but Nordenskiöld had no choice. He had to use an anchorage that was still ice free.

Two days later *Onkel Adam* steamed into Mossel Bay, to discharge its cargo of coal, food, forty reindeer and some three thousand sacks of reindeer moss, painstakingly gathered in northern Norway and Sweden to feed the animals during the winter months. The reindeer were unloaded on the south shore of the bay where there was plenty of grazing land for them, and the four Lapp herdsmen set up their tents, to be near the animals until winter had really set in.

Ashore, the task of setting up housing for the scientists and the crew of *Polhem*, and shelters for the instruments, took up all of the daylight hours. There was no real hurry, for all experienced Norse seamen assured Nordenskiöld that ships could tarry off Spitsbergen's northern coast until late in September, and still return to Norway before the ice closed in. Finally, the work ashore was finished, the two supply ships laid in some ballast for the voyage home, and September 16th was set as their starting date for Norway.

On the morning of September 16, a violent storm blew up from the northwest. Within hours the temperature dropped to well below freezing. Large masses of ice began to drift into Mossel Bay, and by the next morning, when the storm abated, both supply ships, as well as *Polhem*, were frozen fast in sea ice. Overnight, Adolf Nordenskiöld had to face the fact that instead of twenty-six people, the supplies on hand had to suffice for more than twice that number, sixty-seven, for an entire year, until help arrived from home.

There was not even time for him to recover from this blow, when the four Lapps arrived in camp, to report that during the storm all of the reindeer had broken loose and disappeared. These were tame reindeer, unaccustomed to the full blast of an arctic storm, and in all probability they simply ran away in a vain effort to find shelter. After several days' search only one reindeer was found. But ten years later a Norwegian sea captain reported shooting reindeer on an island off eastern Spitsbergen that had marks cut in their ears, a custom of the Lapps in northern Scandinavia: most likely they were survivors of Nordenskiöld's herd.

Somehow, Nordenskiöld had reckoned, by being extremely careful and reducing rations, he would be able to feed all of the extra hands stuck with him for the winter. There was fortunately enough winter clothing to go around. But the loss of his draught animals was a far more cruel blow. He had counted on them to draw the sleds on the dash accros the ice towards the Pole; now the hope of reaching that distant goal was shattered. The future looked dark indeed.

In a matter of hours, the entire outlook of the expedition was changed. Only a few weeks earlier, a wealthy Englishman, Benjamin Leigh Smith, had sailed his chartered fishing boat to the Swedes' anchorage, and called on Nordenskiöld. They discussed the plans for the expedition's attempt to reach the Pole, and the Englishman told Nordenskiöld that he would return next summer, to find out about the results of the season's effort.

In a letter sent by a Norwegian vessel, written shortly after his encounter with Leigh Smith, Adolf Nordenskiöld assured his wife that 'the risks I am facing are hardly worth mentioning, I assure you, and a year will quickly pass.' Leigh Smith liked to spend his winters in Rome, and his summers fishing and hunting in Spitsbergen. As far as Nordenskiöld was concerned, he wrote his wife, he would much rather write a life insurance policy for his Spitsbergen trips, than for his journeys to Rome. The Arctic was a healthy place, and he could not foresee any serious illness for the members of the expedition.

Hard and cruel as the blows struck against the expedition by the unexpected freeze of the bay and the escape of the reindeer had been, one more crisis was to come. Less than a fortnight after the ships were frozen in, and all signs pointed to a severe winter to come, seven fishermen arrived at the camp, having trudged some thirty miles across north

Spitsbergen. They reported that six ships were frozen in at Greyhook, a short distance to the west, with fifty-seven men aboard. Like the Swedish expedition, these fishermen were caught by the exceptionally early onslaught of winter, and their food and fuel were sure to run out in a matter of weeks.

Nordenskiöld and Palander were faced with a cruel dilemma. Since the expedition's supplies, originally calculated for some twenty-five people, had to suffice for sixty-seven, rations for the winter had to be cut substantially. If another fifty-seven were added, not even half rations would last out the winter, and starvation would be a distinct possibility. It occurred to Nordenskiöld that the Isfjord Company had completed a permanent building on the west coast of Spitsbergen, supplied with food and fuel. In a letter addressed to the captains of the Norwegian fishing vessels, and signed by Nordenskiöld, Palander and Krusenstjerna, commander of *Gladan*, they volunteered to look after a small number of men if no other solution was found, but suggested that some of the crew members should make an attempt to reach western Spitsbergen, and spend the winter in the house of the Isfjord Company. He also requested the skippers, if they managed to reach Norway, to forward a telegram to Oscar Dickson, reporting on what had happened, and stressing the fact that the expedition's supplies would not last beyond the following spring. It was essential, he wrote, that relief be sent as soon as possible.

The telegram did eventually reach Dickson, for two of the Norse ships managed to free themselves from the ice, with thirty-eight men aboard, and after a stormy and dangerous journey, landed in Tromsö on Christmas Eve. Seventeen men decided to take the Swedes' advice, and made the trek to the Isfjord Company's house on the west coast of Spitsbergen. Only two men stayed behind at Greyhook on the north coast, one of the captains, Mattilas, and his ship's cook. Mattilas had sailed the waters off Spitsbergen for forty years, had spent several winters there, and was confident that he could survive. It was, to him, a matter of saving his ship and the catch of the season in her hold.

The fate of the missing ships, both the vessels of the Swedish expedition and of the Norwegian fishermen, caused great concern at home. Oscar Dickson, realizing that Nordenskiöld faced the winter with rations barely sufficient to ensure the survival of his men, offered a large sum, one hundred thousand kronor, to the Navy towards the costs of a relief ship. But the Navy refused, claiming it was too late in the season to send a ship to Spitsbergen.

Norway considered matters in a different light. On November 21, when the ships had failed to return, a small steamer, specially chartered by the Norwegian government, left Tromsö for Spitsbergen, but was unable to get even near its coast. On the return journey, storms were so severe that the ship was unable to land in north Norway and, driven far off its intended course, finally made port a thousand miles to the south in Christiansand. A second vessel sailed from Tromsö on January 2, but only managed to reach Bear Island, half way to Spitsbergen, and was stopped by heavy drift ice. A third attempt was made in late January, when a German shipowner chartered a relief ship. On this trip, the vessel got to within fifteen miles of the west coast of Spitsbergen, but had to return before attempting to send men ashore, for fear of being crushed by ice.

Unaware of the attempts to bring relief, the members of the Swedish expedition settled down in their winter quarters. The months ahead looked grim as they awaited the long, dark Arctic winter.

XI. NEAR-TRAGEDY IN SPITSBERGEN – 1872-73

The prospect facing the Swedish expedition in the fall of 1872 was dark. Their first problem was one of surviving the winter on reduced food rations: due to the two supply ships being caught in the ice, sixty-seven persons had to make do with supplies intended to support twenty-two. If the past was to be any guide at all, even if the reduced rations held out until help arrived from Sweden, they were still confronted with the dreaded disease of the Arctic explorers, scurvy.

Scurvy is a disease caused by the lack of vitamin C, ascorbic acid, in the diet. The vitamin is most highly concentrated in citrus fruit, but it is also found in fresh berries and vegetables. Absence of the vitamin brings with it at first mental depression, a tendency to spend the greater part of the day sleeping or simply slumped in a chair. In more severe cases the gums start to bleed and teeth loosen and often fall out; hemorrhages occur, especially in the lower limbs, making it difficult or even impossible to walk without a cane or crutches. Unless the sick person has access to vitamin C., in the form of citrus fruit, lemon or lime juice, or some berry with a high vitamin content, hemorrhages continue, the entire body deteriorates, and death will result.

Scurvy was first observed in the Middle Ages, on the sea voyages undertaken by crusaders to the Holy Land. During the Age of Discovery, the 15th and 16th centuries, the ravages of the disease were appalling: on many voyages half or more of the crew died of it. It was a scourge of the early Arctic explorers, too, and the first signs of the disease were always awaited with dread by all members of these expeditions.

Dr. Envall, physician of the 1872-73 Swedish expedition to Spitsbergen, submitted a report to the Swedish Board of Health on his return. It is a model of lucidity, describing not only the strictly medical aspects of the wintering in the Arctic but discussing, in terms comprehensible to the layman, environmental and dietary conditions that were of importance.

The prefabricated house, set up on shore according to plan, was to have provided shelter for twenty-two people. By crowding beds, the entire crew of *Polhem,* including the officers, and the scientific staff, managed to install themselves there. The house had a separate kitchen, and a living room, where the men could spend their free time, on such hobbies as wood and metal working. Captain Palander maintained a carefully worked-out daily routine, and Dr. Envall stressed the fact that 'no one was allowed to sleep by day without special reason or permission.'

The supply ships, now anchored in the midst of ice in the bay, were supposed to return to Sweden in the fall, and neither was specially equipped for the Arctic winter. *Gladan's* deck was covered over with a roof made of sails, that soon froze into a completely rigid surface, and allowed men to come on deck and get fresh air while still protected from the elements. On the *Onkel Adam* they made a wooden roof over the deck, to allow space for outdoor exercise. Cabin floors on both ships were covered with reindeer hides, the outside walls with felt and extra boards, to conserve as much heat as possible. Stoves were installed, and as a result indoor temperatures both in the house on shore and on the two supply ships were kept between 50 and 55 degrees, Fahrenheit.

Gladan was a naval vessel, and its commander maintained the regular daily routine of a man-of-war, but *Onkel Adam* was a merchantman, and the crew were pretty much left to do as they pleased. Dr. Envall insisted in his report that men who led a well-ordered life, with tasks to perform every day, tended to be in far better health than those who were self-indulgent and spent their days in a shiftless, aimless manner. The statistics in his report do confirm this: the number of days lost because of sickness was exactly twice as high among the crew of *Onkel Adam* than among the men of *Polhem.*

As far as the daily diet was concerned, Dr. Envall held most preserved meats in low esteem, and insisted on the importance either of freshly killed game when available, or of pemmican, for a well-balanced diet. Fresh bread, baked daily throughout their stay, provided a welcome addition, with its fresh taste relieving the monotony of preserved or dried meat, fruit, and vegetables. Lime juice, first used on British ships in the mid-eighteenth century to prevent scurvy, was available, but Dr. Envall reserved his highest paise for cloudberries.

Cloudberries are a member of the rose family, they grow on a low, earth-hugging plant that is found in Norway and Sweden, as well as through much of northern North America. The berries have an exceptionally high sugar content, that enables migratory birds to complete long flights, having previously eaten a large quantity of the berries. Thus the golden plover is able to fly, during the fall, from the Aleutians to Hawaii, a non-stop flight of more than two thousand miles. But the cloudberry has also been known to Scandinavians for many generations as a powerful antidote of scurvy, and Dr. Envall reported that a daily dose of three or four large spoonfuls of the berries – preserved unboiled and without sugar in barrels – brought about rapid improvement in cases of scurvy.

For scurvy did occur among the members of the expedition. Twenty-eight cases in all were observed, and had it not been for the arrival of fresh food supplies in early summer, there may have been quite a number of fatalities. However, only one death attributable to disease occurred during the winter, when one of the sailors died of pleurisy. Another man wandered off to gather firewood during a storm, lost his way, and probably died of exposure, but his body was never found.

By the latter part of October, winter had begun in earnest. The sun disappeared on October 21, and stayed below the horizon for four months; only on nights when there was a full moon was the landscape fully illuminated. The routine of the camp was well set. Close to the living quarters three small shelters were put up, to house instruments. Since there were some three thousand sacks on hand, filled with reindeer moss that was to have fed the reindeer through the winter, these were put to use. Some of the moss was stuffed into the walls of the living quarters of the ships in the bay, to provide insulation, while the rest, still in sacks, was used to build a small shelter, to measure atmospheric electricity.

Temperature, direction and strength of the wind, and cloud cover were observed every hour of the day throughout the winter. In the geophysical observatory, hourly records were kept of the changes in terrestrial magnetism, measured by special instruments. Kjellman, the expedition's botanist, carried out dredgings in the bay even after it froze over, by drilling holes for nets and probes to go through.

One of the more remarkable phenomena observed by Kjellman, and other members of the group who went on walks across the sea ice or along the shore, was the presence of tiny phosphorescent creatures in the ice or snow. Nordenskiöld described it in the following words:

'As we walked along the shore during the winter, near the water's edge where the tides would be felt in spite of the sea ice, at every step we took we could observe an extremely intensive, beautiful blue-white phosphorescence. This light would appear in snow that was completely dark, until our steps stirred it up, it remained for several seconds afterwards, and was so intensive that we felt we were walking into a sea of fire. It was a curious feeling to walk on a dark and bitter cold winter day in this mixture of snow and flames, which would rise at every step and shone with such a strong light that one was just about ready to get scared lest one's boots and clothes would catch fire.'

Nordenskiöld added that the phosphorescence, due to the presence of tiny crustaceans, occurred only at times when the temperature of the mixture of snow and sea ice remained above fifteen degrees Fahrenheit, minus ten degrees Celsius. Yet, even though temperatures dropped considerably below that level, once they rose again, the phosphorescence returned, indicating that the invertebrate creatures responsible for it were able to hibernate at very low temperatures, and became active once more when conditions were right.

Besides assuming his share of the scientific observations, Adolf Nordenskiöld had a special project during the months of winter darkness. Ever since he first published a short article on the great 18th century Swedish chemist, Scheele, he was fascinated by the history of science. Knowing that there were going to be many hours during the winter in Spitsbergen when darkness and storms would prevent any outdoor activity, he packed a complete set of the Transactions of the Swedish Academy of Sciences in his bags, intending to prepare an article on the history of science in Sweden. The Academy was founded in 1739 and its papers provided Nordenskiöld with a full record of the accomplishments of his predecessors.

The article Adolf Nordenskiöld wrote on the shores of Mossel Bay in Spitsbergen, during the long winter of 1872-1873, was published four years later by one of Sweden's leading popular journals, under the title: 'A page from the history of Swedish natural science.' After pointing out that Sweden made no notable contribution to early science at the time when it was the leading power of Northern Europe, Nordenskiöld continued in a remarkably frank vein, seldom found among his contemporaries, to assess Swedish history after the ruinous wars that ended with Sweden's defeat by Russia, in 1721.

'A different age had dawned. Our short-lived dream as a great power came to a bloody end. All that was left of once powerful Sweden was a mutilated territory, bled white by constant wars, with only a small population. No longer could Sweden be great, brilliant, honored by others in world affairs. Instead, we dedicated ourselves to the peaceful competition of science, and there made such progress that hardly another country could match our record."

Sweden did produce great pioneers in many fields of science during the eighteenth century. Linnaeus, founder of taxonomy, the classification of species and genera, is the best known of this galaxy of scientists. But there were others: Wallerius, author of the first modern treatise of mineralogy; Celsius who invented the centigrade scale of temperatures;

Scheele, discoverer of a whole group of elements; Bergman, who introduced some of the basic methods of analytical chemistry. Summing up their accomplishments, Nordenskiöld underlined for his fellow Swedes the importance of peaceful pursuits, and the glory shed on a nation not by ephemeral conquests, but by lasting contributions to the knowledge of our world.

Winter closed in in early December, and by Christmastime only a narrow band of light appeared on the southern horizon. Darkness was so complete, even at midday, that it was impossible to distinguish the outline of the hills, less than a mile away from the beach where the expedition's house stood.

Christmas was duly celebrated with a tree and small presents for every one. In a letter written to his wife not long after Christmas, and delivered by a Norwegian vessel late next summer, Adolf Nordenskiöld wrote that he and his colleagues had drunk a special toast to her on January 12. It was the tenth anniversary of their sleigh drive in Finland, when he had asked Anna to marry him: he thought of the years they had spent together and thanked her for her love.

As the winter wore on, the health of the crews began to show alarming signs of deterioration. Several cases of scurvy occurred, and the doctor was using his medical supplies as well as extra rations of lime juice and berries to improve their conditions. Then, on January 30th, it appeared that the two supply ships might be able to break loose, reach open water, and return home. Ever the optimist, Nordenskiöld even believed that there would be open water to the north, allowing the party selected for the poleward push to be carried further north and put ashore there.

But once more nature crossed his calculations. While attempting to tow *Gladan*, a sailing vessel, towards the narrow band of open water outside Mossel Bay, another violent storm came up and before it was over, there was real danger of the ships being driven on shoals and sinking. Had that occurred, supplies of food, as well as shelter offered by the ships would have been lost, and Nordenskiöld admits in his official report that many, if not most, of the men would have died of exposure and scurvy. Fortunately the storm abated, and though all three ships were damaged to some extent, none sprung a leak. The day after the storm was over, both Mossel Bay and the waters outside it were once more covered with a solid mass of ice, and the expedition settled back into its winter routine.

In mid-February, the sun appeared again over the horizon and was greeted with enthusiasm, as a sign that spring could not be far away. There were still sick men, unable to walk except with the aid of crutches, weakened by scurvy, but all of *Polhem's* crew was in good health, and once more Adolf Nordenskiöld's thoughts turned to the north. True, he could no longer rely on draught animals since only one reindeer was left from the herd, but Englishmen had managed to make deep inroads in the Arctic by dragging sleds themselves, and Swedes surely could do no less. On April 24, a small party, consisting of Nordenskiöld, Palander, and nine crewmen started out towards the northernmost tip of Spitsbergen.

At first, the reindeer drew the sled loaded with food and a tent. Once fodder for the reindeer ran out, it was slaughtered, and provided a good supply of fresh meat for several days.

On May 17, they reached Phipps Island, one of the small islands to the north of East Spitsbergen, and looked out over the Arctic Ocean. Twice before, in 1861 and 1868, Nordenskiöld had been to Phipps Island, both times aboard ship. Both times he saw a vast, level icefield to the north. This time, the entire surface of the ocean was covered with great blocks of ice, making a sled journey just about impossible, for many of these blocks were ten to fifteen feet high, and the party would have had to climb each and every one in an attempt to make progress.

Even Nordenskiöld, stubborn optimist that he was, had to admit that any further progress northward, toward the distant pole, was impossible. But it is also typical of him that, instead of turning back towards his base camp, he decided to embark on a long journey on foot, to explore the unknown interior of Northeastland, the great eastern island of the Spitsbergen group.

Nordenskiöld, Palander, and the nine sailors who made up the party walked over two hundred and fifty miles across ice and snow, crossing crevasses, camping out in depressions created by the wind, to describe and map Northeastland. The journey lasted seven weeks. Each man took turns at the many tasks on hand: dragging the sled with their supplies, cooking meals, and setting up camp. Throughout the entire time they made observations of latitude and longitude, of elevation above sea level, and of the weather. They accomplished all this on reduced rations: the carefully calculated diet, suggested by the Navy, simply could not be followed, since supplies were running low by the time they left their winter station.

The daily routine never varied. At daybreak, a fire was started in the tent where it was protected from the wind, coffee was prepared, and each received his morning ration of 1/2 pound pemmican, 1/4 pound of bread, and 4 ounces of butter. After breakfast, the party started out, roped together most of the time, lest a man disappear in a crevasse covered by light snow before he could call for help.

On they trudged for five hours, taking a fifteen minute break every hour and a half, until it was time for a midday meal. It consisted of 1/4 pound of bread, a piece of salt pork, and an ounce of brandy. After another five hours' journey, they set up their tent for the night, cooked a thick soup made from pemmican, made tea, and rounded out their evening meal with brandy. Afterwards they blew up their rubber mattresses, each man climbed into his sleeping bag, a single heavy blanket was spread out over the entire party, and within minutes all fell asleep from sheer exhaustion.

Nordenskiöld was forty years old when he undertook this demanding and hazardous journey, the first crossing of a polar ice cap. His report on the crossing of Northeast Spitsbergen contains some of the earliest observations on the nature, genesis, and processes of glaciers in the Arctic and many of its details have been fully confirmed by later explorers. The sheer effort of making this traverse remains impressive; coupled with his pioneer scientific observations, it becomes a landmark in the exploration of the polar regions.

During Nordenskiöld's and Palander's absence, the men left behind at the winter station attempted to get word to the outside world that help was badly needed. Late in May, a dog appeared at the camp, and was recognized as belonging to Mattilas, the skipper who had remained at Greyhook, a short distance to the west. At the beginning of June, von Holten, one of the naval officers, took off in a rowboat for Greyhook, but found Mattilas and his young companion dead, under a makeshift tent. Nearby they found a cairn, with a note that a Norwegian fisherman was on his way with news and supplies. On June 7, the ship arrived, bringing not only letters and newspapers, but a small supply of flour and butter sent by Nordenskiöld's old friend, the Tromsö merchant Ebeltoft.

The news from Norway was grim. There was no word of a relief ship, bringing fresh food, and when the officers at the Swedish station asked the Tromsö skipper for help, he refused, saying that he could not leave until he had filled the hold of his ship with fish. By this time all but one of the people aboard *Onkel Adam* had come down with scurvy, and half of the crew of *Gladan*, too. Even if all of the ice had magically disappeared from Mossel Bay, setting the ships free, there just were not enough men available to sail them home. Dr. Envall wrote later that the hope of getting help from home kept the men going, but that the absence of any sign of relief from Sweden brought about a serious worsening of their condition.

It is difficult to understand the reasons that kept Sweden from sending help to the expedition. The fact that nearly seventy people had been stranded for nine months in the Arctic was well known. There was not a scrap of news from them, yet no one in Sweden moved a finger.

On July 2, Anna Nordenskiöld wrote von Otter. One of Adolf Nordenskiöld's friends told her that the Navy was planning to send a ship to Spitsbergen, and she inquired, anxiously, whether such a move was really under way. 'It is possible that the ships were crushed by the ice' – she wrote – 'or that some other accident occurred, yet I continue to hope that all is well and that we shall soon have definite news that the men are alive and in good health.'

It was not Sweden that brought the much-needed fresh food to the men stranded in Spitsbergen. On June 11, when the future looked dark and hopeless, a steam-driven yacht and a smaller sailing vessel landed at Mossel Bay. Leigh Smith, the English yachtsman and hunter who had met Nordenskiöld the previous fall, and told him that he would return in the summer to find out how the expedition had fared, fulfilled his promise. When he saw the conditions under which the men had lived, he immediately offered fresh potatoes, vegetables, meat, lime juice, tobacco and rum, enough to last for over two weeks.

On June 29, Nordenskiöld returned from his journey across Northeast Spitsbergen, and on the same day the ice went out from the bay. *Gladan* and *Onkel Adam* immediately prepared to sail home, their crews restored to health by Leigh Smith's generous assistance and the prospect of getting home. On July 13, Anna Nordenskiöld received a telegram from Krusenstjerna, *Gladan's* commander, sent from Tromsö: 'Greetings from Nordenskiöld. All are well. The ships were freed from ice on June 29. Nordenskiöld will sail northward on *Polhem* as far as the ice allows, then shall return home.'

With his two supply ships on their way south, Nordenskiöld turned once more northward, but the attempt was thwarted by heavy ice. After making several stops along the shores of Spitsbergen to collect more specimen, *Polhem* visited Isfjord on the west coast, only to get word of one more Arctic tragedy. The seventeen Norwegian fishermen who had became icebound at the same time as the Swedish expedition, and had then trekked southwest to spend the winter in the mining company's house at Isfjord, were all dead. Even though the building was well provided with food and fuel, every last man came down with scurvy, and died before spring came.

As *Polhem* sailed past the south tip of Spitsbergen bound for Norway, Nordenskiöld tried to draw up a balance sheet of the year 1872-1873. In his own judgment, he had failed to fulfill the goals he had set for this, so far his most ambitious effort. Thwarted by the ice, he could not even begin to make the dash towards the North Pole that his sponsors had hoped for. True, he managed to bring back all but two of his crew, but sickness had taken a heavy toll among the others.

In the long run, though, he did not fail. He brought back a mass of valuable scientific data that were unique, gathered at a spot further north than any where a comparable series of observations had ever been taken before. The Swedish expedition made Spitsbergen the best known part of the polar world, and many of the observations made there would be applied in later years to other parts of the Arctic. Most important, he knew what a winter in the Arctic meant to men and to ships, and that a carefully planned expedition could, with a bit of luck, not only survive but return with a valuable cargo of new knowledge gained.

Speaking to one of his young colleagues, shortly after his return in 1873, Adolf Nordenskiöld said: 'We shall return to Spitsbergen when we are old men.' Alfred Nathorst, the Swedish geologist, telling this story adds that he had later teased his distinguished mentor: 'Look, your hair is snow white, and I haven't much left on my head; when are we going to Spitsbergen?' Nordenskiöld only laughed, and quickly changed the subject.

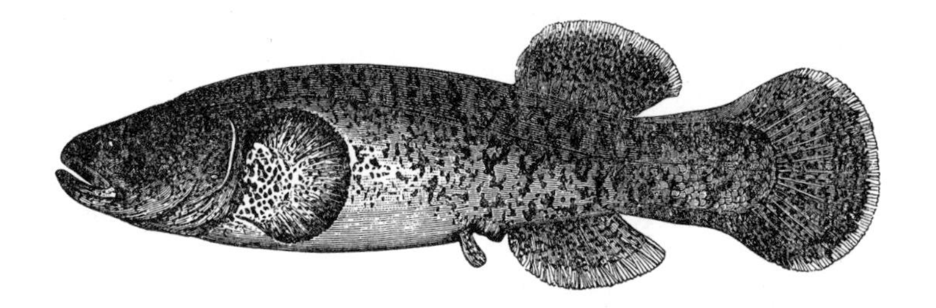

XII. PLANNING FOR THE NORTHEAST PASSAGE --1873-74

When Adolf Nordenskiöld returned to Tromsö after more than a year's absence, in early Agust, 1873, a telegram from Oscar Dickson awaited him. Dickson, who had contributed the lion's share to the costs of the 1872-73 expedition, welcomed the members of the expedition home, regretted the difficulties they had encountered, and expressed his satisfaction that important scientific results were achieved. He added: 'Finances are my responsibility', trying his best to relieve Nordenskiöld of any worries about the additional expense created by the forced wintering of two ships and their crew.

There was another item of news, that claimed Nordenskiöld's attention. He had already learned while in Spitsbergen that King Carl XV of Sweden and Norway had died during his absence. In Tromsö he found out that the successor, Oscar II, had just been crowned in the ancient cathedral of Trondheim. Oscar II had served as a youth in the Swedish Navy, and shared with Nordenskiöld a strong interest in Arctic exploration. The knowledge of having the ruling sovereign so closely concerned with these matters must have given Nordenskiöld a measure of confidence, badly needed after the defeat he had just experienced at the hands of a polar winter.

On August 29, *Polhem* anchored in Göteborg harbor, and Oscar Dickson was on hand to greet the staff and crew. 'Well, what are we going to do next?' he inquired of Nordenskiöld, setting his mind at ease, and once more assuring him of continuing support. Later that year, when the costs for the 1872-1873 expedition were totalled, Dickson reported on the amount, a very considerable sum, and added: 'I can only say that I would have to provide a much larger amount of money before I would give up my support of these expeditions!'

The scientific results of the 1872-73 Swedish polar expedition were, to be sure, worthy of note. Yet Nordenskiöld was far from satisfied, and his old friends in Finland thought that he might be willing to give up exploring the Arctic, and apply once more for the chair of geology and mineralogy in Helsingfors. That chair remained unfilled, and though Nordenskiöld's appointment was vetoed by the Russian authorities in 1867, his friends in Helsingfors University refused to give up hope, and approached him once more.

This time, Adolf Nordenskiöld's answer was a clear, unqualified refusal.

'I am convinced that I cannot apply for a chair at Helsingfors University . . . It would be best to forget about the whole business. I doubt that I would be a good lecturer, and right now I have two other projects on my mind, anyway. One is a major work in mineralogy, the other is to undertake a journey by the Arctic Ocean to Bering Strait and to prove, at the same time, that it is possible and practical to open a seaway between the Atlantic Ocean and the mouths of the Ob and Yenisey rivers (in Siberia). These two tasks will keep me from leaving Sweden now. As for doing it later, that is difficult to answer. On the one hand, I am still strongly bound to my old fatherland, to home, to my family. On the other hand, it is not easy to leave the work I have been doing here for nearly twenty years, nor should I forget the hospitality I was offered in Sweden. I have truly become a Swede, and I was a Swede by descent, even when I came here as a Finlander, seventeen years ago.'
Adolf Nordenskiöld did, at last, make up his mind. Sweden had been good to him, honored him, and had given him an opportunity to do what he wanted: to be a scholar and an explorer. Adolf and Anna Nordenskiöld kept their close ties with family and friends in Finland. But Sweden was their home, Sweden was the place where their children were born, where they now belonged.
In one respect, though, his letter to Finland was misleading. Throughout his life Adolf Nordenskiöld apologized for only one thing: he felt he was a poor lecturer. He never enjoyed teaching, or public speaking of any kind, for that matter. Yet it is a fact that for twelve years in a row he was selected as the featured speaker at the formal annual meeting of the Swedish Academy of Sciences. The text of these addresses was always printed in one of the leading Stockholm newspapers, and in this way Nordenskiöld's colleagues paid tribute not only to his scholarship, but to his ability to present new and important scientific developments in a manner that would interest the general public.

The year in Spitsbergen was over, and routine duties now kept Adolf Nordenskiöld busy at home. There was the formal report of the 1872-73 expedition to be written, the backlog of correspondence that had accumulated during his absence, the care of the mineralogical collections at the Museum in Stockholm. In the summer of 1874 he took off to visit interesting mineral finds throughout Sweden. His journey took him south, this time, and while there he visited the estate of Count Arvid Posse and described it to his wife.

Count Posse was one of Sweden's wealthiest landowners, a man of strong political ambitions, leader of the Agrarian party and, in politics at least, an outspoken opponent of Nordenskiöld, who was a Liberal. But he threw his house, Charlottenlund, open to the distinguished visitor, and received him most cordially. 'As you know, the powerful and influential owner of this place is the political leader, the uncrowned king of the landowners' – wrote Nordenskiöld – 'I am sure he would be most pleased to have a scientist among his followers . . . Charlottenlund would certainly suit your tastes. It is on the seashore, a beautiful and comfortable estate with a magnificent view, surrounded by lovely trees and bushes and well-kept lawns.'

At that time Anna Nordenskiöld and her children spent the summers on her mother's estate in southwestern Finland. It was with an almost audible sigh that her husband ended his letter: 'It would be nice if we had our own place in the country!'

But back in Stockholm there was work to do. Dickson was willing to support another Arctic venture. The question was: whither to turn? Spitsbergen was out, and so was another attempt to reach the North Pole. The odds were against making any real advance towards the Pole, and the experience of 1872-73 was definite proof, in Nordenskiöld's own mind, that he better seek success somewhere else.

When *Polhem* lay at anchor in Tromsö during the summer of 1872, awaiting Nordenskiöld's arrival before starting northward, the officers and scientists aboard became acquainted with their opposite numbers on the *Tegethoff*, berthed next to them. *Tegethoff* was a ship specially designed to withstand the dangers of Arctic waters; she flew the Austrian flag, and was built to explore the Arctic east of Spitsbergen. The two commanders of the Austrian expedition, Weyprecht, a naval officer, and Payer, an army lieutenant, had already made a trip the previous year into the Barents Sea, the waters north of Norway and Russia. The eastern limit of the Barents Sea was the island of Novaya Zemlya. Beyond that lay the Kara Sea, dreaded because it was icebound most of the year, and beyond that the unknown expanse of the Arctic Ocean, as far as Bering Strait.

But when the Austrian ship *Tegethoff* sailed into the Barents Sea in 1871, as far east as Novaya Zemlya, the waters were completely ice free. The ship's commanders, Weyprecht and Payer, believed that they could go beyond, and in due course reach Bering Strait. What they were thinking about was to explore the Northeast Passage, the way north to the Orient.

The Northeast Passage was a dream much older than the quest for the North Pole, and it began in a practical fashion. When Spain and Portugal divided the world between them, following Columbus' first voyage to the Americas, they also controlled the great seaways that led to the fabulous riches of the Indies. France, England, Holland, the nations who joined later in the great sea voyages, found the easy ways to the Indies barred. The best geographers and mapmakers of the time gave them hope, though, by pointing out that there were two other ways to reach the Indies from Europe. The ships could sail northwestward, around North America, or northeastward, around Asia; eventually they would reach a strait that opened to the Pacific and the Indies. Thus began the quest for those elusive seaways, the Northeast and the Northwest Passage.

In 1872, Payer and Weyprecht were confident that they could achieve their aims of sailing ever eastward, to Bering Strait. But their plans came to naught: the *Tegethoff* was caught in the ice, and drifted northwestward through the cruel winter of 1872-73. True, they discovered, as a result of their involuntary voyage, the archipelago of Franz Josef Land, the northernmost islands of the Arctic, but they failed in their quest just like Nordenskiöld did, in Spitsbergen.

It is impossible to establish a priority of plans and ideas, to state whether Nordenskiöld or the Austrians first thought of making the attempt to open the Northeast Passage. There are, however, several facts, that indicate that Adolf Nordenskiöld had been thinking of sailing northeast for some time. Siberia had been on Nordenskiöld's mind since his youth: he had planned a trip across Siberia in 1854, when he spent a winter in the Ural mines as assistant to his father. Two years later, applying for a travel grant to Helsingfors University, he had proposed a field trip to northern and eastern Siberia, to study geological and mineralogical matters. Finally, in his autobiography he wrote of a proposal he had submitted to the Russian government; 'Several years earlier (before 1875) I turned to Russia to promote a hydrographic and scientific expedition to those areas, but in vain.'

Adolf Nordenskiöld was as interested and concerned with observations made by non-scientists, by seacaptains and fishermen, as with the carefully documented reports of his colleagues. Over the years he became a close and trusted friend of Norwegian whalers and fishermen, and listened to their stories and experiences with care. It is typical of Nordenskiöld that he acquired the logbooks of skippers from Tromsö and valued them as highly as the rare books and atlases he collected in his library.

After long years of intense hunting, whaling and fishing, the resources of Spitsbergen showed definite signs of exhaustion in the 1860's and the fishermen of northern Norway looked for new and richer grounds. They started to sail eastward across the Barents Sea, towards Novaya Zemlya, and even beyond. Traditionally, fishermen are a silent lot, unwilling to reveal any information on newly discovered lands or seas that might help their competitors. But the Norwegians who started to explore the Barents Sea behaved differently. It was, wrote a contemporary Norwegian writer, as if rubbing shoulders with the Swedish scientists in Spitsbergen suddenly made them observe nature much more sharply than heretofore; at the same time they started collecting specimens that, earlier, they would not have thought worthy of even a look.

In 1868, Nordenskiöld had a long talk with one of the youngest Tromsö skippers, Edvard Johannesen, then only twenty-four years of age. The following year, 1869, Johannesen sailed across the Barents Sea, northward along the coast of Novaya Zemlya, crossed the strait that divides that island into two halves, cruised around the Kara Sea, and returned to Tromsö. He brought back not only a good catch, but a set of observations on winds, currents, and water temperatures. No doubt Nordenskiöld had provided him with instructions and instruments as well.

Captain Johannesen sent his observations to the Swedish Academy of Sciences, and the Academy in turn awarded him a special silver medal. 'Now, if you were to sail clear around the entire island of Novaya Zemlya' – wrote Nordenskiöld to Johannesen half in jest – 'you will get a gold medal.' The following year, 1870, after filling the hold of his ship with fish during his cruise east of Novaya Zemlya, Captain Johannesen set sail to the north, rounded the northernmost point of Novaya Zemlya, and returned to Norway. It must have been a happy day for Adolf Nordenskiöld when the Swedish Academy of Sciences fulfilled the informal promise he had made a year earlier: Captain Johannesen was awarded the Linnaeus gold medal.

The following year, 1871, Captain Carlsen of Tromsö, the man who had already accomplished the considerable feat of sailing around the whole of Spitsbergen, excited by the possibilities of fishing in the Kara Sea, sailed from Norway directly for the northern tip of Novaya Zemlya and started southward along the island's east coast. There he made a remarkable discovery.

In 1596, Captain Willem Barents of Amsterdam, veteran of Arctic voyages who had, a year earlier, discovered Spitsbergen, sailed into the Kara Sea, bent on opening up the Northeast Passage. The Dutch government offered a princely reward, twenty-five thousand guilders, to the discoverer of that seaway, and Barents, having already made one trip to the Kara Sea, felt confident of success. But the Arctic winter once more interfered, the Dutchmen were caught in the ice on Novaya Zemlya's east coast and were forced to winter there. Many of the men, including Barents himself, died of scurvy. The story of the expedition had been published on the return of the survivors, and contemporary engravings illustrated the printed account.

In 1871, 275 years after the death of Barents, Captain Carlsen discovered the Dutch winter camp, in a perfect state of preservation: even the clock on the wall, shown in the engravings of the contemporary account of the expedition, was in place. The furnishings of the Dutchmen's cabin can now be seen in the Netherlands; Carlsen had made a major contribution to the history of discovery.

Northeastward the next expedition would sail, that much was certain, and the preparations began in the late spring of 1874. Oscar Dickson offered to finance the undertaking, once more giving tangible proof of his faith in Nordenskiöld's judgment.

The two men were drawn together by their common interest, and each was rewarded according to his desires. Dickson was a man of great wealth, ambitious to be recognized by society and by the world of science. There is no doubt but that a grateful Nordenskiöld threw his own, not inconsiderable, weight behind Dickson's ambitions. For Nordenskiöld, nothing could be more important than to continue Arctic exploration, and achieve the success he was denied by the fiasco of 1872-73.

Dickson's share of achievements really began after the 1872-73 expedition. Early in the spring of 1874, he wrote to Nordenskiöld: 'I would, of course, be very much flattered to become a member of the (Swedish) Academy of Sciences, but possibly the statutes would not allow such an ignoramus as I to be elected.' Shortly thereafter, the Academy did elect Dickson to membership, and so did other scientific organizations. On April 18, 1875, he wrote to Nordenskiöld: 'I know I have you to thank for being able to write F.R.G.S. (Fellow of the Royal Geographical Society of England) after my name.'

There had been recognition from foreign governments, too. Lieutenant Parent, of the Italian Navy, was a member of the 1872-73 expedition, and some months after his return to Rome, Dickson was pleased to tell Nordenskiöld that he had received a personal letter of thanks from the Italian Minister of the Navy and, on the heels of the letter, a decoration from the Italian government.

Last but by no means least was the fact that his generous support of the cause of science made Oscar Dickson well known all over Europe, and a much sought-after person. Edward, Prince of Wales, sportsman and principal royal personage in a country vitally interested in exploration, invited Dickson to be his guest on numerous occasions, starting in the mid-1870's. It was after his first visit to the Prince, in December of 1874, that Dickson asked his expert friend Nordenskiöld for a memorandum on Spitsbergen. The Prince of Wales wanted to visit the islands, on a voyage that would also touch on Iceland and northern Norway, and Oscar Dickson felt he could offer advice from the man who knew Spitsbergen better than anyone else.

The advice was not scientific this time. It had to do with the best time of year to see Spitsbergen, what there was to see, what kind of sport could be pursued and where, and how long the Prince would have to stay in the islands to get an idea of the scenery and enjoy some good sport. The voyage was postponed, Dickson wrote later, and it may never have taken place, but somewhere in Edward VII's papers there ought to be a memorandum on Arctic sport, written by one of the great Arctic explorers of all time.

By the fall of 1874 preparations had gone far enough for Adolf Nordenskiöld to prepare a description of the project for an 'Expedition to the Yenisey'. He proposed that the scientific staff sail aboard a Norwegian fishing vessel in June, 1875 to the Kara Sea. After carrying out studies in the geology, botany and zoology of the coastal area and of the sea, and possibly also some ethnographic investigations of the aborigines of northwest Siberia, the plan called for penetration to the eastern part of the Kara Sea, to the mouths of the Ob and Yenisey rivers. Several well-perserved skeletons of the mammoth, a prehistoric elephant, had been found in that area, and Nordenskiöld was truly anxious to bring back a specimen for Sweden's geological collections.

It was in planning the second half of the voyage that Nordenskiöld, introduced a new element: he announced that, unless sea ice kept the ship from doing so, he planned to enter the mouth of the Yenisey. There the expedition would break up into two sections: the ship would return to Tromsö, whilst he himself would attempt to sail upstream by rowboat on the Yenisey, deep into Siberia, and return to Sweden by land, across Siberia and European Russia.

This time, as in 1870, Oscar Dickson paid all of the expedition's costs out of his own pocket. Nordenskiöld's good friend in Tromsö, the merchant Ebeltoft, found a small but well-built fishing vessel, the *Pröven.* Seeing it the first time, Adolf Nordenskiöld must have remembered his first voyages to the Arctic, for *Pröven* was truly a small craft, less than half the size of *Sofia* or *Polhem*, and provided with sails only.

Pröven's skipper was Captain Isaksen, who sailed with Nordenskiöld to Spitsbergen in 1864. Among the eleven Norwegian crewmen, the youngest, Hans Daniel, had had such a memorable Arctic experience that he was singled out in the formal report, written by Nordenskiöld on the expedition. In 1872, Daniel, then only fourteen years old, had sailed to Spitsbergen aboard one of the Norwegian fishing vessels that was caught in the ice that year. When his shipmates decided to leave their ship behind at Greyhook, on the north shore of Spitsbergen, and try to get home aboard another ship that was closer to open water, young Daniel, being ill, had been left behind in the care of the veteran skipper, Mattilas. But the next day Daniel, feeling much better, decided to follow his shipmates, walked some thirty miles across ice in severe cold, and was among those fortunate enough to have returned to Norway that autumn. Had he stayed behind with old Mattilas, he, too, would have died of scurvy as did that veteran of many an Arctic winter.

The scientific staff consisted of two botanists and two zoologists, one of whom, F. Kjellman, had spent the winter of 1872-73 in Spitsbergen with Nordenskiöld.

In May, 1875, Adolf Nordenskiöld travelled to London at Dickson's request. Captain Allen Young, an officer of the British merchant marine with considerable polar experience, was getting ready to sail across the Atlantic to the waters off northern Canada, to try his luck at opening up the Northwest Passage. Nordenskiöld met Young, inspected the equipment the British expedition planned to take along, and reported to his sponsor that he was satisfied with the manner in which his own Swedish group had prepared their voyage.

On June 8, 1875, the small sailing vessel *Pröven* was towed out of Tromsö harbor and started on its journey to the northeast.

XIII. TO SIBERIA BY THE ARCTIC OCEAN - 1875

As the little sailing vessel *Pröven* was sailing eastward to the Kara Sea, the thoughts of the men aboard turned towards their goal, Siberia. It was not an unknown area in 1875, but neither was it fully known. Its vast expanse, greater than all Europe, had been traversed by merchants and missionaries and government officials for nearly three centuries before Nordenskiöld first planned his expedition.

The word 'Siberia' describes the northern third of Asia: it was first entered by Russians at the turn of the 17th century. Taking advantage of its vast and closely interconnected system of rivers and portages, the Russians crossed the entire Asiatic continent in record time. Barely half a century lapsed between the founding of the first Russian settlement east of the Ural Mountains, traditional boundary between Europe and Siberia, and the building of a fort on the shore of the Sea of Okhotsk, part of the North Pacific Ocean. Building trading posts and forts as they went eastward, the Russian pioneers traversed an area more than twice as wide from west to east as the United States, and imposed their rule on the small, scattered tribes of Siberian natives. Hunters, fishermen and reindeer herders, speaking a variety of tongues and far from warlike, these tribes posed no problem to the Russian conquerors, and by the end of the 17th century Russia ruled North Asia from the Urals in the west to Bering Strait in the east.

Close on the heels of the pioneer, the trader, the missionary, and the tax collector came the scientist-explorer. The conquest of Siberia was completed during the reign of Peter the Great, the emperor who introduced Russia to Europe and European science to the Russians. It was Peter the Great who founded the Russian Academy of Sciences, and first sent out scientists to follow in the pioneers' footsteps, to study and describe the geography, and the plant and animal life of Siberia.

Explorer-scientists, Russians, Frenchmen, Germans, employed by the Academy of Sciences, criss-crossed Siberia and reported their findings not only to Russia but to the rest of Europe as well. Anxious to get as accurate an image of their vast Siberian domain as possible, the successors of Peter the Great continued to support exploration there. The Danish sea-captain, Bering, working for the Russian government, mapped the strait separating Siberia and Alaska that now bears his name and in 1741 discovered and mapped the Aleutians and southern Alaska. Yet so primitive a land did Siberia remain, nearly a century after its conquest

by Russia, that Bering took nearly two years to travel from St. Petersburg to the shores of the Sea of Okhotsk, where he built his ships for the exploration of Alaska.
As Russian rule over Siberia was consolidated, the routine of travelling cross-country, slow and difficult as it may have been, became firmly established. The 'Great Siberian Trail' was only a set of rutted tracks, but it did guide the traveller from Europe all the way to the North Pacific. In the 1860's, an electric telegraph line was built following the old trail, that connected the widely spaced cities and towns of Siberia with European Russia. By the time Nordenskiöld and his companions were approaching the Siberian shores of the Arctic Ocean, the map of Siberia was drawn, even though some of the details were not filled in until well into the 20th century.
From the beginnings of Russian conquest and exploration, the very existence of Russian rule in Siberia depended on the use of the river systems. It was to these great Siberian rivers that Nordenskiöld turned his attention: the Ob, the Yenisey, the Lena, and their tributaries beckoned to ships, offering the only feasible way to penetrate inland, and at the same time providing an outlet to the world ocean.
Adolf Nordenskiöld never lost touch with the realities of his world, the world of rapid industrial development in Western Europe and North America, continuously in search of new markets, of new merchandise to enter world trade. His judgment failed him more often than not in his own business ventures, yet in the long run he was vindicated again and again. Thus, his view of the rivers of Siberia as giant feeders of commerce between Europe and Russian Asia, using the Arctic Ocean as a seaway, is fully accepted in our time, subject only to the restrictions imposed upon it by the harsh realities of a long winter and a short navigation season. It was to demonstrate the feasibility of waterborne commerce between Siberia and Europe that Nordenskiöld devised his plan to enter the vast mouth of the Yenisey River and sail upstream, until he reached settlements and areas of some economic development in South Siberia.
To reach the Yenisey, the expedition had to traverse the Kara Sea; to reach the Kara Sea from the west, they had the choice of several routes. The barriers between the Kara Sea and the Barents Sea are the twin islands of Novaya Zemlya and, to the south, the small island of Vaigach. The first and most difficult route to the Kara Sea, since it was ice-bound most of the year, was around the northern tip of Novaya Zem-

lya. The second, popular with Norwegian fishermen, was Matochkin Strait, the winding passage that separates the north and south islands of Novaya Zemlya. If that, too, was icebound, ships had the choice of reaching the Kara Sea passing either north of Vaigach Island, by Kara Strait, or south of it, by Yugor Strait.

Floating ice prevented *Pröven* from using the more northerly of the seaways, and it was through Yugor Strait that the vessel slipped into the Kara Sea, on August 3. The scientists aboard were now in territory where few observations had ever been made regarding the sea itself, its temperature and currents, or its fauna. Nor was there much knowledge of the shores of the Siberian mainland, and as *Pröven* was slowly moving eastward, they landed often, observing and collecting in each place.

The natives of this part of Northwest Siberia, then called Samoyed, now referred to as Nenets, are wandering hunters and fishermen. At the time, Russians had lived among them for well over a century, and the natives' dependence on factory-made cloth, salt, tea, sugar, and firearms was fully exploited by the Russian traders. Nordenskiöld compared their fate with that of the natives of North America: they too, traded furs and fish not only for everyday necessities but, above all, for Russian-brewed alcohol. Their summer garments were mostly of Russian manufacture, only in winter did they still use their fur-lined parkas and boots, to protect themselves in constant subzero temperatures.

On August 13, *Pröven* reached its goal, the wide mouth of the Yenisey River. The men landed on a small island, facing the Kara Sea to the north, that provided a well-protected anchorage on its south side. Nordenskiöld named it Dickson's Harbor, in honor of the expedition's patron. 'I hope' – he wrote – 'that this harbor, now deserted, shall in the near future become, if only for a short time during the year, a meeting place of many ships, which will engage in trade not only between Europe and the basins of the Ob and Yenisey, but between Europe and northern China as well.' Nearly half a century later the Soviet government built a settlement on the mainland side of the Yenisey estuary, across from Nordenskiöld's original anchorage, and named it Dickson. It is one of the command posts of the Soviet northern sea route, the seaway that now connects Europe and the Pacific by way of the Arctic Ocean.

The expedition split up at Dickson Island. The ship *Pröven* readied for the return voyage to Norway, with the botanist Kjellman in command, while Nordenskiöld, two of the scientists, and three Norwegian sailors loaded a large rowboat, named *Anna* in honor of the leader's wife, with supplies for the voyage upstream on the Yenisey. They carried enough bread, coffee, sugar, and butter for six weeks, salt meat and canned meat for two weeks, planning to live off the land until they reached permanent Russian settlements. On August 19, the two parties separated, and the boat set its small sail, taking advantage of the winds of the estuary, and disappeared from sight. *Pröven* made a successful trip back to Norway, collecting meteorological and oceanographic data all the way, and anchored at Tromsö on October 3.

The boat *Anna*, meanwhile, made its way slowly up the mighty Yenisey. Soon after leaving the mouth of the river they came upon the first sign of former Russian occupance, a fishing camp consisting of buildings used as dwellings, with space for rendering whale blubber and storing fish, but long since abandoned, as fishing on the lower Yenisey yielded smaller and smaller returns. Here the river flows across the trackless tundra, the Arctic desert, with only low bushes and moss covering the lee slopes of hummocks and hollows in the ground. It was late in August and the men found, to their great joy, masses of cloudberries and lingonberries ripe on the ground, the first fresh fruit since leaving home.

On the fourth day of their journey, Nordenskiöld and his companions met the first Russians, out to gather berries on the tundra. One of them, employed by a merchant to look after his fishing station, offered to serve as a river pilot, and under his direction the *Anna* proceeded slowly upstream, gradually leaving the Arctic barrens behind and entering the vast forests of north-central Siberia. The islands in the river were covered with luxuriant vegetation, and whenever they stopped at a fishing settlement, they were able to purchase excellent fish, that helped to vary their diet of canned or salted meat.

Nordenskiöld planned to sail upriver, until he caught up with one of the small steamers that plied the Yenisey and would bring them to south Siberia, where the road to European Russia crossed the river. After ten days' journey, alternately rowing and taking advantage of favorable winds, they met the last steamboat of the season, the *Alexander*.

The *Alexander* was neither a passenger boat nor a freighter. Rather, it was a steam-driven 'store', a floating emporium. Her master, Ivan Mikhailovich Yarmeniev, was a genial and friendly merchant, who concerned himself with business rather than with matters of seafaring. The foreward cabin was arranged as a store, with shelves for merchandise along the walls, and a desk. The aft cabin was used as an office and stateroom for the master, and was also filled to overflowing with goods, casks of spirits and general merchandise. There was no place for passengers aboard, and when the boat, with its Swedish flag hoisted on the mast, came alongside, the master did not offer them much of a welcome. But Nordenskiöld never gave up easily. With the help of the Russian pilot who steered their course up to their encounter with the steamer, and using a dictionary, he explained who they were and what was the purpose of their voyage. The master immediately offered them space aboard, and turned out to be a most pleasant and accommodating host.

A small cabin in the foreward part of the boat was emptied of its contents and made into a stateroom for Nordenskiöld and his two fellow-scientists; the three Norwegian sailors were bedded down in the engine room. Later in the journey the three scientists transferred to a roomier cabin and the sailors occupied the small foreward stateroom.

It was quite a journey, going upstream on the mighty Yenisey aboard a floating business establishment. Two mates, of stately and original appearance, clad in long Russian coats, steered the boat, sitting on a high stool by the wheel, smoking cigarettes and exchanging jokes with people in smaller craft who were on their way downstream. A man stood in the bow at all times, constantly sounding with a pole. In order to avoid the strong current of the river, the craft did not follow the main channel; rather it hugged the shore as closely as possible. At times it would have been possible to jump ashore, and the expedition's boat, towed by the steamer, was occasionally dragged over dry ground. The steamer also had two lighters in tow, used to store fish bought during the journey, as well as several small rowboats, since there weren't any landing stages on the banks of the Yenisey.

The steamer's engine, like that of other steamboats used on Siberian rivers, was a wood burner and frequent stops were made while fuel was taken aboard. To carry all that was loaded aboard the steamer, as well as dragging the lighters and boats attached to it, meant that the journey upstream was a slow process: it took a month to cover the distance to Yeniseisk, about a thousand miles.

But Nordenskiöld and his men were not in a hurry. There was plenty of food aboard, they had shelter, and they enjoyed the leisurely trip across Siberia. To most people, Siberia was the exiles' land, covered with snow and ice, a barren wilderness. But though they were still north of the Arctic Circle, Nordenskiöld reported that they rarely saw any snow, unless it was on the north-facing slopes of a deep valley. On the contrary, the banks of the river and the islands within it were covered with luxuriant vegetation.

One of the Norwegian sailors, a man who owned a small bit of ground among the mountains of northern Norway, remarked with envy that the Lord had certainly given some splendid land to the Russians. The soil appeared fertile, the pastures lush with grass, yet no scythe mowed that grass, neither did any cattle graze on it. Time after time did the Norwegians and Swedes exclaim over the seemingly endless and empty lands of Siberia along the Yenisey as it traversed the virgin forests, and later at the sight of the immense expanse of rich blackearth on the plains further south.

During the summer of 1875, three groups of Russian experts travelled in Siberia, and drew up a plan for improving inland water transport in that immense area. There were no good roads in Siberia then and no railroads, the rivers offered the only possible means of mass transport. The Russian engineers drew up a plan that is yet to be put into effect: they proposed that the three great river systems of Siberia, the Ob, the Yenisey, and the Lena, be interconnected and thus opened up for steamers. Nordenskiöld, who learned of the plan when he and his companions left their riverboat in Yeniseisk, was struck by its vast dimensions, and by the possibility of exploiting the untouched resources of Siberia. True, he wrote, 'part of this immense drainage basin lies north of the Arctic Circle, but here are the largest and finest forests of the earth, while south of the forests extend level plains covered by most fertile soils that only wait for the farmer's plough to yield abundant harvests.' In southernmost Siberia grapes will ripen in the open and, Nordenskiöld added, he had a bunch of splendid Siberian grapes in front of him while writing his report. 'May the future see communications by river and sea established between these lands and Europe!', he exclaimed with enthusiasm.

Adolf Nordenskiöld was a true naturalist, interested not only in geological formations and minerals, but also in the flora and fauna of the regions he saw in his travels. In his report of the 1875 expedition, he gave a description of the vegetation of the Yenisey valley that has never been excelled, contrasting the meadows on the low, westerly bank with the great forest that covered the higher, eastern bank of the river.

'On September 7 we had a chance to go ashore on the western bank of the river. It was a meadow, some of it covered with an extraordinarily lush carpet of grass, some overgrown with a bushy vegetation from six to eight feet in height. There were close thickets of beautiful straight-stemmed willows, level patches of vivid green grass, small streams, and the impression created was that of a carefully tended and watered park, free even of dry branches and dry grass.

On the east bank, in contrast, the primeval forest began right at the water's edge. Nature here had quite a different aspect, grand and gloomy. The woods consisted mostly of firs, many of them huge, many grey and half dead from age. The ground between the trees was covered with fallen trunks, some still fresh, others half mouldering, still others already changed into humus. One could advance only with difficulty, at the risk of breaking a leg, among the logs. The fallen logs were covered, some almost hidden, by an unusually heavy growth of moss, while lichens were conspicuously lacking: the tree trunks still upright were smooth, and the bark on the birches scattered throughout the forest shone dazzling white. If one were to wander into this monotonously uniform forest a short distance from the river, he ought to make sure to know his directions, for a mistake in orientation may lead him on for hundreds of miles without encountering a settlement.'

Wherever the river steamer stopped, Nordenskiöld and his companions went ashore, to visit settlements and get acquainted with the inhabitants. He remembered some of the Russian he had learned as a youngster in Finland; he wrote his wife that although his knowledge of the language was limited, he still had to be interpreter for his five companions, who did not speak a word of Russian.

As the craft progressed slowly upstream, it left the tundra, inhabited by the Samoyeds, behind, and entered the forests and meadows where the Ostyaks dwelt, the Siberians natives now called Khanty. They dwelt in conical tents covered with birch bark, and made their living mostly from fishing. An Ostyak settlement is always overrun with dogs, Nordenskiöld wrote, used to draw sleighs in winter, boats in summer. The natives use dugouts, hollowed out from the stem of a tree, and the dogs, harnessed to a long line, pull these primitive craft along the riverbank.

Most of the Ostyaks were nominally Christians, yet in their burial customs they had preserved their ancient ways: the coffins of the dead were placed on a platform made of branches, with an icon and cross at the head, but on a nearby bush relatives hung up some of the dead person's clothes and a sack filled with dried fish, food for the journey to the afterworld.

Many of the Europeans living in the remote reaches of the Yenisey were exiles, sent there for religious or political reasons. One of the villages where the river steamer made an extended stop was peopled entirely by followers of the Russian sect called *Skoptsi,* a fundamentalist branch of the Orthodox Church. Interpreting the Gospel in their own way, the *Skoptsi* renounce all pleasures of the flesh by undergoing voluntary castration: thus the survival of the sect depends on attracting new converts. Many of the people in the village came from easternmost Finland and Nordenskiöld, a better linguist than he would admit, was able to talk with them in Finnish. They told him that they had been driven from their homes, imprisoned, whipped and sent to northern Siberia 'for the sake of righteousness'. By hard work they managed to establish themselves in those inhospitable surroundings, and bore their fate with resignation, certain that they were to be richly rewarded in the next world for their privations, sufferings, and hard luck in this one.

There were political exiles, too, but their fate was seldom as hard as that of the religious dissenters: they were allowed to keep their books, to be joined by their families, to continue their studies in many instances. One of these, an ardent student of photography, took a picture of the members of the expedition: Adolf Nordenskiöld sent it home, certain that his wife would be able to pick him out from among the bearded gentlemen shown on the print.

At last, the *Alexander* docked in Yeniseisk in early October. The owner of the vessel refused to accept any money for their passage, and Nordenskiöld finally presented him with the expedition's sturdy boat in lieu of payment of fares.

But the men were still three thousand miles from home, and some means had to be found to provide for their return trip. On this one occasion Nordenskiöld had failed to plan ahead: he had had so little faith of actually being able to accomplish the long voyage from Europe to the Yenisey, and thence upstream into Siberia, that he did not carry any Russian currency with him.

A temporary solution to the problem of getting the stranded Swedish expedition on the road was found by the merchants of the town of Yeniseisk. They were so impressed with the feat accomplished by the group, and so enthusiastic about the prospects of direct trade with Europe that Nordenskiöld presented to them, that they made a cash loan to him. With the money thus made available, Adolf Nordenskiöld purchased two carriages and on October 3, the men bade farewell to their hosts and started on the long journey home.

After two days, the group arrived in the town of Krasnoyarsk, where the

Great Siberian Trail crossed the Yenisey River. A telegraph line, paralleling the Siberian Trail along its course to the Pacific, was opened in the mid-1860's, and Nordenskiöld sent a plea for help to Oscar Dickson, in Göteborg. Two days later a money order arrived by telegraph, and the expedition was in funds once more, ready to start out westward.

Travel in Russia a century ago was truly an adventure. It was possible to go by railroad from the imperial capital, St. Petersburg, to Moscow, and to continue by rail for another two hundred odd miles east, to the city of Nizhny Novgorod, now called Gor'kiy. Beyond that, the traveller faced five thousand miles of the Great Siberian Trail. The government maintained a network of post stations along this, the only overland link between European Russia and its far-flung possessions in Asia. The post stations were spaced twelve to sixteen miles apart; their function was to provide fresh horses for travellers.

Before leaving for Siberia, every traveller had to obtain a government order, entitling them to a change of horses at these stations. Nordenskiöld had the foresight to request a high-priority document, called a 'crown order', for himself and his companions. However, this document only assured them of mounts, they had to purchase their own conveyances.

Since there were six men, two carriages were needed to transport them and their baggage from Siberia to Europe. One of the carriages was a telega, described by the zoologist of the expedition, Stuxberg, as a notorious instrument of torture. 'Four huge wheels, the back wheels being nearly half again as big in diameter as the front ones; two rough-hewn axles; a brittle shell, made up of boards, in the shape of a kneading trough: that is a *telega.*' Besides the coachman, only one other person could ride in a *telega,* for there were no seats inside.

The other carriage was a *tarantas,* somewhat better made: it resembled a covered wagon, and was rugged enough to survive the innumerable potholes of the Siberian trail. Both *telega* and *tarantas* were drawn by three horses. The lead horse was harnessed in front, and wore a bow-shaped piece of wood over its neck; the bow was hung with bells to announce the wagon's approach to the post stations.

At the post stations, Nordenskiöld presented his 'crown order', fresh horses were harnessed to the wagons, and the travellers were once more on their way. To make better time, the group travelled night and day between the widely spaced towns of Siberia, and averaged about 125 miles a day, stopping only long enough to have meals.

'The *tarantas* is the home of the traveller in Siberia' – wrote Stuxberg – 'he spends his days and nights in it until he reaches his destination. The distances are so great that the traveller has to keep going without stop, unless he wishes to waste time. One doesn't try and spend the night in a post station, it is far better to sleep in the wagon. The bottom of the wagon is covered with hay several feet deep, to help absorb the bumps and the pain caused by the vehicle rattling over rough trails. In fact, in none of the post stations and only a few of the towns can one find a bed. There are hotels in the larger cities, where one can find a restaurant, a café with current newspapers, even a billiard room, but hardly a trace of beds for the convenience of travellers. It is only when one approaches the borders of Europe that this necessary item can be found.'

Nordenskiöld and his companions rattled for six weeks over the rutted trails of Russia, covering two thousand miles from Central Siberia to where the railroad to Moscow began. At the time of their journey, in 1875, people in the United States could cross the country from coast to coast in the comfort of the Union Pacific railroad; another quarter of a century was to pass before the rails span the breadth of Siberia, from Europe to the Pacific.

During the crossing of Siberia, Nordenskiöld found that the hospitality of the Russians they encountered was heartwarming, and their stops in the larger cities were always marked by festive dinners in their honor, visits to the local places of interest, and long discussions with resident scientists. The only difficulty, he wrote his wife, was to keep track of his three Norwegian sailors. They were true seamen, supposedly lost on dry land, yet they had an unerring instinct for finding the nearest tavern at every overnight stop. Nordenskiöld tried to keep them on a meager allowance, yet somehow the three sailors always managed to find some Russians who were only too happy to provide the proper quantity of vodka, to entertain their visitors. It was only the Norwegians' fear of the Russian police that kept them out of serious trouble.

Reading about the slow and jubilant progress of Nordenskiöld and his party across Russia, Anna Nordenskiöld's sister-in-law, Countess Hélène Mannerheim, described their journey in these words: 'Adolf was honored all along his journey with speeches, champagne breakfasts, dinners in private railway cars. The only point I did not hear brought up in those speeches was that the Russians had once expelled him from the Empire. Now they feel that he had rendered incalculable services, and not only of scientific interest. I can see Adolf, an absent-minded and genuinely good man, accepting all this homage.'

On his arrival in St. Petersburg, Adolf Nordenskiöld received more honors still. He adressed the Imperial Geographical Society at its annual meeting, and was made an honorary fellow of the Russian Society of Natural Scientists. He was wined and dined throughout his stay in the capital, and lived in the home of the most distinguished Swedish resident of St. Petersburg, Alfred Nobel.

Finally, late in November Nordenskiöld and his companions embarked on the last part of their long journey, first to Finland and then on to Sweden. His fellow Finns received him with enthusiasm and full honors. Even the watchful Russian police approved of his behavior: in a secret report, the commander of the Russian police in Finland reported to St. Petersburg that 'though Professor Nordenskiöld was given an enthusiastic reception everywhere in Finland, he was duly restrained in his speeches. After arriving in Helsingfors, he paid his compliments to the Governor-General, as if he wished to show in this manner his completely changed attitude towards Russia.'

One is inclined to doubt any real change in Adolf Nordenskiöld's views of the Russian autocracy that held his native Finland so strictly under control, but it is possible to recognize in his behavior the diplomacy and tact becoming a famous person. For it was as a famous person indeed that he was welcomed on his arrival in Stockholm on November 30, and a week later in Göteborg, on Oscar Dickson's home grounds.

There was a banquet at the Göteborg Stock Exchange, in the grand Swedish tradition: there were songs and speeches and toasts, but the high point of the evening came when the expedition's patron, Dickson, offered his toast. This was one of the few occasions when Anna Nordenskiöld accompanied her husband, and Oscar Dickson honored her as much as Adolf Nordenskiöld. 'There is someone here tonight – 'said Dickson' – who has had a greater share of worries than any of us, who welcomed him back with greater enthusiasm than we did; it is to her, who with a spirit of self-sacrifice worthy of a daughter of Sparta gave him up to his task, to struggle amidst ice and darkness, to the noble, unselfish wife, that I have the honor to offer this toast!'

XIV. THE MAN BEHIND THE STATUE: NORDENSKIÖLD AS SEEN BY HIS CONTEMPORARIES

In January, 1876, Adolf Nordenskiöld received word that the French Academy of Sciences elected him Corresponding Member: he was to occupy the seat left vacant by the death of the greatest explorer of Africa, Dr. Livingstone. This was the highest honor Nordenskiöld had yet received: the whole world of science began to recognize him for his achievements in Arctic exploration.

Within less than five years, Adolf Nordenskiöld's name was to become a household word throughout the world, a legend in his own lifetime, a monument to his own triumph. Those who wrote about him celebrated what he had done. Few ever tried to describe the man behind the monument.

August Strindberg, one of Sweden's greatest writers, first knew Nordenskiöld when he was teaching in Stockholm. 'I remember him' – wrote Strindberg – 'from his lectures in chemistry at the Academy of Sciences, in the early 1860's. As a professor at the age of twenty-six, among the old men of the Academy, he attracted a great deal of attention. With his fine head, his uncommonly keen eyes, his brisk, undaunted ways, he charmed all of us who attended his lectures. He was a dashing man; if an experiment was not successful, he was not annoyed, he did not claim to be a magician, he just went on with his lecture.'

There are people still living in Stockholm who remember Adolf Nordenskiöld from their childhood. They see him as a big man, rather formidable-looking, but whose blue eyes were never forbidding when children were around.

For he loved children, his own and all others, too. In her memoirs, the Swedish novelist Hedvig Swedenborg describes a visit to the Nordenskiöld country place, near Stockholm. She was a friend of the younger daughter, Anna, and on a summer day in 1882 she travelled in the company of Adolf Nordenskiöld, by steamboat and carriage, to spend a short vacation with the family.

'There was a high wind when the little steamer left Stockholm, and Lake Mälar was all stirred up, like a tremendous witches' cauldron.

Uncle Nordenskiöld was pacing the deck, with a rolling gait, his hands behind back. Now and then he stopped and looked at me with merry eyes below his tufted grey-yellow eyebrows. I must have looked rather

pale about the gills, for suddenly he asked me whether I was seasick.
'No – said I – don't believe I am.'
'Believe' – and now he was laughing – 'I tell you that if you were seasick, you wouldn't believe anything, not even in God and all his angels.' Well, then I knew that I was not seasick. And when he added that I was a brave little girl – he, the great circumnavigator of the globe – it would have been all the same to me even if the boat had turned somersaults!'
One of his friends wrote in later years that Adolf Nordenskiöld grew to manhood in the Arctic, on the decks of small ships fighting its violent moods. There, a man was worth his own courage, his own skills, whatever his background and upbringing may have been. Nordenskiöld never lacked courage, and proved it on many an occasion. When he was forty, an advanced age by Victorian standards, he slugged for two months across Arctic snow and ice, alongside with men half his age. When past fifty, he was on the Greenland icecap, walking through mushy snow, hell-bent on proving his theory that deep in the interior of that barren island there was green vegetation, even woods.
He loved nature, and was fascinated by all of its aspects. Though his principal interest was mineralogy and geology, he never failed to observe closely all manner of phenomena. Wildlife, weather, ocean currents, vegetation, all this was of equal interest to him: in a sense, he was one of the last great naturalists.
Adolf Nordenskiöld had an affinity with nature. From his friends, the harpooners and pilots and mates of Norwegian ships, he learned to recognize the changing moods of Arctic weather, to look for telltale signs of solid ice or ice-free water. When he was over fifty years old, he still insisted on climbing to the crow's nest of his ship, to look for an open channel through the coastal ice off Greenland. His colleagues and his crew said that he could 'smell ice', a tribute to his skill of observation, sharpened by years of experience.
His years in the Arctic also taught Adolf Nordenskiöld to appreciate men for their own qualities, to disregard public opinion. One of August Strindberg's early works was the novel 'The Red Room', a scathing, merciless attack on the mores of the Swedish middle and upper classes. After its publication, the author became a target for personal as well as literary criticism. When, a year or so after the publications of his controversial novel, Strindberg was invited to a formal dinner by Nordenskiöld, he wondered whether the great man was acquainted with his book.

His doubts were soon over. One of the guests, a cabinet minister, Strindberg wrote, 'noticed my humble self, my Bohemian appearance must have caught his eye. Looking at me he asked Nordenskiöld in a whisper: 'Who is that?'. Nordenskiöld shouted: 'It is Strindberg!' 'Which Strindberg?' – the minister whispered, to lower the tone of the conversation. 'The "Red Room" Strindberg, of course', came the loud reply. Nordenskiöld considered all men equal, and liked to mix with all of them.'

Even though few men of his time were so honored by reigning monarchs, who bestowed all manner of decorations on him, grand crosses and diamond-studded stars meant little to Adolf Nordenskiöld. During that same evening when he introduced the young 'revolutionary' writer Strindberg to his distinguished friends, the question of decorations came up in an unexpected manner. The guest of honor at the dinner party was a prince of the imperial family of Japan, who wore an impressive looking star on his tailcoat. Another guest, a Portuguese diplomat, a good friend of Nordenskiöld, seeing the host's bosom and coat bare of any sign of distinction, urged him to put on at least one decoration. 'But which one shall I wear?' – asked Nordenskiöld. 'You must, of course, wear a Portugese decoration, since I am here as the representative of Portugal.' Nordenskiöld disappeared, and when he returned, he did indeed wear a grand star, but not the Portuguese one. He really was not interested enough in his decorations to bother to tell them apart.

Looking over the roster of men who worked with Nordenskiöld in the Arctic, one is struck by the fact that many of them accompanied him on more than one voyage. 'His confidence, his composure, his indomitable energy inspired all who were with him with a feeling of security,' wrote Carl Forsstrand, who as a young scientist had participated in Nordenskiöld's last Arctic voyage. 'When going ashore on some unknown coast, we were all carried away by his eagerness to use the time well, to carry out as many investigations, and to bring back as rich a set of collections as possible. He was always among the first to go ashore, and was not satisfied with being geographer and geologist: he was also ethnographer, zoologist, and especially entomologist.'

Describing Nordenskiöld when he was already a world-famous explorer and scientist, Carl Forsstrand said: 'In spite of all honors he was still the simple, straightforward scientist, and on board ship still the vigorous leader, unspoiled by high society. One of the first impressions Nordenskiöld made on his collaborators was a feeling of confidence and security. One could not always follow his plans, nor could one always accept his opinions or his, often sanguine, conclusions. But in his company we felt physically secure. It is very true that his impulsive nature, his, at times, boiling temper made people around him somewhat nervous. But one got quickly used to his impatience and to his temper, which never lasted long, for soon his usual calm, good-natured, friendly mood returned. His mood in fact was responsive to a good meal, or even to such an unpretentious source of pleasure as a cup of coffee. But the coffee had to be good and strong, and the cook aboard our ship remembers its exceptionally refreshing effect on what, aboard ship, was called the Chief's morning mood.

During the Arctic summer there is always daylight, and as is well known, people lose their sense of the difference between day and night. At sea, one takes advantage of every chance to work that is offered by favorite conditions of the weather, of the sea, of ocean currents. Thus it can easily happen that day and night become all mixed up, and people choose their hours of work and rest whenever it seems most convenient. As a result, life becomes rather irregular, something we tried to overcome by setting definite hours for our meals. Still, the way this worked out was that people were awake and at work at different hours, according to the nature of our work and the opportunites for carrying on.

But it so happened that Nordenskiöld, who spent most of his time at sea working and writing in his cabin, followed the 'civilized', or non-arctic schedule, and no matter how light it was during the night, he slept then. He also rose very early, walking the deck at 3 or 4 o'clock in the morning, when the others were asleep in their cabins. Then he would get mad, complaining that the ship was going too slowly, that the staff were stupid, that no one was really interested in his work, and so on.

He would mutter a curse, but even that would not sound unpleasant in his lilting speech. But his mood would change quickly when he was served a steaming cup of coffee, lit up his cigar, and found someone to talk to.'

Adolf Nordenskiöld's demands in matters of food and drink were quite modest while in the Arctic, but at home, and travelling abroad, he enjoyed good food, good drinks, and a good cigar. When he was able to afford it, he ordered French vintage wines and Spanish sherry by the case, Havana cigars by the hundred.

Always a gallant companion of ladies, he was a true Victorian, preferring the society of men. His favorite haunt in Stockholm was the 'Idun' society, that he had helped found in the 1860's. Anders Zorn, the leading

Swedish painter of the time, immortalized the club, and two of its distinguished members, in a canvas called 'A Toast at "Idun"'. One of Nordenskiöld's close friends, Wieselgren, dominates the painting, but the great explorer is also part of it, with his snow-white head, and his piercing eyes under bushy eyebrows.

Throughout his life Nordenskiöld managed to keep busy, and never was known to have suffered from boredom. He was always thinking about his next book, his next voyage, or someone else's adventure that he was supporting. It was inevitable that a man with so many irons in the fire would acquire the reputation of being absent-minded.

Many a story about the absent-minded Professor Nordenskiöld made the rounds of Stockholm, and quite a few of them can be easily recognized as classic tales about men of his stature and preoccupations. One of his friends, in a short memoir published after Nordenskiöld's death, tells a story that throws light as much on his absent-mindedness as on his disregard of danger. It seems that, returning from one of his expeditions, he left his ship at Tromsö, and rode on horseback across northern Norway and Sweden to the railhead, near the Gulf of Bothnia. On his return home, several of his friends came over to Nordenskiöld's apartment, to help him unpack. Among his luggage was a bag that he carried, slung over his shoulder while riding. Opening it, it was found to contain gunpowder, matches, and some paper.

'You mean to say that you jogged along on horseback with this bag hung from your shoulder?' – asked his friends.

'I certainly did, and why not?'

'Look at this dangerous mess you had in it: gunpowder, paper, and matches!'

'But these matches aren't any good' – Nordenskiöld answered – 'Look, you'll see!' With that, he took a match and struck it on the seat of his pants. Right away, an impudent little blue flame appeared and shone on him, full of reproach. He stood there for a moment, crestfallen, like a schoolboy caught barehanded. At least that was the way he seemed to his friends, and the room was filled with laughter.

His unselfish support of scientific fieldwork and research by others earned him the admiration of many a young scientist. Throughout his long career, he was always ready to support the cause of younger men who tried new ways, and new means, to wrest the Arctic's last secrets away. Fridtjof Nansen, the great Norwegian explorer, freely admitted how much he owed to Nordenskiöld's encouragement when he first started his polar journeys. Then and later, Nordenskiöld was always ready to counsel, advise and support men who set out for Arctic conquests.

The Swedish engineer S. A. Andrée, whose ill-fated balloon expedition was the first attempt to reach the North Pole by air, tells in his autobiography of the night in Stockholm when he was asked by Nordenskiöld to accompany him home, after a scientific meeting. Nordenskiöld was already fascinated by the possibilities for scientific work offered by lighter-than-air craft, and when Andrée described his plan of flying to the Pole, the great explorer listened carefully, and finally burst out, saying: 'Yes, that is really good, keep working and you may certainly count on me!' And it was Nordenskiöld's support that helped Andrée round up the means to finance his expedition.

Nordenskiöld was a Finlander, and like his Finnish-speaking countrymen, he too had that trait of the Finnish character, *sisu:* an inner drive towards the goal they set for themselves for life, a refusal to bow before seemingly hopeless odds, a single-minded determination to overcome all obstacles.

A close friend and colleague of Nordenskiöld once said, talking about him with another scientist: 'Nordenskiöld is a born scientist, and a determined one. You and I, we creep forward, step by step. Nordenskiöld goes straight ahead, his sights set for his goal, and for that only.'

And in 1876 Adolf Nordenskiöld needed all the energy, all the drive he could muster. The successful voyage to the Yenisey received acclaim in many places, and in a letter waiting for him on his return, Oscar Dickson told him of press stories and reports in scientific journals in Germany, in England, in France, celebrating his exploits. But Dickson also warned him that some influential people were already saying that the successful trip to the Yenisey, during the summer of 1875, was a lucky break, and that no one can be certain that the Kara Sea can be entered in any one year.

Dickson added: 'My reply – though my voice does not count for very much – was that the state of the polar ice has no bearing on navigation to the Yenisey, and that the real secret of your success was in counting on the influence of the warm waters of the Siberian rivers on the ice, opening a seaway to the mouths of those streams.'

This, indeed, was the core of Nordenskiöld's argument, that the waters of the Ob and Yenisey melt enough ice along and near the Arctic coast to make possible the passage of ships from north and northwest Europe to the mouths of the great rivers of Siberia. Thus assured of the success of the first leg of the voyage, he felt he could look forward to planning the conquest of the Northeast Passage.

But theories were not convincing to those who considered that the voyage to the Yenisey in 1875 was merely a fortunate accident, and that in most years the dreaded ice of the Kara Sea would keep merchantmen from reaching north Siberia. The best way to silence the critics was to undertake a second voyage to Siberia, immediately following on the success of the first one, and thus prove the feasibility of the project.

Oscar Dickson was willing to advance the costs of the trip, when additional support was offered from an unexpected quarter. On the return voyage from Siberia in November, 1875, Nordenskiöld and his companions had been guests at a dinner in Moscow, given in their honor by the Russian society for the development of merchant shipping. In his reply to the toasts celebrating his trip, the first voyage by ship from northern Europe to Siberia, Nordenskiöld replied that this was but the first step. Now that the Yenisey had been reached, he was ready to go even further, and open the Northeast Passage, the way to the Pacific Ocean.

The Russian newspapers reported Nordenskiöld's speech in detail. Among those who read it with great attention was a young Russian businessman, then in his late twenties, Alexander Sibiriakoff, heir to a vast mining and business fortune. The mines of the Sibiriakoff family were in Siberia, and the ores had to be hauled by a long, hazardous route to European markets. Alexander Sibiriakoff saw the proposal to develop merchant shipping to northern Siberia as a heaven-sent opportunity to enlarge his own business: the great rivers of Siberia could then be used, cheaply and easily, to ship farm products as well as ores to the Arctic Ocean, there to be transferred to ocean-going ships on their way to Europe.

By the time Adolf Nordenskiöld had returned to Stockholm, a telegram was waiting from him: Alexander Sibiriakoff offered the substantial sum of twenty-five thousand rubles (about 12,500 dollars of the time) as his contribution towards the costs of a second voyage from Scandinavia to the Yenisey. The two had never met, yet the forceful presentation Nordenskiöld had made to the businessmen of Moscow was enough to convince Sibiriakoff that he had found a man worthy of support.

This time, though scientific studies were still to be carried on by the staff of the expedition, business matters, too, were given attention. Both

Nordenskiöld and Dickson requested the support of the Swedish government, and in May, 1876, Nordenskiöld was advised that the Russian Treasury would allow his ship free entry to Russian waters, and duty-free import of goods destined for northern Siberia.

About the same time, Nordenskiöld received a letter from Yarmeniev, the Russian trader in Yeniseisk, in central Siberia. It was on Yarmeniev's river steamer that Nordenskiöld and his companions had travelled up the Yenisey the previous summer, and the good 'captain' recalled with pleasure the many days they had spent together. Getting down to business, he wrote that Nordenskiöld's planned voyage to the Yenisey was known all over Siberia, and that he would try his best and meet the Swedish ship at the mouth of the river. He added that, while furs were not likely to be available during the summer, he could ship a substantial quantity of rye downriver, as well as some wheat, and some Siberian vodka. As for his own needs, he asked Nordenskiöld to bring him a pump for his gold-dredging operations, and added that he would buy from him just about anything that would sell in Siberia.

Nordenskiöld, in the meantime, tried to obtain manufactured goods for shipment to Siberia, and to drum up trade from the Russian end, too. As he put it in a telegram sent to a Moscow business acquaintance: 'I want to furnish practical proof that shipping to Siberia is possible.'

The plan for the 1876 expedition differed from that of the previous year in one important respect. Nordenskiöld was to sail for Siberia from Norway, while a second party, consisting of scientists, was to go by land to the upper Yenisey, go downriver, and meet Nordenskiöld in the estuary of the Yenisey. The 'land party', consisting of five Swedish and Finnish naturalists, had been given the charge of making a survey of navigation on the Yenisey, with special emphasis on soundings in the tidal, lowermost part of the river. In this manner, thought Nordenskiöld, when he and his ship arrived at the mouth of the river, his colleagues had already made a careful study of the lower reaches of the Yenisey and could serve as pilots, guiding him upstream to the little port of Dudinka, chosen as the place where merchandise from Europe and goods from Siberia were to be exchanged.

This time, a steamer was chartered for the voyage, the *Ymer*, well supplied with coal for its boilers, and with enough food for fourteen months, if the vessel were forced to winter in Siberia. Kjellman, a botanist, and Stuxberg, a zoologist, were to sail with Nordenskiöld, leaving Norway in mid-July. The 'land party' was led by the zoologist

1a. Borgå: lithograph c. 1850 - - *a* marks the ‘gymnasium,’ identified by Nordenskiöld on the margin

1b. Nordenskiöld in 1863

1c. Anna Mannerheim Nordenskiöld, c. 1863

Om

Grafitens och Chondroditens

Kristallformer,

Akademisk afhandling

med den vidtberömda Fysisk-Mathematiska Fakultetens
vid Kejserliga Alexanders-Universitetet i Finland
tillstånd

under inseende af

Dr Adolf Edvard Arppe,
Professor i Kemin,

för vinnande af

Licentiatgrad i Fysisk-Mathematiska fakulteten

till offentlig granskning framställd af

Nils Adolf Erik Nordenskiöld,
Fys.-Math. Kandidat,

i Hist.-Fil. Lärosalen den 28 Februari 1855

p. v. t. f. m.

Helsingfors, J. C. Frenckell & Son, 1855.

2. Title page of Nordenskiöld's first published work, 1855

3. Officers and crew of *Sofia*, 1868: front row, first from left, von Otter; third from left, Palander

4a. Eskimo dancing, Umanak, Greenland: from photograph by Th. Nordström, 1870

4b. Block of iron from Disko Island, Greenland; now at National Museum of Natural History, Stockholm

5a. Interior of Eskimo dwelling, Greenland; sketch by Th. Nordström, 1870

5b. Godhavn, Greenland: sketch by Th. Nordström, 1870

6a. Church at Khabarovo: photograph by L. Palander, 1878

6b. Louis Palander photographed aboard *Vega*, winter 1878–1879: courtesy Maritime Museum, Göteborg

6c. From left to right: Stuxberg, Nordquist, Hovgaard, aboard *Vega*, winter 1878–1879: photo by L. Palander

7a. *Vega* in winter quarters, on Siberian coast, 1878–1879: photograph by L. Palander

7b. *Vega* in Napels, February, 1880

8. 'All to the Vega!' - - *Illustrazione Italiana*, March 14, 1880

9a. Scientists and officers of *Vega*, with Italian hosts at Pompeii, February, 1880. Front row, left to right: Kjellman, Nordenskiöld, Negri, Palander, Brusewitz

9b. Crew of *Vega*, photographed at Naples, February, 1880

10a. Alexander M. Sibiriakoff: from 'Voyage of the *Vega*'

10b. Oscar Dickson: from 'Voyage of the *Vega*'

10c. Nordenskiöld, 1880: the '*Vega*' photograph

11. Scientists, officers, and supporters of the *Vega* voyage; lithograph, 1880

12a 'The heroes of the *Vega*' in the Arctic and at a banquet in Italy: from *La Mosca*, February 22, 1880

12b. Banquet offered by the city of Naples to the scientists and officers of *Vega*: from *Illustrazione Italiana*, March 14, 1880

13a. Ruins at Brattahlid, Greenland, August, 1880: photograph by O. Kjellström

13b. *Sofia* at Ivigtut, Greenland, June 23, 1883: photograhp by O. Kjellström

14a. Lars Tuorda and Anders Rossa start eastward on the Greenland icecap, July 22, 1883: photograph by O. Kjellström

14b. Second camp, Greenland icecap, July 5, 1883: photograph by O. Kjellström

15. Tomb of Adolf and Anna Nordenskiöld, Västerljung churchyard

16a. Gustav Nordenskiöld, c. 1894 16b. Erland Nordenskiöld, c. 1928

Théel, who had been with Nordenskiöld on the trip up the Yenisey the year before.

With the help of Oscar Dickson, a substantial cargo was rounded up for *Ymer*, consisting of merchandise both from Sweden and from England. The ship's manifest shows a varied load, ranging from cotton cloth to hardware, from inexpensive furniture to china and glass. At the Siberian exchange point, grain, hides, and vodka were to be the principal goods ready for loading.

The 'land party' left Stockholm on April 29, 1876, and after a difficult journey by ship, train, river steamer, and Siberian cart, reached Krasnoyarsk, on the upper Yenisey, on June 8. The group led by Nordenskiöld could not leave until mid-July, for the Kara Sea was not likely to be open to shipping until sometime in August. Adolf Nordenskiöld took advantage of this circumstance, and accepted an invitation to visit the United States. The Centennial Exposition of Philadelphia was about to open, and he was asked to judge the exhibits in the china and pottery section of the Exposition.

On May 11, 1876, Adolf and Anna Nordenskiöld sailed from Liverpool on the steamer *City of Berlin* for New York, and travelled on to Philadelphia. He was given an enthusiastic reception by scientists who knew his work, invited to the best clubs of Philadelphia, and spoke before the American Philosophical Society. Anna Nordenskiöld enjoyed the sights of New York and of Philadelphia, and had a most pleasant reunion with one of her old friends, an American woman who had been her classmate at a Swiss boarding school, when they were both in their teens.

The Nordenskiölds spent five weeks in the United States, and returned to Europe on the same steamer, leaving New York on July 1. From Liverpool, they went by steamer first to Oslo, then on to Trondheim, in central Norway. Anna Nordenskiöld said goodbye to her husband there, and returned to Stockholm, to her children, while Adolf boarded the steamer *Ymer*, all ready to sail for the Kara Sea.

The voyage from Norway to Siberia was uneventful, and *Ymer* entered the mouth of the Yenisey on August 15. In six weeks, Adolf Nordenskiöld travelled from New York to Siberia, a respectable achievement even today, and just short of the unbelievable when one realizes that for nearly half that distance, he was on board a small steamer capable of not more than 6 knots per hour!

By making the journey from Tromsö to the Yenisey in record time, and without interference from pack ice, Nordenskiöld made his point. It was indeed possible to establish a regular shipping route between Siberia and Northwestern Europe. Now he could turn his whole attention to the much greater task ahead, the conquest of the Northeast Passage.

As to the other, business aspects of this, his second voyage to Siberia, just about everything turned out wrong. The 'land party', under Théel, did set out on the downstream voyage on the Yenisey, but never made contact with Nordenskiöld and his ship. The scientists became so engrossed with the phenomena of Siberian nature that their main task, making a detailed survey of navigation possibilities on the great river, was completely forgotten. And when they finally arrived on the lower Yenisey, Théel turned out to be a poor administrator. He could not find a riverboat for hire that would take him, his colleagues, and the many specimens they had collected, downstream, and after useless talks and frustrating negotiations with the local Russian and native officials and rivermen, the entire party turned around, went back by steamer to the upper Yenisey, and thence by land to Moscow, St. Petersburg, and Stockholm.

Nordenskiöld cruised aboard *Ymer* up and down the vast estuary of the Yenisey, sending out native scouts to look for his colleagues, all in vain. A local medicine man, seeing the distress of the Swedish party, consulted his magic drum and reported that the missing group was less than sixty miles away, working their way down river, and would arrive within five days.

The medicine man was right at least in one respect: at the beginning of September, the 'land party' was less than twenty miles upstream from where the *Ymer* had anchored, and unloaded its merchandise. But Théel's fear of bad weather kept his party marooned on shore, while Nordenskiöld, fretting over the possibility of being frozen in by an early storm, decided to return to Norway.

As a business venture, the voyage of *Ymer* was something less than a success. But this mattered little to its sponsors: Sibiriakoff was encouraged by the smoothness of the voyage, while Dickson felt that he could now counter any argument doubting the possibility of sailing from Norway to Siberia with ease.

Ymer anchored in Tromsö harbor on September 22. Adolf Nordenskiöld spent several days talking with old friends among the Norwegian captains and pilots, and summed up his judgment of the voyage in his report, dated Tromsö, September 27, 1876:

'I am convinced, and this conviction is shared by the fishermen and sealers with whom I spoke here, that regular sailings between Siberia and northern Europe present neither greater difficulties nor greater perils than those met by sailors on seaways used by thousands of ships every year.'

XV. FINAL PREPARATIONS FOR THE NORTHEAST PASSAGE - 1876-78

Nordenskiöld's two successful trips from Scandinavia to the shores of northern Siberia made quite an impression on businessmen, both in Russia and in western Europe. Now they were convinced that a seaway between the mouths of the Ob and the Yenisey and northern and western Europe was a real possibility. True, there was still an element of risk involved, but this did not deter the promoters: in the summer and early fall of 1877, two ships made the round trip to and from Siberia, and a third vessel sailed all the way to St. Petersburg.

An English vessel, *Louise,* sailing from Hull on the east coast of England, reached the mouth of the Ob in the late summer of 1877, sailed upstream almost half the length of the river, unloaded its cargo, took on a shipment of Siberian wheat, and safely returned to its home port. A Swedish vessel, *Fraser,* chartered by Sibiriakoff, the Russian businessman who had contributed to the expenses of Nordenskiöld's trip to Siberia in 1876, sailed to the mouth of the Yenisey, loaded graphite from Siberian mines, and returned to its point of departure in Norway.

It was the third ship, sailing that year from Siberia to Europe, that for a short while attracted all the attention of press and business circles, temporarily even obscuring the successes of Adolf Nordenskiöld. Sibiriakoff, eager to impress Russian business and government circles with the feasibility of seaborne trade between Europe and Siberia, decided to stage a truly spectacular voyage. A Russian sea-captain, Schwanenberg, purchased on Sibiriakoff's account a small sailing vessel, built in Yeniseisk, on the upper Yenisey. It was manned by Schwanenberg himself, two mates, and a crew of two, men who were exiles in Siberia. The little vessel, scarcely the size of a fishing smack, named *Utrennaya Zarya, (Dawn)* left Yeniseisk on August 13, 1877, and stopped at the mouth of the river to take on a small cargo of furs, fish, and graphite, sample products of Siberia. On September 11, the ship reached north Norway, on October 31 it stopped in Kristiania, and continued thence to Göteborg. Instead of sailing around Sweden, Captain Schwanenberg crossed Sweden via the Göta Canal, that links Göteborg and Stockholm, and on December 3 anchored in St. Petersburg harbor. The *Dawn* thus became the first ship to reach the Russian capital from Siberia, and for a short while at least, its officers were the toast of St. Petersburg.

Adolf Nordenskiöld was well aware that his voyages to the Yenisey

River, impressive as they seemed to his contemporaries, were but a prelude to the real performance, the crossing of the Northeast Passage. He was certain of Oscar Dickson's support, and though he had yet to meet his Russian well-wisher, Alexander Sibiriakoff, in person, the Russian assured him that he would contribute to the costs of such a voyage. What he needed now was the support of the Swedish government: the privilege of recruiting volunteers for the crew from the Navy, expert help from the Karlskrona Navy yard to get his ship ready for an Arctic voyage, and permission for officers and non-commissioned officers of the Navy to join the expedition.

In 1877, the Minister of the Navy was von Otter, who had commanded Nordenskiöld's ship, *Sofia,* in 1868. It would have been natural for von Otter to support the project presented to the Navy by an old friend, yet the opposite happened. In spite of Adolf Nordenskiöld's successful trips to Siberia in 1875 and 1876, von Otter was completely opposed to Navy support for a voyage through the Northeast Passage.

In November, 1876, Oscar Dickson wrote Nordenskiöld about a series of conversations he had had with von Otter, during a house party on the estate of a mutual friend. 'For two days I kept after him, begging him to let you use a naval vessel for your voyage to Bering Strait. He repeatedly stressed that the whole thing was *impossible*, something I simply could not accept, in view of what you had told me. Finally, after he definitely refused to provide a ship that would have Bering Strait as its destination, I pointed out to him that a Swedish expedition could barely move a single mile east of the Yenisey without bringing back a rich harvest of scientific and geographical results. Confronted with that argument, he said he would provide a ship if the Academy of Sciences requested it, "to continue Nordenskiöld's geographical explorations east of the Yenisey". But he added that he would give strict orders to the ship's captain to turn back as soon as he encountered any ice, something he was absolutely certain would occur even before the ship could reach Cape Chelyuskin (the northernmost tip of Asia).'

Why did von Otter oppose the attempt to traverse the Northeast Passage, an attempt that, if successful, could bring glory to Sweden? Two explanations suggest themselves, either or both could have been on von Otter's mind.

First, there was the matter of passing the northernmost point of Asia, Cape Chelyuskin. There have been throughout the ages certain landmarks that men believed impassable. Cape Bojador, on the northwest coast of Africa, was such an obstacle, dreaded by sailors, until the intrepid Portuguese captains of the early 15th century overcame it, and went on to explore and circumnavigate Africa. Cape Chelyuskin, too, was a dreaded headland, surrounded by cold and ice, the fogs and storms of the Arctic. No ship had ever sailed past it, and this gave it an aura of fear and invincibility. Von Otter was not alone in his belief that no one could overcome the dangers of the Northeast Passage: William Dall, of the Smithsonian Institution in Washington, one of the great Arctic authorities of the time, wrote to a colleague in Sweden, in 1878: 'not even the courage and audacity of Nordenskiöld and his brave companions will avail anything against the ice barriers at Cape Chelyuskin!'

At the same time, it can be assumed that von Otter also took a dim view of Nordenskiöld's failure, in 1872-73, to have completed his dash to the North Pole from Spitsbergen. The fact that this expedition almost ended in tragedy must have convinced von Otter that Nordenskiöld's judgment was not to be trusted, and that his plan to traverse the Northeast Passage was bound to fail.

What happened next must have been a surprise to Nordenskiöld. Von Otter's decision, opposing the planned expedition, was appealed to the King of Sweden. It seems likely that it was Oscar Dickson who decided to call on King Oscar II for help, knowing the monarch's keen interest in seafaring. King Oscar had served in the Navy, aboard sailings ships. He knew and loved the sea, and his poems about the glory of the Swedish Navy of old were very popular. Dickson felt that there was an excellent chance to appeal to his love of the sea and his concern with the Navy, and to ask for his support of an exciting adventure in polar seas.

In January, 1877, when his own estimate of getting official support for the expedition was very low indeed, Adolf Nordenskiöld received an invitation to a dinner at the royal palace in Stockholm. The elegantly printed card, with the crown and the royal cipher, asked him to dine at the palace on January 26, 1877. Later, he was to call the day the 'birthday of the *Vega* expedition'. On the back of the card, he noted: 'royal support of voyage to Bering Strait assured- am authorized to rely on it and on Dickson's influence'.

King Oscar invited one of the royal princes of Denmark, Hans, to the dinner as his guest of honor; they shared a strong interest in sailing adventures. Von Otter was present, and so was Dickson, but the king also extended his hospitality to the scientists who had participated in the two voyages to Siberia in 1875 and 1876. The dinner ended in an informal agreement: King Oscar promised not only to use the prestige of the crown to ensure the support of the Swedish government for the voyage, but pledged financial support of it as well from his own, private means. Adolf Nordenskiöld was now ready to go ahead, and make a formal application to Parliament, asking for the support of the Swedish government.

Eight times during the preceding twenty years had Adolf Nordenskiöld journeyed to the Arctic, first as a scientist participating in expeditions, later as the chief, in charge of ships and men. He was as familiar with the Arctic as any man of his time, he knew its mood and dangers, he knew that planning for an Arctic expedition demanded not only knowledge but imagination as well. It was not enough to know what equipment was needed along the way, what foods had to be taken aboard, one also had to know that an Arctic voyage demanded more of a safety margin than any other venture at sea. During the year and a half that followed the dinner at the royal palace in Stockholm, Adolf Nordenskiöld planned his expedition to the Northeast Passage. Never before was an Arctic voyage so carefully laid out in advance.

The first step was to find a ship strong enough to withstand the pressure of pack ice and, in case the expedition was frozen in, survive the months it was beset in ice. Oscar Dickson put his own business organization to work, and within a few weeks after royal support was promised, two ships were brought to Nordenskiöld's attention. On March 23, 1877, Dickson advised him by telegram that a British-built, steam-driven yacht, *Pandora,* and a German-built fishing and whaling ship, *Vega,* were available.

It quickly became evident that *Pandora* could not be used for the expedition: her hold was too small, and could not possibly carry enough coal and supplies for two years, in case the expedition was forced to winter in the Arctic. *Vega* on the other hand seemed to be well suited for the purpose Nordenskiöld had in mind, and he had asked the man he wanted to command the ship, Louis Palander, to look the ship over.

In the spring of 1877, although royal support was assured for the voyage, Nordenskiöld had not yet submitted a formal request for Navy support, and his plans remained unofficial. Foremost among these was the hope that the Navy would be willing to appoint Lieutenant Louis Palander as commander of the *Vega.* Palander had been second in command of *Sofia* on her successful trip to the north of Spitsbergen in 1868. He had commanded *Polhem,* Nordenskiöld's flagship in 1872-73, and shared the trials, crises, and disappointments of that harsh winter. No other naval officer had the experience and the qualifications of Palander, and it was as the choice of both the expedition's principal supporter, Dickson, and its chief, Nordenskiöld, that Palander journeyed to Germany, to take a long, hard look at the ship that was to carry the hopes of Sweden to the Arctic Ocean.

Palander's report was enthusiastic, and Oscar Dickson advanced the sum necessary to purchase *Vega*, 150,000 Swedish crowns. *Vega* was launched in 1873, in Bremerhaven, Germany. She was a wooden ship that had been built of oak, but the hull was covered with an extra 'ice skin', a protective sheeting of greenheart, hardwood from an exceptionally strong tropical tree. *Vega* measured 38 meters, 125 feet, along the keel; 43 meters, 142 feet, on her deck; her beam was 8 meters, 26 feet, wide, and her capacity was rated at 357 tons. She was fully rigged, with pitch pine masts, steel wire rigging, and extra strong sails; under sail she could make nine to ten knots per hour. There was also a steam engine on board, rated at sixty horsepower; under steam, the ship was capable of six to seven knots per hour.

By the standards of the time *Vega* was a powerful and a well-equipped vessel. Besides two longboats, a steam-powered picketboat, or barge, was also part of the equipment; there was a steam winch to hoist heavy loads aboard, and a reserve rudder and reserve propeller for the engine.

Vega is no longer afloat: she was sold after the voyage to a Swedish fishing firm, sailed for over twenty years in the North Atlantic, and sank off western Greenland after being caught in the ice. But one of her longboats, with the name '*Yenisey*' still visible, is preserved at Nordenskiöld's country estate; and the steam picket boat is stored near Stockholm.

For advice on what to take aboard for a voyage that could very well include a winter in the Arctic Adolf Nordenskiöld turned to his old shipmate, Dr. Envall, who had served as surgeon to the Spitsbergen expedition of 1872-1873. Dr. Envall drew up a set of standard menus that served as a basis for planning for the commissary. Canned foods as well as fresh were to be aboard; pemmican for winter journeys on ice and on land; fresh potatoes, from Italy; cranberry juice from Finland; and cloudberries that marvellous anti-scorbutic, high-vitamin fruit, preserved in barrels, from north Norway.

Clothing, too, was given special attention, since, if the expedition had to winter in the Arctic, the men had to work outdoors when the temperature dropped to between 10 and 25 degrees below zero, Fahrenheit. Winter clothing consisted of woollen undergarments, heavy wool trousers and jacket, a sailcloth blouse as windbreaker, a parka, and leather-soled canvas boots, that were stuffed with hay. Nordenskiöld pointed out that leather boots become heavy and drenched with moisture in deep snow and are hard to dry, while canvas boots and hay would easily dry overnight.

Headgear for the winter consisted of a cap with ear-flaps and a heavy felt hood. The men used sealskin mittens, lined with sheepskin, and fastened to a string passed around the neck. Last but not least, every man was issued snow glasses, to protect against the glare of sun on snow. 'One must have lived in the Arctic' – wrote Nordenskiöld – 'during winter and spring, after the sun returns, to realize how indispensable it is to be protected from the glare that meets the eye in every direction. The inexperienced, even though forewarned, seldom observe the necessary precautions and pay for it by becoming snowblind, not a very dangerous condition, but always extremely painful, lasting several days.'

While supervising and directing preparations for getting ship and provisions ready, Adolf Nordenskiöld also spent a great deal of time preparing a memorandum, addressed to the Swedish government, setting forth his views on the feasibility of the voyage and asking for the government's support. He surveyed virtually all the available literature on past attempts to master the Northeast Passage, and attempted to gather as much current information as possible on the navigability of northern waters. In his investigations he consulted books, journals, and memoirs, as well as observations made by skippers who had journeyed to Arctic waters in the 1860's and 1870's. Over twenty log books of Norwegian ships are preserved in Nordenskiöld's papers, detailed records of the state of wind, water and ice made by captains who had sailed to Novaya Zemlya and beyond in search of fish.

The Russians, who had ruled Siberia since the early 1600's, made several attempts to sail through the Northeast Passage. In 1648, a little band of men, led by Dezhnev, went by small boats along the coast of Northeast Siberia as far as Bering Strait, crossed the strait south to the Bering Sea, and landed on its western, Siberian shore. Dezhnev, without realizing it, had actually discovered Bering Strait, that separates Asia and North America. But his voyage was completely forgotten, and it was not until a century later that any record of it was printed, when the Russian government once more became interested in navigation in the Arctic

Ocean. Today the easternmost point of Asia, on Bering Strait, bears the name of Cape Dezhnev.

Between 1736 and 1743 a series of expeditions were sent to the Siberian Arctic, under the auspices of the Russian Academy of Sciences: one of their tasks was to sail along the entire Siberian coast eastward, to the Pacific. Led by naval officers, these attempts succeeded only in part. Using flat-bottomed barges, sleds in the winter, or slogging on foot, small groups of Russians reached the northernmost point on the mainland of Asia, named after its discoverer Cape Chelyuskin; explored the waters off the coast of east Siberia, named after the commander of that group the Laptev Sea; and surveyed the coasts and islands of northeast Siberia and northwest North America, where both the strait separating the two continents, and the sea uniting them, commemorate the name of their explorer, Captain Bering.

By the early years of the 19th century, the Russians had come to know a good part of the coastline of Siberia, yet no ship had ever succeeded in making the journey from Europe to the Far East through those waters. At the same time, British and American vessels had been exploring the Arctic, entering into its waters from Bering Strait, mostly in search of whales and fish. What remained to be done was to prove that it was possible to sail around the northernmost cape of Asia, and thus connect Atlantic and Pacific.

Nordenskiöld, however, was not content to rest his case on the fragmentary record compiled by earlier explorers. He spent a good deal of his time in 1876 and 1877 writing to people who might have had current information on the state of the Arctic Ocean along the shores of Siberia. For these reports he relied on his Russian patron, Sibiriakoff, who contacted merchants, officials and priests throughout northern Siberia, asking for their views.

One of the letters Sibiriakoff received was from Ivan Platonovitch Kolesev, a merchant in the Siberian city of Yakutsk. Yakutsk was the administrative center of northeast Siberia, and Kolesev was well aquainted with conditions throughout that vast territory. He wrote: 'It is true that the shore of the Arctic in northeast Siberia is clear of ice, often from late May into October, but it is almost impossible to define the period open for navigation. Often, open water extends as far as the eye can see, but there is to the north a white line on the horizon, to remind you of eternal ice. With just a breath of the north wind, those masses of ice are driven onto the shore, and woe to the vessel that cannot hide in a sheltered bay... Attempts to sail in the Arctic Ocean along the Siberian coast have been successful in a way: our Cossacks, in their clumsy, flat-bottomed boats, sailed all the way to Bering Strait. But everything depends on the state of drift ice: it is not dangerous when the weather is calm, but the slightest wind can spell disaster for ships, piling up ice against the coastline, where it mercilessly destroys anything in its way.' Kolesev ended his report by saying that a northern sea route between the Atlantic and the Pacific would indeed be desirable, but that he had serious doubts as to its future, unless either the climate changed in the far North, or powerful icebreakers could be built, to open the way for ships.

Another of Sibiriakoff's correspondents, writing from Siberia's capital, Irkutsk, stated that the summer of 1876 was indeed an open one, most of the Siberian coast was ice-free. He considered the period August-September best for sailing across those waters. He added that if a ship managed to pass Cape Chelyuskin, it stood an excellent chance of completing the voyage and reaching the Pacific.

But Nordenskiöld was aware of the presence of others besides Russians in the extreme northeast of Siberia. Captain Cook, the great explorer of the Pacific, had sailed through Bering Strait into the Arctic Ocean, and others followed in his wake. One ship was the American naval vessel, *Vincennes,* that entered those waters in 1855. Nordenskiöld found out that the officer who had commanded the *Vincennes*, Rear Admiral Rodgers, was stationed in Washington, as Superintendent of the Naval Observatory, and wrote him requesting his views on the navigability of the waters off northeast Siberia.

Admiral Rodgers replied that in August, 1855, he had sailed as far as longitude 176 degrees east of Greenwich, more than four hundred miles west from Bering Strait, until he had found pack ice. Anxious to provide up-to-date information for Nordenskiöld, he forwarded the inquiry to the United States Navy's Bureau of Navigation. The Bureau, in turn, sent out an officer, Lieutenant Washburn Maynard, to interview whalers and ship's captains on the New England coast.

Maynard's report, sent on to Adolf Nordenskiöld, stated that Bering Strait is rarely free of ice before the first of July, and is often impassable until the latter part of that month. The ice is described by the whalers as 'field ice', there being but few icebergs. This field is driven to the north by southerly winds which prevail during the months of June, July, August and a part of September, sometimes evidently to a considerable distance, since some ships have been as far north as latitude 72 degrees without seeing ice in any direction. (Bering Strait is at the approximate latitude of 66 degrees.)

Lieutenant Maynard added that most of the American whalers entering the Arctic Ocean follow the Alaskan coast, but a trading schooner, owned by the Alaska Commercial Company of San Francisco, usually called at places on both the American and the Siberian shores of Bering Strait.

Following up Maynard's report, Nordenskiöld contacted the Alaska Commercial Company. William Miller, president of the company, replied to the inquiry, and quoted a letter from the captain of the American whaler *Massachusetts*. 'Capt. Williams is of the opinion from his observation that, usually after the middle of August, there is no ice south of 70 degrees, nor west of 175 degrees, until the first of October. There is hardly a year but that you could go as far as Cape North (Cook's farthest landfall on the Siberian coast), which is at longitude 180 degrees, during the month of September. If the winds through July and August have prevailed from the southwest, as is usual, the North Shore will be found clear of ice.' The report ended by assuring Nordenskiöld that the charts made by the U.S. Navy expedition, in 1855, are quite correct, with the exception of some details in the shore line, and that the headlands were shown correctly, and the soundings were reliable.

Encouraged by the information he received, Nordenskiöld summed up the situation in these words: 'That the ocean lying north of the north coast of Siberia between the mouth of the Yenisey and Chaun Bay (about 600 miles from Bering Strait) has never been ploughed by the keel of any proper seagoing vessel, still less been traversed by any steamer specially fitted out for navigation amidst ice;

that the small vessels with which it had been had attempted to traverse this part of the ocean, never ventured very far from the coast;

that an open sea with a fresh breeze was as destructive for them, indeed more destructive, than a sea covered with drift ice;

that they almost always sought some convenient winter harbor just at that season of the year when the sea is freest of ice, namely late summer or autumn;

and that notwithstanding the sea from Cape Chelyuskin to Bering's Straits has been repeatedly traversed, none has yet succeeded in sailing over the whole extent at once.'

In conclusion, he wrote: 'It seems probable to me that a well-equipped steamer should be able, without meeting too many difficulties from ice, to force a passage this way during autumn in a few days, and thus not only solve a geographical problem of several centuries' standing, but also, with all the means that are now at the disposal of the man of science in geography, hydrography, geology and natural history, survey a hitherto almost unknown sea of enormous extent.'

Pointing out that King Oscar of Sweden, Oscar Dickson and Alexander Sibiriakoff had offered to support the expedition, Nordenskiöld made the following specific requests:

'That the steamer *Vega*, bought for the expedition, already in very good order, may at the Navy yard at Karlskrona be made completely seaworthy for the object in view; may be provided with the necessary stock of coal and provisions for at most two years; that the officers and men belonging to the Navy who take part in the expedition as volunteers may be allowed, during the time they take part in the expedition, sea pay and other privileges in the same way as during a Navy cruise; and that the expedition, since its ship will be commanded by an officer of the Navy and manned by men of the Navy, may obtain the right to fly the flag of a man-of-war.'

Parliament granted all of these requests, but the Navy balked at letting *Vega* fly the Navy ensign. Instead, Nordenskiöld obtained permission to hoist the flag of the Royal Swedish Sailing Society: Sweden's colors, with a triple 'S' and the royal cipher.

In another, more important matter the Navy did agree to Nordenskiöld's original request, and assigned Lieutenant Louis Palander to duty as commander of *Vega*. His second in command, Lieutenant Erik Brusewitz, had also had considerable seagoing experience, and served under von Otter on the ship that, in 1871, brought Nordenskiöld's meteorites from Greenland to Scandinavia.

In selecting his shipmates, Adolf Nordenskiöld followed his old principle, making the group representative of Scandinavia as a whole. Besides the commander, his second officer, and the crew, all of whom came from the Swedish Navy, *Vega* also had one Danish and one Finnish officer and, to make the group truly international, an Italian officer as well.

Lieutenant Andreas Hovgaard, of the Danish Navy, was recommended to Nordenskiöld by a Danish acquaintance: he was astronomer, meteorologist and geophysicist of the expedition. Lieutenant Giacomo Bove of the Italian Navy, suggested by Nordenskiöld's old friend, Commander Negri, President of the Italian Geographical Society, was *Vega*'s navigator and hydrographer. The Finnish member of the group, Lieutenant Oscar Nordquist, had graduated in the spring of 1878 from the Finnish Military Academy, and had been commissioned in the Finnish rifle regiment of the Imperial Russian Army. He was described to Nordenskiöld as a brilliant linguist, whose knowledge of Russian was considered essential for the expedition's contacts with Russian authorities. To obtain permission for Nordquist to join the expedition, Adolf Nordenskiöld wrote to the President of the Imperial Geographical Society in St. Petersburg, asking him to intervene with the Russian authorities on Nordquist's behalf. Leave was granted to Nordquist, proof of the importance Russia attached to the *Vega* voyage.

Vega's crew was selected from Swedish Navy volunteers: Palander and Brusewitz picked two noncommissioned officers and fifteen enlisted men. Several of the crew had had experience in Arctic waters, two of them had been with Nordenskiöld in Spitsbergen in 1872-73. Just before sailing, three Norwegian harpooners, chosen from among the best in northern Norway, joined the ship.

The scientific staff of *Vega* consisted, besides Nordenskiöld, of a botanist and a zoologist. Frans Kjellman, the botanist, had worked with Nordenskiöld in Spitsbergen in 1872-73, and had sailed with him to the Yenisey in 1875. Anton Stuxberg, the zoologist, was something of an Arctic veteran, too, who had participated in both the 1875 and 1876 expeditions to the Yenisey. The two scholars were assisted by the ship's doctor, Ernst Almquist, by Lieutenant Nordquist, who was something of an amateur zoologist, and by an expert taxidermist and laboratory assistant, Boström.

Officers, scientists, and crew numbered thirty men. Their ship was being readied at the Navy's Karlskrona shipyard, after Parliament had voted special funds for the expedition. When King Oscar gave his approval to the *Vega* voyage, in January, 1877, it was agreed that Oscar Dickson would act as treasurer for the project. In terms of cash contributions, Dickson provided the lion's share, 62% of the total net cost. Alexander Sibiriakoff contributed 15% of the net costs, King Oscar II, 10%, while the Swedish treasury, in addition to providing equipment for the vessel, contributed 13%. The total advanced amounted to 710,000 Swedish kronor, 185,000 dollars at the time.

The *Vega* expedition was conceived, from the beginning, with a double purpose: to prove the feasibility of a Northeast Passage from Europe to the Pacific, and to gather scientific data in an area largely unknown at the time. But the expedition's Russian sponsor, Sibiriakoff, insisted that the commercial side of the venture should also be kept in mind. In addition to his contribution to the costs of the voyage, he had equipped three ships to accompany *Vega* part of the way, to carry coal and supplies for the expedition, and goods destined for Siberia.

The most ambitious vessel of Sibiriakoff's little squadron was the steamship *Lena.* It was designed by a Finn, Robert Runeberg, and built in Sweden, with a hull strong enough to withstand ice pressure; its destination was the great river of East Siberia, the Lena. The second ship, one that had already sailed to and from Siberia, was the small steamer *Fraser,* while the third was a sailing vessel, *Express,* whose job it was to carry coal as well as commercial cargo. The destination of *Fraser* and *Express* was the lower Yenisey, they were to discharge their cargo there and pick up products of Siberia for the return voyage.

The manifest of goods carried to Siberia was varied: nails and iron bars, horseshoes and sheet iron, petroleum and salt, a complete iron barge, and a portable rivet forge, all merchandise from the advanced industrial nations of West and North Europe to the remote markets of North Asia.

The captains of *Lena, Fraser* and *Express* were Norwegian and Swedish merchant marine officers, all three with considerable experience in Arctic waters. But Alexander Sibiriakoff insisted that his own representative, a Russian mining engineer, Serebrennikoff, make the journey to Siberia with the squadron, a reasonable request since contacts with Russian authorities were likely to present some problems.

On June 22, 1878, *Vega* lifted anchor at Karlskrona, and started out toward Göteborg. While *Vega* was passing through the Sund, near Copenhagen, a German man-of-war signalled her, asking for her destination. Captain Palander's reply was brief and to the point: Bering Strait!

On June 27, *Vega* arrived in Göteborg, and all scientific equipment was loaded on board. Nordenskiöld was present, and so was his old Italian friend, Commander Negri, to wish godspeed to the expedition and to his compatriot, Lieutenant Bove. Oscar Dickson entertained the officers and the scientific staff at dinner in his home, and on July 4, at 3 in the afternoon, *Vega* sailed out of Göteborg in lovely weather with a light westerly wind. Dickson and Governor Ehrensvärd saw the ship off, but Nordenskiöld had already left by rail, to join his wife and his older son, Gustaf, who were to accompany him as far as Tromsö.

Nordenskiöld knew that this was going to be a long voyage: even if all went well, and *Vega* arrived at Bering Strait before the fall freeze-up, plans called for the ship's return by way of the Far East, India, the Suez Canal and the Mediterranean. At best, he would not be back for a year, and he asked Anna and his son to see him off.

Vega and *Lena* arrived in Tromsö together; the two other ships were already on their way to the Kara Sea. Nordenskiöld's family said goodbye to him and left for home. At 2:15 in the morning, on July 21, 1878, as *Vega* steamed out of Tromsö Sound, Nordenskiöld and his companions started out towards their distant goal.

XVI. JOURNEY OF THE 'VEGA' TO EAST SIBERIA – 1878

The northern seas always had a fascination for Scandinavians. Writing in the thirteenth century, the anonymous author of one of the oldest Norwegian chronicles of seafaring, the 'King's Mirror', summed up the motives of men bound for the Arctic in these words:

'One is fame and rivalry, for it is in the nature of man to seek places where great dangers are to be met and thus to win fame. A second motive is curiosity, for it is also in man's nature to wish to see and experience the things that he has heard about and thus to learn whether the facts are as told or not. The third is desire for gain: for men seek wealth wherever they have heard that gain is to be gotten, though, on the other hand, there may be great dangers, too.'

Curiosity was foremost on the minds of the men aboard *Vega*, the desire to sail across unexplored seas. Fame, too, drove them on, the desire to be the first to succeed where others had failed for more than three centuries, to open a seaway north by east to the Orient. And it is quite obvious from Adolf Nordenskiöld's own writings that he envisaged, as the ultimate aim of the expedition, the exploration of a seaway that would give access to Siberia and all its resources.

After being delayed by strong winds off North Cape, the northernmost tip of Norway, *Vega* made the passage across the Barents Sea without delay, and on July 31, ten days out of Tromsö, the four ships met at Yugor Shar, the strait leading into the Kara Sea. There is a small settlement there, Khabarovo, a place Nordenskiöld had visited during his first trip to Siberia, in 1875. All of the men went ashore except the ship's cook. He had no interest in foreign lands, and managed to remain aboard ship during the entire voyage.

The first chore Nordenskiöld attended to while ashore was to check the ship's chronometer: he had determined the location of the church at Khabarovo during his first visit, and could thus check the chronometer's accuracy against the longitude he had measured earlier. Palander meanwhile took a picture of the weatherbeaten little church, with its Russian crosses, against the lonely tundra.

Khabarovo was a market town, where the native Nentsi traded skins, walrus hides, and walrus tusks for ammunition, tea, bread, sugar and rum with the handful of Russians who came to visit the place during the summer. The Swedes were more interested in acquiring native curios, and

Nordenskiöld bought several small stone carvings representing native idols. One of the Russians, seeing the visitors' interest in local lore, offered to take them to a place where the natives still made sacrifices to their old gods. The next day, Nordenskiöld and several members of his staff crossed the narrow Yugor Strait on a steam launch and were led by their guide to a small hill, overlooking the sea. A stone cairn marked the sacred place. Here the natives brought their carcasses of bears, reindeer, wolves, and foxes, smeared the blood on the idols' faces, and left skull and bones on the ground.

The Nentsi idols were wooden sticks of various lengths. The top of the stick was crudely carved to represent a face, usually with a prominent nose. The Swedes collected a number of the little figures, and on the advice of their Russian guide, left a couple of small silver coins by the cairn, to put the spirits at ease.

The Russian guide then took Nordenskiöld and Captain Nilsson across a small inlet, to show them a Nenets grave. It was in the form of a stout wooden box, carefully fastened to the ground by means of stakes and crossbars, to protect it from marauding animals. Opening the box, they found a skeleton, surrounded by all manner of household implements and tools, put there to accompany the dead to the next world. While Captain Nilsson managed to take the Russian guide for a short walk, Nordenskiöld quickly removed skeleton and implements from the grave, and closed the box, stuffing everything in a sack he had carried with him. He later justified his actions in a letter to his wife, saying that so little was known of the natives of North Siberia that the skeleton would provide valuable information for anthropologists trying to determine the physical characteristics of the race.

From Khabarovo the ships sailed on eastward and, on August 6, anchored in the lee of Dickson Island, at the mouth of the Yenisey River. First, as much coal was transferred from *Express* to *Vega*, as could be stored in her hold. With the coaling completed, *Express* and *Fraser* sailed up river, to discharge the cargo they had brought from Europe. This time, everything went on schedule: the two ships picked up wheat, rye and tallow, returned to the mouth of the river, and without any mishap or delay reached Göteborg, in mid-October.

After taking leave of their companions, *Vega* and *Lena,* too, got ready and on August 10 weighed anchor at Dickson Island, ready to face the unknown waters ahead. Up to their arrival at Dickson Island, the ships had crossed waters well known and, on the whole, adequately charted.

The voyage ahead, rounding the Taimyr Peninsula that juts northward from Siberia, and sailing past the dreaded Cape Chelyuskin, was another matter.

The Russian explorers who had reached Cape Chelyuskin by land, more than a century earlier, had made some sketch maps that survived. But these were too general, and on too small a scale to be relied upon, and Palander, ever the careful seaman, would not take any chances with the ships under his command. *Vega* and *Lena* kept close to the coastline, and took frequent soundings to avoid running aground. This took time, and further delay was caused by the fog that often completely surrounded the ships.

The first day out of Dickson Harbor, *Vega* hove to off a small island during a foggy spell. Nordenskiöld, Kjellman, Almquist, and Nordquist rowed ashore in a dinghy, to take a close look. It was a barren and utterly desolate place, Nordenskiöld wrote, a low rock, with cliffs rising in a few places above the sea, the surface broken up by frost and covered with a thick growth of lichen. In low, protected spots the bedrock was covered by gravel that, through alternate freezing and thawing, became divided into small hexagonal shapes. In the cracks between these shapes there was a scant growth of mosses and a few flowering plants. There were no mammals in sight, not even the usual inhabitant of lonely Arctic islands, the polar bear.

The visitors found only six species of birds, foremost among these were snow buntings, that prefer these desolate places for nesting. They fluttered around, twittering, as if showing off their nests protected by small mounds of stones. Down by the water's edge, wading birds were busily running to and fro, catching insects. The naturalists were fascinated by the fact that the birds they shot had their crops full of parts of insects, while they themselves spent hours finding only a few tiny gnats. Obviously, the birds had better eyesight, were faster on their feet, and caught their prey on the wing.

Vega and *Lena* continued northeastward, cautiously following the coastline. The fog, drifting around the ships, became so heavy at times that the captains' only means of signalling to each other was by steam whistle. The sea was mirror-smooth, drift ice was often in sight but did not slow down the ships' progress. By the afternoon of August 14, though, the fog became so thick that the ships anchored in a well-protected inlet. Nordenskiöld named it Actinia Bay, after the numerous sea anemones, Actinia, they found on the bottom of the bay.

The ships spent four days in Actinia Bay, waiting for the fog to lift. Nordenskiöld, anxious to leave messages behind, reporting the expedition's progress in case other ships stopped in the same vicinity, had the sailors build a cairn of boulders, half a mile from where *Vega* was at anchor, and placed a message, put in a tin can, inside the marker. The message was brief: 'The Swedish Arctic expedition of 1878, consisting of the steamers *Vega* and *Lena*, left Dickson Harbor on August 10, and sailed in almost ice-free waters. The expedition anchored here on August 14, and have remained, waiting to continue their journey in a westerly, then northerly direction around Taimyr Island, as soon as the prevailing thick fog will allow it. All is well. Please forward this message immediately to His Majesty the King of Sweden.'

The date of the message was August 17, 1878. Ninety-two years later, in the early fall of 1970, a Soviet hydrographic vessel, *Sekstan*, anchored in the waters of Actinia Bay and the pilot of the ship, Vladilen Troitskiy, noticed a boulder on shore that seemed unusually tall and placed in an upright position. He went ashore and discovered that the boulder was part of a cairn, and found a tin can inside, with a barely legible message written on a yellowed piece of paper.

The message was carefully placed between blotters, and after the ship's return to European Russia, the staff of the Soviet Academy of Sciences managed to restore the Swedish text of Nordenskiöld's message. Of the Russian text, written on the back of the paper, only a few words could be read. After the message was fully restored, it was placed between plastic sheets and permanently sealed, and on May 14, 1971 the Soviet Ambassador to Sweden presented it to King Gustav VI Adolf. It is now kept with the Nordenskiöld papers in the Swedish Academy of Sciences, in Stockholm.

The fog lightened a little after three days at Actinia Bay, and on August 18th the two ships steamed on towards the north. By the next afternoon the navigator's calculations showed that the expedition was approaching Cape Chelyuskin, but fog prevented any view of the coastline. Suddenly, the fog lifted and the two ships found themselves in a bay, with the vast, dark mass of the famed headland dead ahead.

The log of *Vega* recorded the event in these words: '19 August 1878. Anchored at 6 p.m. off Cape Chelyuskin, latitude 77 degrees 36 minutes 36 seconds north, longitude 103 degrees 25 minutes east, in four fathoms water. Raised flag on mainmast. Fired five shots from cannon. Issued extra rations to crew: two ounces cheese, five ounces sugar per man.'

Nordenskiöld showed much more enthusiasm in his comments. 'We have now reached a great goal' – he wrote – 'sought after in vain for centuries. For the first time, a ship lay at anchor off the northernmost cape of the Old World.'

Lieutenant Hovgaard made a drawing of the arrival at Cape Chelyuskin. *Vega* has just fired a salute from her cannon; *Lena*'s smoke is rising from her stack; while in the foreground a large polar bear contemplates the happenings from atop an ice floe. The bear kept running back and forth on his perch, looking out to sea, sniffing uneasily, trying to find out who were these remarkable visitors to his realm. A boat put out to shoot the bear, but he was so scared by the five-gun salute that he took to his heels and was not seen again.

Members of the expedition picked up rocks from the Cape to carry home as souvenirs. One of the rocks, carried home by Nordenskiöld, ended up at La Jolla, California, where his great-grandson is a member of the faculty of the University of California. When a group of Russian scientists visited his home in the 1960's, their host asked them whether they knew where the northernmost point of Asia lay. 'At Cape Chelyuskin, of course!', said the visitors. 'Not at all' – replied the host – 'it is right here, on the mantelpiece in our living room!'

The crew set up a cairn on the Cape, similar to the one in Actinia Bay, and placed a message in a tin can inside it. The message listed the names of the expedition members, and of the ships, and the date, August 19, 1878. This message, too, was found much later, in 1936, by sailors from a Soviet vessel, and the find was reported in Soviet and Swedish newspapers.

In his book on the *Vega* voyage Nordenskiöld described Cape Chelyuskin. 'Asia's north cape forms a low promontory, divided by a bay, the eastern arm of it projecting considerably further north than the western one. A ridge with gently sloping sides runs inland from the east arm of the bay and rises within sight of the western arm to a height of a thousand feet. The summit of the ridge, like the lowland at its foot, was almost bare of snow. Only on the hillsides, in the deep furrows carved out by meltwater, and in low spots on the coast were there large masses of snow. There was also snow in many places along the water's edge. But no glacier rolled its bluish-white ice down the slopes, there were no lakes, no sharp cliffs, no high peaks that would lend any natural beauty to this landscape. It was the most monotonous, the most desolate place I have ever seen in the Arctic.'

In contrast to the monotonous landscape, the vegetation showed great variety: much of the ground was covered with moss and lichens, and on the tip of the Cape there was a profusion of wildflowers. It looked, wrote Nordenskiöld, 'as if many of the plants of the region had attempted to migrate further north, but on meeting the sea had stopped, unable to go farther, unwilling to turn back.' As the men were walking about, suddenly a very large flock of wild geese appeared overhead, coming in from the sea, flying southward. Did these birds come from land lying north of Cape Chelyuskin? Nordenskiöld would have liked to pursue the matter, but his course lay to the east, and it was time for his ships to weigh anchor, and continue on their quest for the Northeast Passage.

In 1913, thirty-five years after *Vega*'s visit to those northern waters, Adolf Nordenskiöld's guess that there was land north of Cape Chelyuskin was confirmed. Two Russian naval vessels, commanded by Captain Vilkitskii, discovered an archipelago due north of the Cape, now called North Land, Severnaya Zemlya.

After their stay at the Cape, *Vega* and *Lena* continued eastward. The ships encountered patches of drift ice, but it was fog that constituted the greatest hazard as they were moving on, along an unknown coastline.

'It is barely possible' – wrote Nordenskiöld – 'for anyone who had not had that experience to have any idea of the optical illusions produced by fog in places where the size of an object visible in the fog is not known and its distance cannot be determined. Our guessing at size and distance becomes wholly undependable. Furthermore, the ignorance of the beholder changes the obscure outline of objects concealed by fog into whimsical fantasies.

'Once, during a boat journey in Spitsbergen, I had to row to an island several kilometers away. When we started out the sky was clear, but while we were busy shooting some birds for our dinner, suddenly we found ourselves in the midst of thick fog. It happened so quickly that we did not have a chance to take our bearings of the island. We had to row blindly, among drifting ice floes. All of us worked as hard as we could, looking for the island where the beach would offer a safe anchorage. Suddenly we saw a dark line on the horizon. We took it to be the island we were bound for, and at first did not think it strange that this dark line rose rapidly, for we believed that the fog was lifting, and that we could see more of the island. Next, two white snowfields appeared, that we had not noticed before, one on each side of the islands, but right away all this became a sea monster, much like the head of a walrus, as big as a mountain. But this, too, started to move, and finally shrunk to nothing much more than the head of an ordinary walrus, which lay on an ice-floe near the boat: its white tusks appeared earlier as the snow fields, its dark brown, round head had been the dark line above the horizon. Barely had this will-of-the-whisp gone, when one of the men called out: "Land straight ahead – high land!" We now saw a region of high mountains, with peaks and glaciers, but this, too, disappeared in another instant, and shrunk to a perfectly normal, low ice floe, blackened on top with earth.

'On another occasion, when Palander and I, and nine of our men, made a journey by sledge around Northeast Spitsbergen, in 1873, we met a bear on the ice of Wahlenberg Bay, in foggy weather. We had all seen the bear, and were waiting for it. But instead of approaching us in his usual zig-zagging course, while he was using his nose to decide whether we were fit to eat, just as the marksman took aim the bear spread out giant wings and flew away. We saw him clearly then, it was a small ivory gull. On that same journey, on an occasion when we were resting in our tent, we heard the cook shout outside: "A bear! A big bear! No, a reindeer, a very small reindeer!" Someone fired a shot, and the animal turned out to be a very small fox; the honor of having played the part of a very large animal cost him his life. You can judge from these stories how difficult it was to sail in fog and through drift ice in unknown waters.'

As the ships slowly steamed on, Nordenskiöld tried to reach the New Siberian Islands, lying almost due east of Cape Chelyuskin. But fog and drift ice made that course too dangerous; instead, *Vega* and *Lena* turned south, to follow the coastline. Trawling nets were lowered from time to time, and an exceptionally large haul of marine life was brought on board: sponges, sea spiders, worms, crustaceans. Water temperature was close to, and at times below, freezing point, and the scientists recorded these observations with surprise, this being the first time that such an abundance of marine life was found under what seemed truly adverse conditions, in very cold water that freezes over for as much as eight months of the year.

On August 27, the two ships were off the delta of the Lena River. The escort steamer *Lena* was destined for the middle reaches of the river, for the city of Yakutsk; to start her journey upstream, the steamer had orders to enter one of the branches of the delta, there to pick up a river pilot. On the night of August 27, *Vega* and *Lena* were about to part company.

The captain of the *Lena*, Captain Johannesen, was rowed over to *Vega*, where Nordenskiöld gave him last-minute instructions, and letters of introduction to the Russian authorities, obtained through the help of the Swedish Legation in St. Petersburg. Nordenskiöld asked Captain Johannesen to send telegrams to the expedition's patrons, Dickson and Sibiriakoff, and to Anna Nordenskiöld, as soon as he reached his destination, Yakutsk. These telegrams, and letters that were mailed at the same time, turned out to be the last news anyone had of *Vega* for several months.

Vega sailed eastward, while Captain Johannesen turned *Lena* south, toward the delta of the Lena River, looking for his pilot. His instructions were to look for a flagpole flying a signal flag, marking his rendezvous with the native who was to guide the ship through the labyrinth of the delta to the main, navigable branch of the river.

Captain Johannesen cruised around for four days, searching the delta, but neither flagpole nor pilot was found, because the pilot never left his home base. He was hired for the job by a business associate of Sibiriakoff, Kolesev, in Yakutsk, and was paid an advance on his salary. Finding himself suddenly in funds, the man decided to celebrate, got drunk, and broke his arm. By then he was both unable and unwilling to live up to his assignment, and stayed home.

At the end of four days, Captain Johannesen finally decided to risk the river trip on his own. At first the shallow waters presented quite a problem, but Johannesen persisted, and on September 7th he was on his way upstream. In two weeks' time he reached his destination, Yakutsk, only to find that Kolesev, the man who was to be his host, was not there. Never one to be deterred by the informality of Russian business practices, Johannesen kept on his way and sailed on upstream for another three hundred miles. It was early October by then, winter was closing in, and Johannesen decided to turn back, and laid up *Lena* in winter quarters just outside of Yakutsk. The following summer he returned to Europe with a cargo; *Lena* thus became the first ship to penetrate deep into the interior of East Siberia, joining it to the Atlantic and the world of Europe.

On his first anchoring at Yakutsk, Captain Johannesen entrusted the telegrams Nordenskiöld gave him to the Russian postal service. In three weeks' time, they were delivered in Moscow, to Sibiriakoff, and in Sweden, to Anna Nordenskiöld and Oscar Dickson. Adolf Nordenskiöld was full of optimism: the two ships had passed Cape Chelyuskin on August 19, the sea was nearly ice-free, he was steaming on to Bering

Strait, and requested letters to be sent to Yokohama, Japan.
The letters Adolf Nordenskiöld wrote to his wife and to Oscar Dickson, that had been posted in Yakutsk, arrived in Sweden early in December. In his letter to Dickson, Nordenskiöld stated that with the circumnavigation of Asia's northernmost point, Cape Chelyuskin, one of the main objectives of the expedition was accomplished. The collections of specimens from land and sea were exceptionally rich and of the greatest scientific interest, he wrote; morale on board *Vega* was excellent; and the chances of crossing Bering Strait and making a landfall in Japan before the end of the year were very strong indeed.
As *Vega* continued on a southeasterly course, paralleling the coastline, the first signs of winter began to appear. On the night of September 2, the temperature of the air sank below freezing for the first time. The ship now faced two hazards: when it was too far out to sea, the ice might suddenly become so heavy that it could not be traversed and the vessel would be caught, but if the vessel was too close to the coast, the water might turn out to be too shallow for safe passage.
One by one, *Vega* passed the mouths of the great rivers of northeastern Siberia: the Yana, the Indigirka, the Kolyma. There was a Russian settlement on the lower Kolyma, but the season was late, and it would have taken precious time for *Vega* to call there. Warm water from these rivers was still streaming into the Arctic Ocean and it assured an ice-free, safe channel near the coast.
It was a dull and monotonous coast, devoid of landmarks; inland, the empty tundra stretched on, mile after tedious mile. Birds had already left the far north, southbound on their yearly migration; and there were no seals or walruses in the sea. Life on board settled down to a routine: the crew kept the ship scrubbed clean, the scientific staff carried out observations of temperature and wind. All were quite tired of the surroundings, and looked forward to their crossing of Bering Strait, and to the exotic world of the Far East.
For five weeks, since they had left the small settlement of Khabarovo on the Kara Sea, the men on *Vega* had seen only their own companions, and those on the other ships of the expedition. While they covered hundreds after hundreds of miles on an empty sea, the coasts they passed by were equally empty. They never met a Russian hunter, nor any of the Siberian natives whose presence on these shores had been reported by earlier explorers. Suddenly, on the morning of September 6, when *Vega* passed Cape Shelagskii, that marks the entrance to one of the big bays on the

north Siberian coast, the lookout reported two boats off the starboard bow.

Every man, except the imperturbable cook, rushed on deck to watch the two skin boats approach the ship. The boats were wide, like the 'umiak', or women's boats, of the Greenland Eskimo, and were loaded to the gunwhales with laughing, chattering natives, men, women, and children, all pointing excitedly to the ship, obviously anxious to come on board. The engine stopped, and everyone climbed up on the deck.

The visitors were Chukchi, the natives who live on the shores of the northeasternmost peninsula of Asia, that is named after them. They did not appear to know a word of Russian, but neither were they surprised to see a large vessel off their coast. The reason for this soon became evident: most of them knew the word 'ship', and one youngster could count up to ten in English. It was not until much later that the men aboard the *Vega* found out about the wandering habits of the Chukchi, who roamed along the coasts of the Arctic and of the Bering Sea, and had had business with American whaling ships before.

'Many of them were tall, well-grown men' – wrote Nordenskiöld – 'clothed in close fitting skin trousers and parkas of reindeer skin. They were bareheaded, their hair was cut short, except for a lock that was combed over the brow. Several had caps stuck in their belts, but obviously they felt that the weather was still too warm for any head covering. The women were tattooed, with black and blue-black lines running across their foreheads, noses, and cheeks. Yet their faces were not as homely as those of the Eskimo, or of the Nentsi of northwest Siberia. Some of the young girls were in fact not ugly at all. They looked distinctly cleaner than the Nentsi and had a rather pretty, reddish-white complexion. Two of the men were quite fair, they may have been descendants of escaped Russian prisoners who had settled among the natives.'

For all that the men of *Vega* knew, this might have been their only encounter with the natives of the region. Palander took several photographs, including one of the Chukchi in a remarkable garment, a raincoat made of the gut of seals, looking very much like a modern nylon windbreaker.

At last, the visitors took their leave, and *Vega* continued its lonesome voyage along the coast. There were numerous lagoons, formed by sand spits that separated them from open water. Farther inland, the land rose gradually to low, bare hills overlooking the tundra; some of these

were already covered with a thin layer of light snow. Several small settlements of the Chukchi came into view as the ship sailed along the coast, mostly on the sand spits that separate the lagoons from the sea.
On September 8th, *Vega* was barely five hundred miles from Bering Strait, but its progress became slower and slower. There was drift ice in the sea, the fog at times became so dense that the ship had to heave to, and the offshore waters were so shallow that constant soundings were necessary to keep in navigable depth. Finally, they had to stop.
After nearly three days of waiting for the fog to lift, they sailed on. But progress was painfully slow, and after making barely forty miles, the ship encountered pack ice. It was decided to anchor offshore again, and to wait until a favorable wind would push the floes out to sea. It was the 11th of September. All the reports Nordenskiöld had received indicated that a navigable channel offshore would stay open at least until the end of the month.
Time lay heavy on the hands of the men. They went ashore, visiting the Chukchi villages that were scattered along the coast. Nordenskiöld would have liked to barter with the natives and acquire tools, walrus ivory, possible some fresh seal meat, but he found himself hampered by the lack of articles he could use for exchange. On his earlier trips to Siberia, in 1875 and 1876, he had dealt with natives who were in constant touch with Russian traders, and who preferred Russian currency to barter. This time, he had taken plenty of Russian money with him, only to find that the Chukchi were not the least interested in cash.
The only articles Nordenskiöld could use for barter were on board *Vega* by accident. In 1876, two large boxes of Dutch clay pipes were supposed to have been carried aboard Nordenskiöld's ship to the Yenisey, but the boxes had arrived in Tromsö after his departure for Siberia. He had had them put aboard *Vega*, as a last-minute addition to the ship's stores, and he had also kept two bales of tobacco, intended for shipment to the Yenisey on *Fraser*, for his own use. These items were much in demand. The Chukchi would accept copper coins only if a hole was bored in each, since they wanted to use them as earrings. Silver coins were popular, and Nordenskiöld distributed a large number of Swedish silver crown pieces, thinking that if anything happened to the expedition and, like others before, it vanished in the Arctic mists, the coins would at least show where they had last been seen.
After ten days' waiting, Nordenskiöld and Palander decided that if they were to avoid spending the winter off that inhospitable coast, an attempt

should be made to find a navigable channel and continue eastward. Nordenskiöld climbed a low hill, and found that there was an open channel near the coast. *Vega* started out, but most of the time the water was so shallow that there was only a depth of about a foot under the keel. The next morning they struck a large ice floe. At first an attempt was made to blast through it with gunpowder, but they could not make any headway. The men went down on the ice and hacked away with axes. At last, enough of an opening was cut so that the ship, with its strong prow, could get through.

Slowly, painfully, the ship inched forwards. Finally, on the 26th of September, more open water was encountered. The next day, *Vega* cautiously made its way around Kolyuchin Bay, the last major inlet on the coast before Cape Dezhnev, the entrance to Bering Strait. On the 27th, the ship was anchored to a large ice floe at the eastern entrance to Kolyuchin Bay. Lieutenant Hovgaard went out in the steam launch to survey the waters ahead, and came back to report that there was sufficient depth to continue. One of the Norwegian harpooners climbed a hill, and reported that there was a broad open channel to the southeast. The chances were very good that *Vega* could get past the ice threatening to close in from the Arctic Ocean, and make the final dash to the great goal ahead, Bering Strait.

Darkness came quickly that day. Nordenskiöld and a number of the crew stayed on for a while on the beach. They gathered driftwood, and lit a bonfire, chatting merrily about the trip ahead in seas where heat, not cold, would pose problems, and where ice, continual fog, and unknown shallows would no longer haunt their every move.

'The evening was glorious, the sky clear' – wrote Nordenskiöld – 'and the air so calm that the flames and smoke of the fire rose high against the sky. The dark surface of the water, covered with a thin film of ice, reflected the fire as a straight line, bounded on the horizon by a belt of ice, its irregular outline appearing as the summits of a distant mountain range.' There was no wind, and though the temperature of the air was below freezing, it seemed quite mild.

Early the next morning, on September 28, *Vega* got under way once more, but the channel, reconnoitered the day before, turned out to be too shallow. The ship tried to get further from the coast, but there was so much drift ice that it became impossible to proceed any further. *Vega* was tied up to an ice floe, to await a favorable wind. But the wind never came, and the expedition found itself marooned.

Several months later, in a report he had prepared for his sponsors, dealing with the prospects for navigation in the Arctic Ocean, Nordenskiöld summed up the reasons why *Vega* was forced to spend the winter off the north coast of Siberia. He had believed, on the basis of information he had received from American sources familiar with the waters near Bering Strait, that the ship was unlikely to encounter any ice until mid-October. The information was correct: the day after *Vega* was caught in the ice, an American whaler, the *W. M. Meyer*, was in ice-free waters, barely fifty miles east of *Vega*'s position. The fact that the Swedish expedition was caught in ice was due to an unusual concentration of ice, in the first place. As Nordenskiöld put it, had they chosen an anchorage a little distance further east, a few hours at full steam would have been enough to reach ice-free waters.

There was also the matter of delays all along the route. Strong winds held up *Vega's* departure from northernmost Norway; there was heavy fog, causing the ship to stop, between the Yenisey and Cape Chelyuskin; they ran into fog and drift ice along the Siberian coast east of Cape Chelyuskin.

Above all, he wrote, it was impossible for a scientific expedition, fully equipped to carry out important investigations, simply to sail straight ahead across uncharted seas, without giving the scientific staff on board the opportunity to study the sea and the life in its waters. To hurry ahead would have meant the loss of valuable scientific observations, only to boast that the Northeast Passage could be conquered within a single season. Time has only strengthened Nordenskiöld's reasoning. It was not until 1932 that a Soviet icebreaker, the *Sibiriakoff*, could accomplish the traverse of the Northeast Passage in a single season.

In retrospect, the forced wintering of *Vega* turned out to be a boon to the expedition. For the first time, a fully equipped scientific staff was able to carry out an uninterrupted series of observations, from September to July, of the weather, of terrestrial magnetism, of the aurora, of the conditions of life in one of the most desolate, least known, and least accessible regions on earth. The rich harvest of data on the environment was more than matched by the firsthand reports on the way of life of those Arctic primitives, the Chukchi. Adolf Nordenskiöld and his companions contributed far more to science by spending a winter in the frozen Arctic than they could have realized on that cold Siberian dawn, when the bleak reality of their involuntary stay of nine months first became apparent.

XVII. A SIBERIAN WINTER–1878-79

The prospect facing the men aboard *Vega*, unable to move from their last anchorage, was far from cheerful. True, they were within only a day's sailing of their goal, Bering Strait, but they could not reach it for at least nine months. There was nothing to do except to settle down for the long Siberian winter, hoping that families and friends at home would believe that the ship had been frozen in, and not lost.

Nordenskiöld and Palander took stock of their situation. There were two outposts in this remote region of the Russian empire, Anadyr on the Bering Sea and Nizhne Kolymsk on the delta of the Kolyma River. But Anadyr was nearly six hundred miles away, and Nizhne Kolymsk almost eight hundred miles distant. To reach either of these settlements men would have had to travel through a trackless wilderness, unknown and unmapped, and face the full fury of the Arctic winter without dog teams, and without enough experience in Arctic land travel to have any real chance of surviving the adventure. Worse, were they to accomplish the impossible, and arrive at the Russian outposts, they would find only a Russian official, a priest, a handful of exiles, and a few native families. The Swedish expedition could not possibly count on help from these representatives of the Russian government. They had to last through the winter, save their ship and, hopefully, complete the great adventure the following summer.

Adolf Nordenskiöld had faced an Arctic winter only once before, in Spitsbergen, in 1872. But the lessons of that winter were well learned. This time, Nordenskiöld spent many months trying to plan for every emergency, calculating supplies, clothing, fuel, and food. *Vega* carried all that was necessary to keep thirty men fed, clothed and comfortably housed during an Arctic winter, and for at least six months beyond the end of the winter, until supplies could be replenished. There was enough flour to bake fresh bread every day; thousands of cans of meat preserves; two live pigs, to be slaughtered for the Christmas holidays; nearly two tons of coffee; two hundred gallons of strong brandy and rum; lime juice, cranberry juice, cloudberries, pickles, sauerkraut, to keep the dreaded scurvy under control. Everything was on board to provide a sufficiently varied diet. The coal bins were nearly full, allowing the ship to be kept warm, and still holding enough in reserve to fire the boiler and start the engine when the ice broke up.

The inside of the ship had been completely rebuilt in the Navy yard at

Karlskrona, to provide the greatest degree of comfort, should the expedition have to winter in the Arctic. The center of the aft section was the wardroom, used for meals and as a living and working room for the officers and scientists. It was surrounded by cabins: single staterooms for the senior staff, double ones for the juniors.

Petty officers and crew were housed in the fo'c's'le, and shared the space with the galley. There was a large store room between the two living areas, and further storage space on the engine deck below. On the main deck, a huge canvas awning was spread over the whole area amidships: this quickly froze, became a solid roof, and provided a sheltered space for outdoor exercise.

Wardroom, staterooms, and crew's quarters were heated by large cast iron stoves, that kept the temperature in the living quarters between 12 and 15 degrees Celsius, 52 and 60 degrees Fahrenheit, throughout the winter. At night, when the fires were low, staterooms and bunks tended to get quite cold, and Nordenskiöld noted that on especially cold nights the outside walls of the staterooms became coated with ice. But the first chore of the morning watch was to fire up the stoves, and in a half hour or less heat was circulating through the ship once more.

At first, *Vega* was anchored in very shallow water, with only inches of water under her keel. Concerned lest pressure ridges of ice should build up during the winter and crush the ship, Palander moved her further from the shore during the first day of their stay, when the ice was still thin enough to allow a little room for maneuvering. The ship's log records the gradual change in the ice: 'September 28: moored to ice floes; October 28, moored to ground ice; November 20, 6 a.m., ship frozen solid.'

To provide some protection from winter storms, *Vega* was moored to a sheet of ice, an 'ice island', in the shallow offshore water. The 'ice island' was 37 meters, 120 feet long, 23 meters, 75 feet wide, its highest point being nearly twenty feet above water. The ship was about half a mile away from the shore, and within four days of their arrival, the men could walk over the ice to reach the shore. At first, the ice measured only about ten inches, twenty-five centimeters, in thickness, but as temperatures dropped, the ice cover increased: by mid-May, it was more than five feet, 1.5 meters thick. Yet for the first two months or so there were puddles of fresh water everywhere that were used for drinking, cooking, bathing, and washing. After mid-December, all fresh water was frozen solid, and snow or ice from land had to be melted to get sweet water for the ship.

Part of the supplies and foods was carried to shore in early October and placed in a large cache dug in the ground. If disaster befell the ship, these supplies would have had to support the men until warm weather allowed them to travel on, to reach help.

During the month of October, officers and men worked on shore every day to build a set of structures, where magnetic and weather observations could be carried on. Palander built the magnetic observatory out of ice blocks. The instruments were placed on pieces of wood resting in holes excavated in the permanently frozen ground. Next to this structure, called the ice house, four buildings made of snow served as shelters for the weather instruments, thermometer, wind gauge, and instruments measuring humidity and snowfall. One small snow house was used exclusively to keep the observers' guns and knives, while they were working with the magnetic instruments.

Weather and magnetic observations were made around the clock all winter: every four hours in October, every hour from the first of November to the first of April, then every four hours again, for the rest of the *Vega*'s stay. The observations were made by the nine officers and scientists aboard, with one of the engineers and one of the seamen also taking part. Every man had a six hour watch, most of the time being spent ashore at the observatories. To walk a mile from the ship to the observatories, in temperatures that often fell to thirty-five degrees below zero Celsius, thirty degrees below zero Fahrenheit, and then spend five hours working with instruments in subfreezing temperatures demanded quite an effort. To protect the men on their walk ashore and to assure their safe return during blizzards, Nordenskiöld had a regular fence erected along the entire route, made of pillars of ice and linked by rope, to provide a guideline in the swirling snow when visibility was often zero.

Looking after scientific observations kept the officers and scientists aboard *Vega* busy; besides, the scientists had their own collections of specimens, gathered during the ship's voyage from Norway to easternmost Siberia, to classify, analyse, and describe. But there were eighteen sailors aboard, too, and both Nordenskiöld and Palander were keenly aware of the need for these men to have their own round of work, to keep active and follow a regular routine. Since all of the men were Swedish navy volunteers, Palander followed the regular daily round of duties aboard a warship.

The entries in *Vega*'s log of a typical week during the winter of 1878-

1879 bear witness to the fact that the seamen aboard did not have very much time on their hands. Daily duties included standing regular watches and bringing fresh water, later snow, aboard. Decks were cleared and scrubbed, sand was brought from the shore for ballast, the bilges were pumped out at regular intervals, clothes had to be washed, equipment was kept in good repair. On Saturday mornings, after the decks were cleared, scrubbed, and washed, and bedclothes were aired out, all men stood health inspection by the ship's doctor. Saturday night, all were issued extra rations of rum and sugar. Sunday, Palander inspected the ship and the crew, and held divine service at eleven o'clock in the morning.

Adolf Nordenskiöld knew that if the ship was beset for the winter, the long hours of darkness, when chores could no longer be performed, presented quite a problem. He had assembled a library of nearly one thousand volumes for winter reading, available to staff and crew, and had also contacted several daily newspapers at home, and asked them to donate a year's file of their issues to *Vega*'s library. Every day the men were issued a newspaper, bearing the right date, but published the previous year.

On Sunday evenings, the scientists gave a series of lectures to the crew. The topics included the history of the Northeast and the Northwest Passage, the first voyages around the world, the history of the Austro-Hungarian Polar Expedition of 1872, the changing face of the earth, and many others. 'We even made several feeble attempts' – Nordenskiöld wrote – 'to organize an evening of musical entertainment, but gave up because we had neither instruments nor talent among the men on *Vega*. Nor did we have a suitable director for theatricals aboard, to be presented in the manner of the English expeditions to the Arctic, but even if such a director could have been found, I fear he would have had a job finding enough talent for his show.'

In a letter written in mid-November, and mailed to his wife many months later, Adolf Nordenskiöld described his own daily routine during the winter in Siberia. Meals were served at eight in the morning, two in the afternoon, and half past seven in the evening. He took his daily exercise walking on the main deck, no matter how cold it was outdoors. Always interested in acquiring new skills, he studied Italian with Lieutenant Bove, spending an hour with him every morning. After lunch, he played chess with Doctor Almquist, or had a nap; after supper, he played cards with Palander, Kjellman, and Almquist. At ten in the evening, the card game broke up; Nordenskiöld took one more walk on deck before turning in, and read in bed, often until quite late. He spent most of his time writing up notes taken during the voyage, describing observations made at the winter quarters of the ship and taking his six-hour turn every third day on shore, recording observations made by the instruments.

What made *Vega*'s stay off the easternmost shores of Siberia interesting to the men aboard and truly valuable to science, was the presence of the natives of the region, the Chukchi.

Ranging across much of easternmost Siberia, but especially along the shores of the peninsula named after them, the Chukchi are hunters, fishermen, and herders of reindeer. Some twenty thousand still live in the region visited by Nordenskiöld and his companions nearly a century ago, and their way of life has changed little since that time. They wander in search of food many hundreds of miles each year, from Bering Strait and the shores of the Bering Sea all the way to the lower reaches of the Kolyma River. Nowadays, even their remotest encampments can be reached swiftly by aircraft, but in Nordenskiöld's day sleds drawn by reindeer were their only means of contacting the outside world, and that included the remote and virtually unknown Russian government that ruled their land.

To the Chukchi, the outside world was represented by the English and American whalers who regularly visited their shores. Russian was an unknown tongue to them, but they were acquainted with a few English words, including 'ram', for the rum dispensed by the whalers in exchange for skins and ivory.

Lieutenant Nordquist had joined the expedition to serve as interpreter in meetings with Russian authorities. But the nearest Russians were living hundreds of miles from *Vega*'s anchorage and Nordquist quickly found another task: he devoted his time to studying the language of the Chukchi. He was a talented linguist, and within a matter of weeks he was the 'offical' interpreter in contacts with the natives. His skill in acquiring their language really impressed the Chukchi, for when the American ship *Jeanette* visited the district a year later they were still talking about the stranger who had spent a winter in their midst and spoke fluent Chukch.

Nordquist made a systematic study of the Chukch language, and later published his findings. The others on board *Vega* all managed to pick up a few words of the language, and business with the natives was con-

ducted in a 'pidgin' made of Swedish and Chukch words.
The first Chukch visitors had appeared at *Vega*'s ladder the day after the ship was beset in ice, in late September. After that, not a day went by without its quota of visitors. At first, it was only the natives from the neighboring settlements who came, but the report of the arrival of these remarkable foreigners – wrote Nordenskiöld – must have spread quickly, for soon there were visitors from remote villages. *Vega* became a resting place, where every passerby stopped for some hours.
The Chukchi arrived on foot, if they came only a short distance, or by sled from faraway settlements. Dog teams stood all day in rows before the flight of steps, made of blocks of ice, that led up to the ship's deck. The dogs were fed very little by their owners, and Nordenskiöld saw to it that one of the sailors would spread some pemmican, while the animals waited for their master.
Once on board, the Chukchi always greeted their hosts with the cry: 'I am hungry! I have no food! Give me a piece of bread!' They usually brought pieces of wood, needed for the ship's stoves, but sometimes they had stone carvings with them, and occasionally they brought a fish they had caught. In exchange they were given bread and leftover food, and at noontime the cook would bring up a large kettle, filled with soup and whatever was available around the kitchen. The visitors would crowd around, using spoons, empty tins, their hands, cleaning up every scrap of food.
Beginning in October, members of the expedition began to make excursions on shore, visiting the neighboring Chukchi settlements, often spending the night with their hosts. Nordenskiöld described the curiously shaped 'double tent' of the Chukchi: there was an inner chamber, used for cooking and sleeping, and an outer one, for storing tools and utensils. The tents were made of animal skins stretched over a light wood frame, and when a family decided to move on to another fishing or hunting ground, only the skins ware taken along, the wooden frames were left in place. Chukchi families apparently owned several such tent frames, scattered over quite a large territory, and by taking only the tent covering and their most important tools and weapons along, they could move quickly and easily about.
The Chukch tents averaged about 3.3 meters, eleven feet, in length; 2.1 meters, seven feet, in width; and 1.8 meters, six feet, in height. The walls were of reindeer skin, the floor had a base of twigs and dried grass and was covered with a walrus skin, at night they spread out reindeer skins

for sleeping. Small stone lamps, burning whale oil, provided heat and light. At night as many as eight people would crowd into a tent, their bodies and the oil lamps made the place so warm that even when the outside temperature was at thirty-five to forty-one degrees below zero Celsius, thirty to forty degrees below zero Fahrenheit, men and women inside took off all their clothes above the waist and often slept without clothes, covered only by reindeer skin blankets.

During their winter in northeast Siberia the Swedish expedition managed to acquire a large number of tools, utensils, and bone carvings from the Chukchi. The collection is kept in the Stockholm Museum of Ethnography, and looking at these objects, one is bound to admire the simple but ingenious design of the Chukchi artifacts used for hunting and fishing, preparing food, or scraping skins used for clothing. The bone carvings, representing walrus and seal, bears and foxes, fishes and birds, even small flies and shellfish found in that remote corner of the Arctic, are strikingly impressive. Their strong, simple, impressionistic lines show not only animals but the faces and bodies of human beings: they are as handsome as the now popular works of the remote relatives of the Chukchi, the North American Eskimo.

The Chukchi held a strong belief in the powers of their medicine men, the *shaman*. Nordenskiöld did not, to his great regret, encounter a single one of these medicine men who acted as middlemen between the Chukchi and the world beyond, but the magic drum, the central ceremonial object of the shaman's religious rites, was found even in the humblest of tents. The drums, made of the stomach wall of a seal, were stretched over a wooden frame and struck with sticks made from whalebone splinters. The shamans used these drums to accompany a frenzied form of dancing, that put them in a trance and let them speak to the world of spirits.

To travel across tundra, snow, and ice the Chukchi use light sleds, drawn by reindeer or by dogs. The dogs are harnessed in a long line of pairs to the sled, and though they travelled slowly, the Swedes, going on a number of short trips to the interior by this means of transport, found that they could cover as much as forty miles a day. The Chukchi dogs are of the same breed, if smaller, as the Eskimo use in northern Canada and Greenland; during *Vega*'s stay, however, a new strain appeared in the region. There were two border collies aboard the ship, and during the winter they mixed freely with the local dog population: the resulting puppies, resembling collies more than malamutes, were highly valued by their owners.

Reindeer are the Chukchi's most prized possession. Palander described the scene, on a winter morning, of a herd of reindeer meeting their owner in front of the tent. 'When we came out of the tent, all the reindeer came towards us, in tight marching formation. At the head was an old buck with huge horns, he came up to the master and wished him good morning by rubbing his nose against the man's hand. The rest of the reindeer stood in well-ordered ranks, like the crew in divisions aboard a man-of-war. The owner then went through the ranks and greeted every reindeer, they were allowed to rub their noses against his hand. The man took every animal by the horn and checked him very carefully, looking for parasites in the hides. When the inspection was over, the master gave a sign, and the whole herd wheeled around and in close formation, led by the old buck, returned to their pasture.'

There was not much animal life visible at *Vega*'s anchorage during the winter. Only three species of birds spent the winter there, owls, ravens, and ptarmigans. But there were numerous hares and foxes, and occasionally footprints of wolves and wild reindeer were seen. Several varieties of lemming, seals and polar bears were hunted by the natives. But in the spring, beginning in late April, large flocks of migratory birds arrived: snow buntings, geese, ducks, gulls, shore birds of many varieties. Still later song birds passed by, and some chose *Vega*'s rigging for a resting place. Among the unusual species there was a rare kind of sandpiper, with a curious, spoonlike bill, that breeds in the Arctic and winters in the Philippine Islands.

Hunting in the winter, and observing migratory birds later in the spring, provided a welcome diversion for the men aboard the *Vega*. But Nordenskiöld and Palander also insisted that the monotonous daily routine be interrupted as often as an excuse could be found. The birthdays of the ruling monarchs of every land represented on the ship were such festive occasions, and special dinners were served to celebrate the birthdays of the King of Sweden and Norway, the King of Denmark, the King of Italy, and the Emperor of all the Russias.

The highlight of *Vega*'s winter in Siberia was Christmas, celebrated in true Swedish fashion. There was no real Christmas tree available, for although the expedition's leader thought of nearly everything, he forgot to put a tree aboard. Kjellman found a large piece of driftwood on the beach, and asked the Chukchi to bring branches of willows from the country to the south. The branches were tied onto the driftwood stem, paper painted green simulated leaves, and the whole contraption was covered with candles, decorations, and Christmas presents.

Before the ship had left Norway, a number of parcels had arrived with presents for the staff and crew. Nordenskiöld, anxious that no one should feel forgotten at Christmas, went to the stores in Tromsö and bought a number of small presents, each individually wrapped. At six o'clock on Christmas afternoon, officers, staff and crew assembled in the area between decks, where the Christmas tree was set up. First, presents with names on them were distributed, then lots were drawn for the unnamed ones. One of the crew played his harmonica, and everybody joined in singing Christmas carols.

The special Christmas dinner included ham with rice and vegetables; raspberries for dessert; and special rations of rum, aquavit, and beer. Later in the evening, Christmas punch was served, and toasts were offered for king and country, for the success of the expedition, for all on board, for the families at home, for relatives and friends, and finally for the four crew members who had made and trimmed the Christmas tree.

A lithograph, made from Nordenskiöld's description of their Siberian Christmas and included in his book on the voyage of the *Vega*, shows the festive scene. Adolf Nordenskiöld is easily recognized in the foreground, sitting and chatting with one of the sailors. Palander is talking to another, while young Stuxberg, decked out for the occasion in a frock coat, dashes across the floor. In the midst of the excitement the imperturbable steward, Levin, holds a tray of punch-filled cups, and the candles of the tree and lanterns overhead shed a soft and even light on the scene.

Anna Nordenskiöld surprised her husband by including a photograph of herself in his Christmas gift parcel: she was always reluctant to have her picture taken. Marie made a teacozy for her father – it comes in handy in this climate, Nordenskiöld remarked in his letter home. Gustav made a pencil box, and Anna, a bookmark. About the only thing missing, wrote Adolf Nordenskiöld to his wife, was a picture of his youngest son, Erland, and he asked her to send a photo of the boy to Japan.

The temperature was twenty-six below zero Celsius, fifteen below zero Fahrenheit, outside, when Adolf Nordenskiöld wrote his family, shortly after Christmas. The ship had been beset for more than three months, and the spring thaw was still months away, but Nordenskiöld's invincible optimism took the completion of the great voyage for granted. As always, he was planning ahead, suggesting to his wife that they meet in Europe. He was going to stay aboard *Vega*, so that 'the circumnavigation of the old world will really be accomplished'. Anna, with their oldest daughter, – he wrote – was to travel to Germany first, to visit a childhood friend, then on to Switzerland and Italy. Perhaps she could even go as far as Egypt, and meet *Vega* as she enters the Suez Canal, then sail on with her husband to Italy, Spain, France, and Sweden. It was only a matter of time, in a few months *Vega* would once more be on her way!

By the time the men aboard *Vega* had celebrated Christmas, they had settled down to a steady routine. They knew that they were likely to be icebound until early summer at best, but they do not seem to have had any doubt about surviving their forced wintering. They were far more concerned about getting word to their families and friends at home.

Adolf Nordenskiöld entrusted letters and telegrams to Captain Johannesen of the *Lena*, when the two ships parted company early in September, and he was certain that those messages had reached Sweden within a reasonable time. But the news he had sent home spoke of *Vega* continuing eastward to Bering Strait and Japan: instead, the Swedish expedition was caught in ice. How to get word to the outside world of their forced wintering was the problem.

An opportunity to send a message home came early: on October 6, barely ten days after the ship became icebound, the men on deck saw an extraordinary procession moving towards the ship. Several Chukchi were dragging a sled across the ice, and a man was laying on it. Everyone assumed that he was seriously ill, and was being brought to the ship's doctor. But when the sled reached the ship, the supposed invalid climbed quickly up the ladder, and stepped on deck with the self-assurance of a man of rank. He was a Chukch, dressed in a faded parka and a woolen shirt; he crossed himself, greeted everyone, and announced in broken Russian that he was Menka the 'starost', headman of the Chukchi.

Menka the headman represented the might of imperial Russia in Northeast Siberia. He was invited to the wardroom, properly entertained, and questioned about the district and its people. As it turned out, he knew only a little Russian, could neither read nor write, but was quite at home with a map of the region, and pointed out a number of settlements to his hosts. He brought pieces of roast reindeer as presents to the strangers, and was suitably rewarded with a woolen shirt and some tobacco. When he told the Swedes that he was on his way to the Russian settlement of Anadyr, on Bering Strait, everyone became very excited, since a message sent there could be forwarded to the Russian authorities in South Siberia, and thence to Sweden.

Nordenskiöld composed a letter to the Governor-General of Siberia, asking him to forward news of the location of *Vega* to Sweden, and the Chukch dignitary left, assuring his hosts that their letter was in safe hands. Less than a fortnight had gone by when Menka returned to the ship, this time asking for 'fire water', in exchange for reindeer meat. By then the Swedes had very little faith in his efficiency as a carrier of messages. His reception was much less cordial than on his first visit, and he left in something of a huff.

This was the first opportunity for messages to be sent to the outside world during *Vega*'s wintering, and the men could not help but wonder whether the letter entrusted to the Chukchi headman would ever reach its destination. But Menka did deliver the message to a Russian official at Anadyr, in late February. It took the letter another two months to reach the Governor-General in Irkutsk, and it was delivered to Sweden on May 16, seven months and a week after it was originally composed. In recognition of his help, having carried Nordenskiöld's letter to the Russian authorities, King Oscar of Sweden sent a special gold medal to Menka, the Chukchi headman. It was presented to him in due course and undoubtedly was worn with much pride.

During the fall and early winter of 1878, anxiety about the fate of the *Vega* began to mount in Sweden. Captain Johannesen's telegrams and letters reached Stockholm late in October; after that there was only silence.

The first vague report came to the Swedish Foreign Office on December 27, 1878. The Swedish Consul in San Francisco had spoken to whalers just returned from the Bering Sea, where they had heard rumors of a sizable ship beset in the Arctic Ocean, a short distance from Bering Strait. Two days later a telegram arrived from the Swedish Consul in New York: 'Captain Campbell master American whaler *Norman* left St. Lawrence Bay October 17. Natives from East Cape told having seen man-of-war forty miles north of East Cape. Natives reported reliable, many whalers wintered with them.'

Captain Campbell's report certainly sounded reassuring. St. Lawrence Bay lies on the Siberian shore of the Bering Sea, and the natives' report on the location of the ship made it highly likely that it was the *Vega*.

Further details of Captain Campbell's report were supplied by a letter from the Alaska Commercial Company of San Francisco, sent to N. A. Elving, the American Consul-General in Stockholm. The Company sent several whaling ships to the Bering Sea and the Arctic Ocean every year, and the vessel commanded by Campbell was the last to leave St. Lawrence Bay at the end of the 1878 whaling season. At first, Campbell paid little attention to the natives' story of a man-of-war caught in the ice off Siberia, since he knew that his was the last whaler to sail home and that no steamer had been seen passing Bering Strait during the season. On his return to San Francisco, he found out about the missing Swedish ship, and immediately reported what his native informants had told him.

Captain Campbell even had an explanation for the natives' insisting that the ship frozen in off Siberia was a man-of-war. Three years earlier, in 1875, a corvette of the Russian Navy, *Horseman,* had made a cruise in Arctic waters and created quite a sensation. It was the first time that the natives, so familiar with whalers that they could identify a whaling ship some distance away, had seen a steam-driven vessel, equipped with cannon. They assumed that all steamships were men-of-war.

By the beginning of January, 1879, then, there was a report, confirmed by a reputable American skipper, of a steamer icebound in the Arctic, some distance northwest of Bering Strait. The report appears to have been given full credit in Sweden, at least there does not seem to have been any doubt expressed as to its validity. Family and friends of Adolf Nordenskiöld had full confidence in him, in the officers, scientists, and crew of the *Vega*. They believed that the elaborate preparations he had made for the journey assured its safety during the winter. Evidence certainly points to this view being taken by all in Sweden, including the expedition's two Swedish sponsors, King Oscar and Dickson.

Elsewhere, concern about the fate of the ship and the men aboard was much more evident. Alexander Sibiriakoff, the Russian sponsor of the expedition, sent one of his employees, Serebrennikoff, to Sweden. Serebrennikoff was either to charter a relief vessel, or to have one built in a Swedish shipyard. On January 9 the leading newspaper of Göteborg reported that Sibiriakoff had commissioned Sweden's largest shipyard to build a 380 ton steam-driven vessel, capable of navigating in Arctic waters, and that he had hired a German merchant navy officer, Captain Sengstacke, as skipper of the ship.

But Sibiriakoff was not satisfied with having a relief vessel built. Only a few days after his representative signed a contract for the ship, Sibiriakoff sent a telegram to the Governor-General of Siberia, asking him for help, and offering to underwrite the costs of an expedition, organised at the Russian settlements on the Bering Sea, to rescue Nordenskiöld and his men.

In his reply, the Governor-General wrote that he had already requested officials in Yakutsk and Nikolayevsk, the two towns nearest to the assumed location of *Vega*, to send help. He felt that the distances were so enormous that it might be best to request help from America, since Alaskan settlements were much nearer to *Vega* than Russian ones.

Russian, Swedish, Danish and German newspapers continued to discuss the chances of the Swedish expedition's survival, and interest in their fate was shown in the United States, too. There, James Gordon Bennett, publisher of the New York Herald, who had already purchased a steam yacht for an Arctic expedition, starting in the summer of 1879, offered his services to locate and succour Nordenskiöld.

In Adolf Nordenskiöld's papers there are two letters, transmitted to Anna Nordenskiöld by the American Consul-General in Stockholm, that explain why family, friends, and supporters of the expedition in Sweden took a much calmer view and were willing to await spring and further news. The first of these letters was written by a whaling captain of San Francisco, E. P. Herendeen. Captain Herendeen stated that the men aboard the whaling bark *Norman* were told by natives in Plover Bay – now called Providenniya Bay, on the Russian shore of Bering Strait – that 'there was a Russian man-of-war in the ice, in the Arctic. They did not describe her as being disabled at all, only that she was impeded, and *this is all that anyone knows about it.*'

Captain Herendeen was of the opinion that this report came through the 'deer men and traders, who could easily make that distance in a short time'. His guess as to the actual spot where the *Vega* was beset was less than one hundred miles too far to the west; he believed that the men aboard would surely get through the winter in safety, even if they lost the ship, 'which is doubtful, as she is a well fortified and strengthened ship'.

In the 1850's, the American whaler *New Bedford* had been wrecked within a few miles of *Vega*'s presumed location, the Captain wrote, and 'though they lost everything, the natives cared for them and got them all through the winter in good condition. No doubt is entertained among whalermen that the *Vega* will come out all right.' Captain Herendeen concluded by pointing out that an American, one Charley Chanfelt, was spending the winter of 1878-1879 at Plover Bay on Bering Strait. 'If there is any further news from Nordenskiöld, a vessel going north, touching at Plover Bay – as the traders and whalers do – will get news of the *Vega* and she will probably be reported on the arrival of the first traders from the north, about the last of August, 1879.'

Captain Herendeen's matter-of-fact evaluation of the available news was obtained for Consul-General Elving by William H. Dall, one of the most knowledgeable persons regarding the world of Alaska and the Bering Sea. Dall, a distinguished American naturalist, had served in Alaska in the 1860's with the International Telegraph Expedition, when an attempt had been made to link North America, Siberia, and Europe by a telegraph line across Bering Strait.

In his covering letter, Dall wrote: 'I believe our brave Nordenskiöld will rise out of the snow and ice like a phoenix from her ashes, next spring, and that his achievement will rank with Stanley's travels in Africa in audacity of conception, courage in carrying out, and successful preservation of the results and the explorers. The dog-sledge relief expedition from Irkutsk, which some of the newspapers mention, would be of no use, as the party with sledges could not carry enough supplies to feed themselves, let alone the *Vega*'s party, and I think it will not be attempted. It certainly would be a foolish proposition.'

Dall's letter was received in Stockholm in late February, 1879. On May 15, a telegram sent by Sibiriakoff reached Oscar Dickson, and was immediately printed by the newspapers of Sweden and all over Europe: 'Nordenskiöld reported to Governor-General in Irkutsk, dated September 25, that *Vega* was beset at Serdze Kamen. All is well, all are healthy. Letter received in Irkutsk May 10.' The message entrusted to Menka, the Chukchi headman, had arrived at long last.

Anna Nordenskiöld knew now that her husband and his shipmates were compelled to spend the winter off the inhospitable shores of Northeast Siberia. But the news was eight months old. Did the men survive the winter? Another fortnight went by before she received a second telegram from Oscar Dickson: 'Captain Johannesen reports *via* Irkutsk that he received a letter from Professor Nordenskiöld, dated the eighteenth of February. All are well. Heartiest congratulations.'

The worst of the long wait was over for Anna Nordenskiöld, for the parents and wives, children, and friends, of the men aboard the *Vega*. But when this latest news reached Stockholm, *Vega* was still surrounded by ice, awaiting spring and the chance to move on. Temperatures remained well below freezing; the coast, and *Vega*, continued to be icebound. The only events to provide some variety in the lives of the men aboard were the calls the Chukchi made at the ship, since *Vega* was, as Nordenskiöld put it, 'the only place of entertainment on the shores of the Arctic Ocean'.

On February 20, three large sleds, drawn by dogs and laden with goods, stopped at the *Vega.* The drivers said they came from the east and were on their way to the yearly market at the Russian settlement of Nizhne Kolymsk, on the lower Kolyma. Nordenskiöld decided to try again to send word home, and since the Chukchi would not accept money, he gave them three bottles of rum in lieu of postage. The men promised that they would deliver the letter and would return in May. And they kept their word: they stopped again at the *Vega* on May 8, and reported that a letter was about to arrive, brought by men with the next convoy of sleds. Eagerly the men asked how large was the parcel. 'Very large', said the Chukchi, and were rewarded with a proper amount of rum.

The letter did come the next day, but it was only a short note from the Russian official in Nizhne Kolymsk, reporting that Nordenskiöld's letter had been delivered to him on April 4, and was immediately forwarded. Six weeks later the letter reached Irkutsk, on August 2 it was received in Sweden.

In the meantime the weeks and months dragged by until, in late April, the first migratory birds arrived. There were only a few patches of bare ground on the south side of the hillocks near the coast, and ice still covered the sea when the first snow bunting came, on April 23. Then came large flocks of geese, eider ducks, long-tailed ducks, many varieties of gulls, and several kinds of shore birds and song birds. *Vega*'s deck, Nordenskiöld wrote, was the only bare spot for miles, and the smaller birds settled for a rest in the rigging of the ship. The men were busy, shooting birds and mammals to put together a complete collection of the animals found in this remote, almost unknown corner of northernmost Asia.

Louis Palander, *Vega*'s skipper, kept a diary of events and observations, and excerpts illustrate the sense of awaiting the arrival of summer, and the freeing of the ship from her icy fetters.

'June 19. This afternoon a Chukchi dignitary, one Noah Elisei, the brother of Menka the headman, arrived. He brought a letter from the Russian official in Nizhne Kolymsk. The letter did not say anything, except that its bearer was sent to help us. This was obviously absurd, since the man was on his way eastward, and needed our help more than we needed his assistance. He begged us for all sorts of things, for tea, sugar, rum, tobacco, etc.

June 20. We have been aboard ship for exactly one year. I ordered flags up for the occasion.

June 23. Midsummer Eve. Divine weather. The thermometer read 4 degrees, (40 degrees Fahrenheit), the highest it had registered since the end of last August. In the morning Nordenskiöld, Kjellman and I went for a walk on land. The streams are getting wider every day, the coastal lagoon is deep enough for our steam launch. We are still surrounded by ice, but there is meltwater on its surface.
June 24. Midsummer Day. An unusually clear, pretty and warm day. We can hear the surf from the coastal lagoon. Flags were run up to honor the day, otherwise it was boring enough.
June 28. The natives brought the first egg of an eider duck today.
July 1. Kjellman found the first dwarf birch we had seen on this northern coast of Siberia.
July 4. Especially good weather, warm and wonderful. On land it is really warm, surely at least 20 degrees in the sun or more (68° Fahrenheit).
July 5. The weather is pleasant, but there is hardly any wind at all, and without it only the sun melts the ice. And that will take a long time. So we wait. This is annoying, in fact, more than annoying.
July 6. Flowers are popping up every day. Kjellman has a whole lot of flowers in his portfolio, when he comes back from the shore.
July 11. Cloudy, cool, foggy. We tried to cut a path with explosives, but failed; the stuff was too wet. The ice is getting thinner every day; this is especially noticeable when the wind is from the south.
July 14. The opening around the ship is getting bigger every day, bit by bit we are getting loose. A native reported that there were five American ships to the east. Bove and I went to the nearest Chukchi settlement, Irgonnuk, to try and get sled dogs, to reach the Americans. But no one was willing to let us have dogs, they said that the ice was too thin and the streams were too deep. We came back to the ship, having had a good long walk, at ten o'clock in the evening. It is getting more and more difficult to get to the shore and back.
July 15. Today was the first day all winter that we did not have any native visitors.
July 17. The channel on the seaward side of us has widened considerably.
July 18. We are free! We are free! We are free! Yes, we are really free and on our way. After being imprisoned for nine months and 20 days, we are truly free. All day long there was a strong wind from the southwest. I noticed at 1 p.m. that the open water was widening astern of the

ship... I had the boiler fired, and started the ship backing into the ice that separated us from open water astern of us. At first we moved to the northwest, and soon reached open water, proceeding then forward under steam and sail. We could not say goodbye to our Chukchi friends, for there were no visitors aboard today.'

On July 18, 1879, at 3:30 in the afternoon, *Vega* was once more on her way. At dawn on July 20, the ship was abreast of Cape Dezhnev, as East Cape now is called, and entered Bering Strait at 11 o'clock that morning. *Vega* hoisted flags to salute the strait where the Old and New World meet, and the men aboard shouted four hurrahs for the occasion.

Adolf Nordenskiöld wrote: 'Thus at last the goal was reached that so many nations had struggled for, ever since Sir Hugh Willoughby... ushered in the long series of voyages to the Northeast... Now, for the first time, after 336 years had gone by, and when most experienced seamen had declared that this was an impossible undertaking, the North-east Passage was at last achieved. This was done thanks to the discipline, zeal, and ability of the men and officers of our Navy, without sacrificing a single human life, without any illness among the members of the expedition, without the slightest damage to the ship, and under circumstances that indicate that this same feat could be repeated most years, perhaps every year, within a few weeks' time. We may be excused if, under these circumstances, we saw with pride our blue and yellow flag rise to the top of the mainmast, and heard our men's hurrah, in the strait where the Old and New World reach out towards each other. True, the seaway we had followed is no longer necessary as a trade route between Europe and China. But it was granted to this and to previous Swedish expeditions to open an ocean to navigation, and to offer nearly half a continent the possibility of a seaway to the world ocean.'

Later that year, the American naturalist William Dall wrote Adolf Nordenskiöld, summing up how the world of science viewed the accomplishments of the *Vega* expedition:

'I am sure His Majesty the King of Sweden will be among the most enthusiastic of those who welcome you to home and Sweden; and the foresight, energy, and courage which, through you and your companions, has shed such lustre on Swedish enterprise well deserve all the honors which a king or ruler may have in his power to bestow.

Still, to an explorer or man of science there is something in the congratulations and appreciation of his labor by his co-laborers and scientific colleagues, which is grateful in its way, as the recognition of royalty is in another way. The King may realize the courage, the bold plan, and above all the emphatic and overwhelming success of his devoted subjects. The others realize more fully the labor, the anxiety, the responsibility, the separation from family, kindred, friends, the knowledge of the world's doings and the comforts of civilization, and may appreciate more keenly the accomplishments of our predictions with the certainty of a chemical experiment, which more than anything else fills with joy the heart of the scientific laborer.

My dear sir, I congratulate you most heartily and warmly on your success, which places your name high among the ranks of those who have unlocked the secrets of the Icy Sea, and fairly entitles you to the title of the first of living Arctic explorers.'

XVIII. THROUGH BERING STRAIT TO THE ORIENT – 1879

On July 20th, 1879 *Vega* passed through Bering Strait and thus achieved its objective, the completion of the voyage across the Northeast Passage, from the Atlantic to the Pacific. It would have been natural for Adolf Nordenskiöld to turn the ship's prow southward and reassure the world, by telegrams sent from Japan, that all was well with the men aboard *Vega*. But more than six weeks were to pass before the Swedish expedition reached Japan: Adolf Nordenskiöld was far more interested in exploring the geology, fauna and flora of the Bering Sea and of its shores, than in rushing back to the world of telegraph services and newspapers, and to bask in public acclaim. Though he stated several times in his narrative of the voyage that he was anxious to reach a telegraph station, he did not hurry, but took full advantage of *Vega*'s position in far northern seas to continue scientific studies of that environment.
The boundary between Russian and American territory passes through the Diomede Islands, in the middle of Bering Strait. In Nordenskiöld's time that boundary meant little to the people of the Arctic, who had met and exchanged goods on Big Diomede Island since time immemorial. It would have been interesting to spend a few hours there, wrote Nordenskiöld but he had to push on, for Diomede Island was wrapped in a heavy blanket of fog, due to its location where the warmer, ice-free waters of the Bering Sea meet the cold, icy waters of the Arctic Ocean.
Vega's first stop after leaving its winter quarters was St. Lawrence Bay, on the Siberian shore of Bering Strait. The sheltered part of the bay was still filled with ice, and the ship had to anchor in open unprotected water. The men went ashore to visit the small settlement. The Chukchi who lived there depended entirely on whales for their livelihood, and for their tools and their utensils. The 'ribs' of their tents, that held the animal skin coverings, were of whale bone; they used whale bones drenched in whale oil for fuel; a large whale rib was used over the fire as a pot holder; hollowed-out whale bones were used as lamps, other pieces for runners on sleds and for ice-axes; and whale meat and blubber was the mainstay of their diet.
There was little safety for a ship in St. Lawrence Bay, and there was also the risk of a sudden cold spell that could have frozen the waters of the bay. After a few hours' stay *Vega* crossed over to the Alaskan side of the Strait, and anchored on the south side of the Seward Peninsula.

Her landfall was then known as Port Clarence, it is now called Teller. The anchorage was well protected and, for the first time since the previous August, *Vega* lay at anchor in a real harbor, rather than in the open sea, at the mercy of winds, currents, and ice. Nordenskiöld noted with pride and satisfaction that even though the vessel had been fully exposed to the elements, thanks to Palander's skill and his careful handling of the ship and the efficiency of the officers and crew, *Vega* was not just undamaged, but as seaworthy as when she left the dock at Karlskrona, over a year earlier.

'The whole harbor of Port Clarence was swarming with natives' – wrote Palander in his diary – 'Eskimo, who are as different from the Chukchi as night from day. These are neat and tidy folk, good looking and polite. Their parkas are made of lemming skins, the women carry their babies on their backs, inside their parkas.' Though these Eskimo lived less than a hundred miles from their Chukchi neighbors, the fact that numerous American ships visited this part of Alaska was obvious. The Eskimo used American-made handguns and rifles, their axes and knives were made of steel, and many of them wore cotton clothing underneath their outer garments of skin.

Two of the Eskimo men spoke a little English, one had been to San Francisco, the other as far as Honolulu. In some of the tents the Swedes saw plaited mats and coconut shells, brought from southern seas either by the whalers, or by Eskimo who had worked on whaling ships. All were anxious to engage in barter, and Adolf Nordenskiöld suddenly discovered that he was in an excellent bargaining position. When he had dealt with the Chukchi during *Vega*'s wintering, he had had to be careful, for it was impossible to tell how long their forced stay was going to last, and clothing, tools, food and ammunition were precious. Now a return to ports where supplies were ample was but a matter of weeks, furthermore, the voyage home was to take the ship through the tropics and winter garments were no longer needed.

'I took advantage of my riches by going around to the tents like an itinerant pedlar, carrying sacks full of heavy blankets, felt hats, stockings, and ammunition, and obtained in exchange for these goods a handsome and choice collection of Eskimo articles.' Nordenskiöld's collection included hunting and fishing gear, bone and stone carvings and masks, and a beautifully made kayak of white skins, now displayed in the Stockholm Museum of Ethnography.

The expedition spent four days at Port Clarence while the scientific staff made numerous shore excursions, returning on board with treasures of plants and animals, and gingerly nursing their skin, severely put to the test by hardy Alaskan mosquitoes. After the ship had lifted anchor and turned back once more towards the Old World, one of the sailors brought a sealed letter to Palander that had been left on board by an Eskimo. Upon opening it, the captain found inside the business card of a San Francisco firm, offering their outstanding selection of hunting gear to 'sportsmen in Arctic waters'. 'Only an American firm would spread such advertising among the Bering Strait Eskimo', was Palander's comment.

Vega returned once more to the Siberian shore of the Bering Strait, anchoring in a fjord that was protected by an offshore island from the open sea. Konyam Bay was a spectacular place, with mountains dipping steeply into the water, reminiscent of parts of north Norway, but much of it was still icebound, and thus far from safe. After a short stay, *Vega* set course for St. Lawrence Island, athwart the entrance to Bering Strait. The scientists went ashore to gather specimens of plants and animals for their collections; and Stuxberg made some drawings of the unusual patterns the local Eskimo tattooed on their face and arms. But St. Lawrence Island does not have any sheltered harbor, and ships anchoring offshore risk being driven aground by a sudden storm. Palander was anxious to leave as soon as possible, and so at last *Vega* took a southward course, into the Bering Sea.

Bering Island was the next stop, the largest of the Commander Islands, named after Captain Vitus Bering, Alaska's discoverer. Bering and his men landed on this island in the fall of 1741, on their return from Alaska. All were weakened by scurvy, and Bering and many of his men died during the winter. But several survived, among them the expedition's naturalist and surgeon, Steller, who later wrote an excellent description of the fauna and flora of the island, as it appeared to the first Europeans to have landed there. Nordenskiöld was familiar with Steller's writings, and anxious to visit the place.

Bering Island had remained in Russian hands when Alaska and the Aleutians were sold to the United States, in 1867. But an American corporation, the American Alaska Company, acquired the exclusive rights of seal hunting on Bering Island and the settlement was inhabited by Russian officials, Aleut and half-caste hunters and fishermen, and employees of the Alaska Company.

For the first time in nearly a year the men aboard *Vega* found new people they could talk to. Nordenskiöld and Nordquist met the Russian officials, while the others enjoyed long visits with the Swedes, Finns, and Danes working for the Alaska Company.

Among the animals described by Steller as native of Bering Island was a marine mammal he called a 'sea-cow', it was later named *Rhytina Stelleri*, in honor of its discoverer. Steller found large numbers of these animals pasturing, as it were, on the seaweed that grew in abundance in offshore waters, but indiscriminate slaughter had exterminated the species within less than a century. Offering a sizable reward to anyone who could lead him to a skeleton of the extinct animal, or even to a heap of its bones, Nordenskiöld was able to assemble a nearly complete skeleton of Steller's 'sea cow', something he always considered one of the truly important scientific results of the entire *Vega* voyage.

If Adolf Nordenskiöld had had his way, the ship would have wandered about for another month or two in the Bering Sea and the North Pacific, while he and his fellow scientists spent many happy hours dredging the sea, or collecting plants and animals on bog and tundra. But Nordenskiöld knew that it was time to let the world know that *Vega*, and the men aboard, were safe and sound.

While *Vega* had stopped at Bering Island, a steamer of the American Alaska Company arrived from the nearest Russian harbor, Petropavlovsk. Her captain and crew brought news from home to Nordenskiöld. When Anna Nordenskiöld received word, earlier in the year, that *Vega* was reported beset off northeast Siberia, she wanted to let her husband know that all was well at home. Through friends in Finland and in Russian court circles at St. Petersburg, she sent a message to the Baroness Frederichs, wife of the Governor-General of Siberia, asking her to pass it on to Adolf Nordenskiöld. Mail moved slowly in Siberia in those days, but in due course the message was forwarded to the Pacific coast and, in August, to Nordenskiöld himself.

On August 19, *Vega* left Bering Island, bound for Yokohama, Japan. For the first few days of the voyage the ship was still in cool northern waters, but on August 25, they crossed into the warm 'Black Current', and seawater temperatures suddenly rose to 24 degrees Celsius, 75 degrees Fahrenheit. *Vega* sailed through a series of storms and, on August 31, the mainmast was struck by lightning. No one was hurt, though just about everyone on board was shaken by the violent explosion; the mast was split, and the weathervane on top of it fell into the sea. It was the only time the ship suffered any damage on the entire voyage. At half past eight on the evening of September 2, *Vega* anchored

off Yokohama, Japan. Nordenskiöld and Palander hastened ashore, to find a telegraph office and flash word of their safe arrival to Sweden.
A telegram from Japan to Europe was normally forwarded *via* the Russian telegraph system of Siberia. But there was a major flood in Siberia, the line was broken, and Nordenskiöld was informed that his telegrams had to be sent *via* India, at the cost of 400 U.S. dollars. He did not have that much cash with him, and tried to pay with gold coins from various European countries. The telegraph clerk refused to accept the coins, when a distinguished looking European gentleman, who had watched the proceedings with interest, came up to Nordenskiöld and introduced himself: he was the Russian Consul in Yokohama. As soon as he found out that it was a matter of advising the world of *Vega*'s arival, he offered to pay for the telegrams, until Adolf Nordenskiöld could get some cash at a bank, the following morning.
The first telegram was addressed to King Oscar II of Sweden: 'The Swedish expedition sends greetings to their high patron. Program fulfilled. Northeast Passage executed. An ocean opened to navigation without loss of a single man, without illness, and without damage to the vessel.' The second was sent to Anna Nordenskiöld: 'All well. Adolf.' Other messages went to the expedition's supporters, Oscar Dickson and Alexander Sibiriakoff.
The news was received in Stockholm on September 5. Flags fluttered from public buildings, telegrams were sent to Nordenskiöld from all over Sweden and from the rest of Scandinavia. The long wait was over, one of the last secrets of the planet was unveiled: Adolf Nordenskiöld and his men had crossed from Europe to the Orient by the Northeast Passage.
Nearly eight months were to pass before *Vega* finally returned to Sweden. But even while the ship was still imprisoned off the Siberian coast, Adolf Nordenskiöld had set forth his views on the meaning of his voyage. His report was entitled 'On the Possibility of Commercial Navigation in the Waters off Siberia'. It is a remarkable document. In it, Nordenskiöld showed himself to be both a man of practical views, and a visionary.
The report was dated April 6, 1879. There was not the slightest doubt in Adolf Nordenskiöld's mind that his ship was going to complete the voyage, and he was already looking forward to its practical consequences. He described in detail the problems ships were likely to face on their way from Europe to the mouth of the Yenisey; from the Yenisey, rounding Cape Chelyuskin, to the Lena delta; and from the Lena delta

to Bering Strait. He called for detailed mapping of these Arctic waters, and for the establishment of 'rescue stations' and of a commercial port. In his conclusion, he summed up the prospects of this northern seaway.

'1. A ship, having experienced seamen aboard, should be able to complete the passage from the Atlantic, along the Siberian coast, to Siberia in a few weeks. Yet it is unlikely, from what we know of the Arctic Ocean off Siberia, that *all* of this seaway will become commercially significant.

2. It is now possible to affirm that there are no difficulties whatsoever in the way of developing a regular connection by sea between the Ob and Yenisey rivers and Europe.

3. It is most likely that the seaway between the Yenisey and the Lena, and that between the Lena and Europe, could be used commercially, but a round trip between Europe and the Lena cannot be completed in a single summer.

4. Further studies are necessary to determine whether there is a possibility of establishing seaborne trade between the Lena and the Pacific. But our experience proves that it will always be possible to ship to the Lena, by steamer, heavy machinery and other goods that cannot easily be transported by sleds or carriages.'

Even before *Vega*'s arrival in Japan the Russian press carried a report supporting Nordenskiöld's views. A writer for the Moscow daily, 'Golos', saw three sailing vessels on the upper Ob, built in Siberia during the previous winter, loaded with wheat, tallow, and vodka. The owner, a merchant of Irkutsk, had hired German and Latvian captains and crews, and on August 27 the three ships reached the mouth of the Ob, and were on their way to England.

To many a Russian businessman, and to quite a few in western Europe, the northern seaway to Siberia held a rich promise, of opening up the interior of that vast region. But there was not enough investment capital available, and within a decade the building of the Trans-Siberian railroad began. Once a rail route linked European Russia to the Pacific, interest in the northern seaway just about disappeared.

Half a century went by before Nordenskiöld's vision of the Great Northern Seaway became a reality. The Soviet government, intent upon providing access to those parts of Siberia accessible only by river, devoted time, funds, and considerable energy to the project. Intensive research, as called for by Nordenskiöld, to explore those northern seas, began in the early 1920's. Today Soviet polar stations, combining the functions of 'rescue stations' for the seaway with those of scientific research, are located in all of those places Nordenskiöld had identified, and Dickson Harbor, where his little ship, the *Pröven*, had anchored in 1875, is the nerve center of the entire Northern Seaway.

Nordenskiöld's assessment of the economic importance of the Northeast Passage turned out to be entirely correct: the bulk of the merchandise transported to and from Siberia by way of the Arctic moves between Russian ports in Europe and the Yenisey, and Russian ports on the Pacific and on the Lena. In the last third of the twentieth century, the introduction of fast, shallow-draft vessels that skim on top of the water, thereby avoiding sandbanks and shallows, promises to increase the importance of the Northern Seaway still further, allowing access to virtually all of the rivers of Siberia that drain to the Arctic Ocean.

Years after Nordenskiöld had returned from Siberia, he was interviewed by a French journalist, anxious to print something exciting about that great exploit. But Adolf Nordenskiöld was an honest man. He said: 'I am not a hero. I was not interested in reaching the North Pole. I was merely concerned with finding the way to the Orient, getting my men and myself over there and back home. I am only a practical geographer.' No one could have summed up better the true meaning of the voyage of the *Vega*.

XIX. TRAVELS IN OLD JAPAN

The morning after *Vega*'s arrival in Yokohama, all the mail for the men aboard, accumulated during nearly a year, was delivered to the ship. The news was all good, no deaths or illnesses were reported from home, and there were stacks of newspapers for everyone to read, to catch up on what had happened during the months they were out of touch with the rest of the world.

The first task for captain and crew was to make sure that the ship was fit for the long voyage home. The distance from the Swedish harbor of Karlskrona to Yokohama, by way of the Arctic Ocean, was a little over one-third of the total distance of the projected voyage. The plan was to return from Japan to Sweden by way of the South China Sea, the Indian Ocean, the Red Sea, the Suez Canal, and the Mediterranean. Much of the return trip led across tropical waters, and Palander insisted that copper sheeting be applied to *Vega* below the waterline, for protection against barnacles. The work was done at the Yokosuka shipyard, in Tokyo Bay, and the officers, scientists and crew thus had a well-earned rest for several weeks.

Among the news items of interest to Adolf Nordenskiöld was a telegram from his Russian patron, Alexander Sibiriakoff. The ship he so generously had had built and equipped to go to *Vega*'s rescue, the *A. E. Nordenskiöld*, left Sweden in May and arrived in Japan in early August. On its way to Bering Strait it was shipwrecked on the coast of Hokkaido, the northernmost of the Japanese islands. All of the ship's crew were saved but when *Vega* arrived in Japan, the would-be rescuers were still awaiting transportation to Yokohama and thence back to Europe.

For Adolf Nordenskiöld and his shipmates Japan prepared a heroes' welcome. The Japanese government, the diplomatic corps. and the foreign colony vied with each other for the privilege of wining and dining the leader of the expedition, the officers, and the scientists aboard. A fortnight after their arrival, Nordenskiöld and his colleagues were received in audience by Emperor Mutsuhito, at the Imperial palace of Tokyo.

Barely a decade had passed, at the time of Nordenskiöld's visit, since the building of modern Japan had begun under the rule of the man who received him in formal audience. Although a few ports were opened to foreign ships, as a result of the intervention by the United States in 1854,

Japan continued along her old ways, reluctant to admit foreigners to her shores. But the increasing pressure of the outside world for Japan to open her gates to all led to an internal revolution, and in 1867 Mutsuhito, then a young man of 15, ascended the throne. The reforms brought about under his rule, known as the Meiji reforms, made Japan, then a remote and completely isolated feudal state, a modern nation in barely a third of a century.

Adolf Nordenskiöld was a keen observer of nature, but the pages he wrote about his visit to Japan show him to be an equally good observer of men. He had looked forward to the chance of seeing Japan, for he knew something about the great change that was taking place in that remote island empire. Outwardly, Japan was still quaint and picturesque, as the handful of Europeans who had been there described it during its centuries of complete isolation. Most of the people still wore their traditional native dress, their kimonos and clogs; the Japanese house retained its fragile appearance, looking like a delicately constructed matchbox of wood and paper. In the cities, merchants and artisans went about their business in a leisurely manner, out in the country the farmers tilled their fields of rice and vegetables as they had done for centuries. But Japan was already changing her ways, building new industries, constructing railroads, training and equipping modern armed forces, and the leaders of the nation made it a point to appear, on important occasions, in Western-style clothes.

In a handful of pages Adolf Nordenskiöld gives us a striking portrait of this changing Japan. He was fascinated by the colors, sights, and sounds of old Japan, and apparently spent a considerable sum purchasing the exquisitely finished products of Japanese artisans, lacquer and metal objects, pottery and silks and painted paper screens. The chapters dealing with his visit to Japan that are part of his narrative of the *Vega* voyage are full of charming vignettes of Japanese life.

One of the features of Japan that pleased Nordenskiöld most was the stark simplicity and dazzling cleanliness of the old-fashioned Japanese inns. He was fascinated by their almost complete lack of furniture: only a scroll or a flower arrangement, in one corner of a room, attracted the eye. He found the fact that partitions between rooms were made of thin, movable panels, most unusual; the size of rooms could thus be changed quickly and easily. One night, he wrote, he went to sleep in a very large bedchamber and, being a sound sleeper, did not hear any noises at all. When he woke up in the morning, he found himself in a very small room, the walls having been moved about during the night. Stepping onto the tiny balcony, he looked out over the miniature garden that filled the interior courtyard of the inn, and saw its carefully trimmed *bonsai*, or dwarf trees, tiny ponds, smooth or craggy stones and pebbles, and sandy paths.

Japanese food did not really appeal to Adolf Nordenskiöld, he described it to Anna as 'impossible'. But he enjoyed the ballet-like formality of the tea ceremony, and the exquisite braziers and pots, and cups and saucers, that were as much part of the ceremony as the precise movements of the participants.

The more he saw of old Japan, the better Nordenskiöld liked it. At long last, the formal receptions in his honor tapered off, and through the good offices of the Danish member of the expedition, Lieutenant Hovgaard, he was invited by the Danish Consul in Japan for a week's trip to the 'interior'. They were to visit Japan's most important active volcano, Asamayama, and see as much of the countryside as their time would allow.

Nordenskiöld and his companions employed all of the means of travel then available in Japan: carriages, horses, rickshaws, sedan chairs. At times, they preferred walking to the local ways of transport. They stayed in Japanese inns but, having hired a cook in Tokyo, ate European-style food, although most of that consisted of involved variations on the theme of the single available source of meat, chicken.

The travellers spent several days on the way, and visited the famous hot springs at Ikao and Kusatsu, then, as today, among the most popular spas of Japan. Nordenskiöld described vividly the gingerly way the Japanese, suffering from a variety of ailments, lowered themselves into the huge basins filled with hot sulfurous water; its temperature varied between 45 and 53 degrees Celsius, 113 and 128 degrees Fahrenheit. He witnessed the curious custom, observed at these hot springs, of the patients beating the water with wide wooden paddles in order to cool it, a custom that still persists. The fact that men and women took the baths together stark naked must have seemed strange to a European of the Victorian era, but Adolf Nordenskiöld was a realist. 'Prude English "misses" –' he wrote his wife '– find themselves travelling in a rickshaw drawn by a man who is practically stark naked. In a few days time they find this perfectly natural.'

The worst way to travel in Japan, according to Nordenskiöld, was by *kago*, a form of sedan chair. The lithograph illustrating this form of conveyance shows him decked out in pith helmet and summer clothing, seemingly relaxing in what is really a cloth sling, suspended from two bamboo poles, and carried on their shoulders by two men. 'It is exceedingly inconvenient for Europeans, because they cannot, like the Japanese, sit with their legs crossed under them, and it becomes very tiresome to let one's legs dangle without any support at all.'

His favorite form of transportation was the rickshaw. Travelling over one of the old roads of Japan, he wrote: 'Everyone who has an eye for the beauties of nature and the life and manners of a foreign people must find a journey by rickshaw very pleasant indeed . . . The landscape here is extraordinarily beautiful, perhaps unmatched in the whole world. The road is cut, with great difficulty, across wild black rock, along deep clefts often covered with the most luxuriant vegetation. There isn't any fence to protect the rickshaw, as it rolls rapidly along, from the bottomless abyss by the wayside. One must have strong nerves to enjoy the trip, and trust the sharp eyes and surefooted gait of the coolie. One is surrounded by a maze of high, cleft mountain tops, while deep down in the valleys mountain streams rush along, whose crystal-clear waters are collected into small lakes, confined by steep cliffs covered by a thick growth of plants. The traveller passes over a dizzy gorge by a fragile bridge; later, he sees a stream of water by the wayside, rushing down from an enormous height. Thousands of men on foot meet the traveller, crowds of pilgrims, long rows of coolies, oxen and horses carrying heavy burdens. As they rest at the foot of steep slopes, one has a good chance to observe this motley crowd. There are always happy and friendly faces here, a pleasant impression never destroyed by that coarse speech and behavior one so often finds in Europe.'

Nordenskiöld and his companions did not miss any of the attractions the small Japanese town or village offered to the traveller. Crowded into a few pages are excellent description of the Japanese theater, of Japanese wrestling, of the blind masseurs who announced their approach by singing their off-key tune, much in the manner of a fruit vendor at a Russian country fair.

On the last day of the excursion, the party stopped at a roadside inn near Tokyo. There were half a dozen girls in the courtyard of the inn, washing themselves in a large fountain, combing their hair and brushing their teeth. The three Scandinavians were suddenly conscious of their own appearance, since they were about to make their entrance to the capital of Japan. They took their basket of towels and shaving gear, and proceeded to wash and shave in the fountain.

This created quite a sensation. Everyone wanted to know how Europeans went about their morning toilette, and the girls outdid themselves trying to help the foreigners. One held the mirror, another the shaving brush, a third the soap. Older, married women and men gathered in small knots a little further off, all curious, and eager to observe the proceedings. Later, while Nordenskiöld and his companions had their breakfast on the open porch of the inn, the girls all sat around, laughing and chattering and talking to the visitors. 'It ought to be noted' – wrote Nordenskiöld – 'that though we were not surrounded by any select group, not a single offensive word was heard from the tightly packed crowd of onlookers. This gives us an idea of the general tone of Japanese society, even amongst those lowest in it, and shows that the Japanese, though they have much to learn from Europeans, ought not to imitate them in every way. There is much in Japan worth noticing that is good and old and part of the nation's personality, perhaps more than the Japanese now have any idea of, and certainly more than many a European resident will admit.'

There was still time to do more sightseeing in and around Tokyo, and Adolf Nordenskiöld certainly took advantage of every moment. The Japanese art objects he bought were things of great beauty, and he proudly carried home what was to be the first of many medals struck in honor of his great exploit. It was a handsome, heavy silver piece, with a map of Northern Asia on one side, a long Japanese inscription on the other, praising the men of *Vega* and their pioneer voyage; the inscription was inlaid in gold. The medal was commissioned by the Tokyo Geographic Society and is still displayed, with other mementoes of the *Vega* voyage, in the Stockholm Historical Museum.

Besides collecting Japanese art works for himself, Nordenskiöld took time out to engage in another form of collecting. During his stay in Japan he accumulated a small, yet representative library of Japanese books, dealing with a great variety of subjects, all published during the Tokugawa era, the time of Japan's seclusion that lasted from the 1620's until 1868. The collection, consisting of over one thousand titles, in more than six thousand volumes, was donated to the Stockholm Royal Library on *Vega*'s return; it was one of the first important collections of *Japonica* to be made available to scholars outside Japan. Announcing the purchase in a letter home, Nordenskiöld added: it would be a good thing if one of the librarians started studying Japanese right away. In fact, Sweden ended up by inviting Rosny, from Paris, one of the first European scholars of Japanese language and literature, to compile the full catalogue of the collection.

On October 11, all repairs on the ship having been completed, *Vega* weighed anchor, and steamed towards Kobe, Japan's second port. They had waited for more than a week for good weather: Palander felt that it was best to delay their departure until the season of violent storms was over and the ship could proceed without undue risks towards the China coast. Nordenskiöld was as always eager to see as much as possible, and after anchoring in Kobe, he immediately went ashore, to visit the old imperial capital of Japan, Kyoto. Combining scientific pursuits with plain sightseeing, he and Nordquist made a cruise on Lake Biwa near Kyoto, dredging for specimens of freshwater fish and other forms of life in Japan's inland waters, and then returned to visit the temples and palaces of old Kyoto.

Little evaded his observant eye, and he gives the reader glimpses of the art of the Japanese swordsmith, descriptions of the essentials of Shinto forms of worship, and of Japanese temple architecture. At the end of a long and tiring day of sightseeing, he was taken to a party, given in his honor by the governor of Kyoto, complete with geisha girls. The governor, having thus provided his distinguished guest with a good introduction to traditional Japanese entertainment, followed it up the next evening with a formal dinner in European fashion, complete, as Nordenskiöld put it, with European dishes, wines, and speeches.

The governor, who was also a noted poet, put a delightful Japanese flourish to the occasion. His secretary delivered a scroll to Nordenskiöld the next morning, upon which the governor had written a *haiku,* a formal Japanese poem, celebrating his guest's achievement:

'As far as the sea extends,
The autumn moon spreads its benevolent light'

read the poem, an allusion to the light of the moon that spreads far to the north, to *Vega's* wintering place.

From Kobe, the expedition sailed across the Inland Sea of Japan to make their last stop in Japan at the far western port of Nagasaki. Adolf Nordenskiöld made one more excursion ashore, and collected a number of excellent impressions of fossil plants from recent geological formations found in Nagasaki's surroundings.

The stay in Nagasaki ended with a grand gala dinner where speeches were made in Japanese, Chinese, English, French, German, Italian,

Dutch, Russian, Danish, and Swedish, by local dignitaries, resident foreign businessmen, and officers and staff of *Vega*. As the ship steamed out of Nagasaki harbor on October 27, the crews of two English gunboats saluted it, manning the yard and bulwarks. The long voyage home now began.

'It was only natural that we looked forward to our departure with joy' – wrote Nordenskiöld – 'after fifteen months' separation from our homeland. But there was a feeling of sorrow mixed with that joy, that we were compelled to leave so soon this lovely land and her noble people, never to return. There is a movement among them that will not only give a new awakening to this old and civilized people of East Asia, but will also prepare the ground for European science, industry and arts. It is difficult to foresee what new, hitherto undreamed blossoms and fruit this ground will yield. But those Europeans who believe that it is only a matter of putting modern European dress on an old feudal nation of Asia, are very much mistaken. Rather, it seems to me that the day is dawning on an age when the lands surrounding the East Asian Mediterranean will play a truly important part in the further development of the human race.'

XX. AROUND THE OLD WORLD – JAPAN TO ITALY – 1879-1880

When *Vega* left Japan at the end of October, the worst of the fall storm season was over. There was a steady northeast wind, and the ship made the run from Japan to Hongkong in five days. It was a record run, the fastest of the entire voyage: the log showed an average speed of nearly twelve knots.

It was after sunset that *Vega* sailed into the magnificent harbor of Hongkong, on November 2, 1879, and lights were burning everywhere: street lights in the mainland part of the colony, Kowloon, lights outlining the steep hills of Victoria on Hongkong Island. The harbor was full of Chinese junks, each with its lighted lantern on the poop; the lights in the cabins, and on the mast tops, of merchantmen moored at their berths were reflected in the water. The men stood on *Vega's* deck, admiring the view.

After anchoring on the Kowloon side, Nordenskiöld and Palander went ashore, and took rooms in one of the hotels. But word of *Vega*'s arrival was all over the colony by next morning, and soon invitations for dinners and receptions were delivered to the chief of the expedition. At noon, a smartly uniformed sergeant of the Hongkong police brought a note from the governor of the colony, Sir John Pope-Hennessy, asking the chief of the expedition and the commander of *Vega* to be his guests during their stay.

After lunch, Nordenskiöld and Palander boarded one of the ferries plying between Kowloon and Victoria, and were met by the governor's coach. A short ride took them part way up the Peak, the steep hill overlooking the harbor, to Government House. In his diary, Palander described the magnificent view from the balcony of his bedroom, the superb gardens surrounding the residence, and the fresh breeze blowing from the sea. 'I live like an emperor!', he exclaimed.

There was a state dinner, given by the Governor, and an official reception at Government House. The business community of Hongkong, anxious to express its appreciation to the men of the *Vega,* arranged a meeting in the City Hall. English businessmen in cutaways were seated next to their Chinese competitors, wearing black silk gowns, in the crowded auditorium, listening to the President of the Chamber of Commerce welcome the Swedish explorers. Afterwards, a formal address was presented to Nordenskiöld, bound in red silk, with over four hundred signatures, many written in beautiful Chinese characters. In his reply, Nordenskiöld reminded his hosts that the attempt to find the Northeast Passage was 'the very first germ of the seagoing merchant fleet of England'. He spoke of the expedition of Willoughby and Chancellor that, nearly three and a half centuries earlier, had set out from England to the Pacific, so convinced of success that the ships were, for the first time in English seagoing practice, sheeted in lead to protect them in tropical seas.

He ended his address by saying: 'I am surrounded here by eminent merchants of different nations, and the interest they feel in our undertaking seems to me clearly to indicate that the newly opened way will soon be employed for commercial purposes. I am quite convinced that as the first northeastern voyage, 330 years ago, opened trade between northern Russia and England, so will this voyage open trade between the borders of the Pacific Ocean and Siberia, a part of the globe the importance and natural resources of which are yet only appreciated by a very limited number of practical men.'

Caught up in the social whirl of cosmopolitan Hongkong, Adolf Nordenskiöld suddenly realized that his wardrobe was, in his own words, somewhat shabby. He carried clothes with him that would be comfortable in the tropics, but it seems evident from his letters home that he was not prepared to be lionized, to become the center of formal entertainment. He asked his wife to order a suit of tails and a double-breasted morning coat, with light-colored trousers, 'all rather elegant, I must insist', from his tailor in Stockholm, to be sent to him either at Suez, or at Naples.

Although the expedition planned only a short stay in Hongkong, Nordenskiöld, Palander, and Kjellman were anxious to see at least a small corner of China, and travelled upriver by steamboat to Canton. 'Canton was by far the most interesting city I have visited' – wrote Adolf Nordenskiöld to his wife – 'many of its crowded streets have arcades, with high buildings on either side; the street floors of these buildings are occupied by stores. The streets are so narrow that two sedan chairs can barely pass each other, and people swarm everywhere, as on an anthill. In one section of the city there were Chinese lanterns and European-style chandeliers hung from ropes over every street. They were getting ready for a big celebration, because that part of the city was saved during a recent fire. The only way you can get around in Canton is either on foot, or in a sedan chair.'

The trip to Canton and back took two days, and after another rousing round of festivities, luncheons, receptions, and dinners, at the end of a week's stay *Vega* sailed on November 9 from Hongkong; Labuan, a small island off the north coast of Borneo, was to be the next landfall. Nordenskiöld was particularly anxious to visit Labuan, a place noted for its coal mines; he hoped to collect fossil plants from the coal beds, to be compared with other fossil remains from carboniferous strata in more northerly places.

Vega was now in the very heart of the tropics, since Labuan island lies only five degrees north of the equator. All aboard suffered from the heat and high humidity, and the men in the engine room could only work short watches. Once more, Louis Palander proved to be knowledgeable: he had hired two Chinese seamen in Hongkong to work as firemen, thus relieving the Swedes from long hours in intense heat belowdecks.

The expedition spent only three days on Labuan island. Nordenskiöld collected a number of excellent fossil specimens, while several of the staff made an excursion to the interior: they took the ship's barge up one of the small streams, and visited Malay villages.

Leaving Labuan, *Vega* turned southwest, towards Singapore, on her way to the Indian Ocean. Everyone was hoping to get mail: it had been nearly three months since the first letters from home were picked up in Japan, and all were anxious for more up-to-date news. As soon as the ship docked, a messenger arrived from Barclay Reed, the Swedish Consul in Singapore, with a hefty packet of mail.

The first letters Adolf Nordenskiöld opened were from his wife. The children were all thriving, the elder ones did well in school, everyone enjoyed summer vacation in the country, but they missed Father very much. It seemed like a long time before he would be back home again.

But Anna had other news, too, news from Oscar Dickson, the expedition's principal patron. Shortly after the Nordenskiöld family had returned to Stockholm from their summer holiday, Dickson came to call. It was not a happy encounter. Dickson was very much the business magnate, out to impress the world, or so it seemed to Anna. What was more important was that Dickson had had an audience with King Oscar, shortly before calling on Anna, and the King had told him about preparations being made for the *Vega*'s homecoming.

The King planned to present special medals to Nordenskiöld, Palander, and the officers and scientists of the expedition. The Academy of Sciences, too, was talking about honoring Nordenskiöld. But from what Dickson told her, Anna Nordenskiöld was quite convinced that it was

going to be a quiet homecoming: King Oscar wanted Nordenskiöld and Palander to leave their ship at Naples, and return home by train.
Writing her from Japan, Adolf had hoped that his wife could meet him in Egypt, or at least in Italy. But she felt that the trip would be too expensive. 'Oh, if the King would only provide me with money so that I could meet you in Naples!' – she wrote – 'Wouldn't that be fun!' Instead, there would be only a modest ceremony when Nordenskiöld returned to Stockholm, probably at the railroad station.
'I shall wait for you at home' – wrote Anna – 'The children will want to be there when you arrive; I'll ask one of the gentlemen we know, to look after them. I dot not wish to appear in public.' Anna was disappointed, she knew that her husband deserved more than a halfhearted official welcome.
What made her even more depressed was Dickson's attitude towards the whole matter of the voyage of the *Vega*. On earlier occasions he had been enthusiastic about the results of Nordenskiöld's trips. This time, he was not even convinced that the journey added anything to geographical knowledge. Anna wondered whether it was Dickson's disappointment for not having taken part in the expedition. Whatever it was, Dickson made no attempt to hide his bad mood. He even went so far as to say that he was not prepared to spend his entire fortune, supporting expeditions of this kind.
This was a far cry from the enthusiastic messages that Anna had received when news of *Vega's* crossing of the Northeast Passage had first reached Sweden. Von Otter, who had bitterly opposed the voyage from the beginning, was among the first to send her confirmation of the news that *Vega* was safely berthed in Japan. And King Oscar's telegram spoke of 'the unforgettable victory won by your noble husband, a new Vasco da Gama, as the prize for his perseverance, for toil and hardship.'
If Nordenskiöld was disappointed by the news from home, his letters to Anna never showed it. As for Dickson's attitude, he reminded his wife that Oscar Dickson had indeed spent large sums of money on the *Vega* expedition, and on earlier voyages; but, he added, Dickson got his own reward by becoming well known all over Europe.
He had news for Anna, of recognition of another sort. He was offered ten thousand Swedish kronor, two thousand dollars, a large sum for the time, for the publication rights of his account of the *Vega* expedition, and Macmillan, one of England's leading publishing houses, offered nearly twice that amount for the rights to the English translation.

The Nordenskiölds had lived in pleasant, but far from affluent, circumstances. He was entitled to a good-sized apartment in the building of Sciences in Stockholm, as part of his appointment of Curator of Mineralogy. But the family's sole support was Adolf Nordenskiöld's salary. He had tried more than once to supplement it with extra income, but had not been successful. Now he realized that, with sudden public interest in a popular account of his journey across the Northeast Passage, his book might become a best-seller, and he could earn a sizable amount of extra money. He thought of small luxuries he could not afford before, first and foremost of having a place in the country. Adolf and Anna Nordenskiöld both grew up on country estates, and Anna spent many summer holidays at her family's estate in Finland. Nothing would please Anna more than a country home of her own, where she could have a garden and an orchard.

Adolf Nordenskiöld was fully aware of the interest of scientific circles in the observations collected during the *Vega* voyage, and he planned to start on scientific reports, right after his return to Sweden. He was also very much concerned with the future use of the Northeast Passage for trade, and was already planning to go to Russia soon after his return, to encourage government and business circles to invest in the development of the new seaway. But he was astonished to find intense public interest in a popular account of the expedition.

This public interest in the voyage of the *Vega* was very much in keeping with the spirit of the times, for the eighteen-seventies were a decade of discovery. It all started with Stanley's report of finding Livingstone, the great explorer who was presumed lost, in the heart of Africa. Stanley and others continued to explore Africa from the Sahara to the Congo; Englishmen and Russians travelled far and wide across the interior of Asia; Swedes and Austrians pushed poleward in the Arctic.

Exploration and discovery were front-page news in those days. Maps and pictures, illustrating journeys to the distant corners of the world, were regular features of weekly magazines. The world was shrinking fast, the areas on the map marked 'unexplored' dwindled in size every year. Man believed that technology gave him the keys to his planet, and Jules Verne wrote 'Around the world in eighty days' in that mood, in 1873.

The discovery of the Northeast Passage ranked with the greatest of explorations in the eyes of the world. Adolf Nordenskiöld was elected honorary member of learned societies in France and Denmark, in Japan and Germany, in England, Austria, and Russia. All of this was reported in Swedish newspapers, together with descriptions of *Vega's* triumphal reception in Tokyo, Hongkong, and Singapore. Government circles in Stockholm began to realize that Adolf Nordenskiöld was a world figure now.

The man to whom all of this homage was addressed was as yet unaware of most of it. In his letters home he described the enchanting world of Japan and the exciting and exotic tropics. He spoke of the art objects he had purchased, bronzes, cloisonné, porcelain, even whole suits of Japanese armor. And he did tell his wife of the entertainments organized in honor of the expedition.

Leaving Singapore, *Vega* sailed through the Strait of Malacca and, crossing the Bay of Bengal, came to anchor in Galle harbor, on the southwest tip of the island of Ceylon. Nordenskiöld had advised his family and the Swedish government of his intention to stop there, and he had to wait nearly a week for the arrival of mail from Europe. This time was put to good use by the staff: Nordenskiöld visited districts of Ceylon noted for their sapphires and other gemstones; Almquist climbed the highest mountain of the island, to collect samples of lichens and other plants; Kjellman added to the ship's collection of algae, dredged from Galle harbor.

In a letter written shortly after *Vega* left Ceylon, Nordenskiöld described the island's tropical vegetation of Ceylon, and the infinite variety of fruit, including some that were completely new to him. There were masses of bananas, pineapples, mangoes, oranges, coconuts, and durian, to be enjoyed every day. He also bought Buddhist manuscripts on his visits to the cities and temples of the interior, and sent three sapphires to his wife, to have them mounted in a ring as a souvenir of his visit to the island that has always been famous for gems.

From Ceylon *Vega* pointed straight across the Indian Ocean to the British colony of Aden, at the entrance of the Red Sea. The crossing lasted a fortnight, and the men aboard celebrated both Christmas and New Year at sea. It was a quiet Christmas, the thoughts of everyone were preoccupied with their return home, but on New Year's Eve the officers and scientists were surprised by a delegation from the crew. They were dressed in parkas and boots, and their leader spoke in the pidgin of Swedish and Chukch that everyone had used during their Siberian wintering. The men spoke of the year just past and wished everyone well for the year to come. Their only complaint was that, true men of the north that they were, the heat of the voyage across the tropics was hard for them to bear.

Aden was an important coaling station for ships plying between Europe and India, and a key outpost of the British Empire. But it was a barren place, and Nordenskiöld described it as unlike any other he had ever seen. 'There isn't any place in the Arctic, not the granite cliffs of the Seven Islands or the pebbles and rocks of Low Island in Spitsbergen, nor the mountainsides of Novaya Zemlya, or the barren ground of Cape Chelyuskin, that is so bare of vegetation as the surroundings of Aden, and those parts of the east coast of the Red Sea that we saw. Nor can one compare the richness of animal life in the Arctic with the poverty of species of these southern regions. Animal life in the coastlands of the farthest North, where high mountains are surrounded by deep waters, is far more numerous than in the south: this is true not only of the vast bird colonies and great numbers of game, but even of the abundance of lower forms of life in the sea. At least, the dredgings we made during the voyage from Japan to Ceylon gave a very scanty yield when compared with what we found north of Cape Chelyuskin.'

Vega stopped at Aden to fill her bunkers with coal. There was an Italian warship in the harbor, and the officers and scientists of *Vega* spent an enjoyable evening, dining aboard the *Esploratore*. In the mail-bag awaiting the expedition, there was a letter from Oscar Dickson to Nordenskiöld, reflecting a change of heart of the Swedish government. Instead of treating the *Vega* voyage as just another of Nordenskiöld's Arctic adventures, Sweden was now concerned about the best way to express its appreciation of the accomplishments of the expedition.

It has long been customary in Sweden to bestow decorations on public figures of distinction. Ten years earlier, in 1868, when Adolf Nordenskiöld had made headlines establishing an Arctic record aboard Sofia, he was offered the decoration, 'North Star', by the Swedish government. Nordenskiöld had refused, for he considered the awarding of decorations an outmoded system of recognition, not to be practiced in a modern democracy. Though he was subsequently decorated both by Italy and Spain, he never spoke of these honors, and kept them secret, to the extent of not reporting them to the Swedish government, as he was required by law to do.

Nordenskiöld's well-known stand against accepting awards or decorations put the government in an awkward position. If he refused these honors, none of the other members of the expedition could be decorated, neither could its principal patron, Oscar Dickson. In his letter, Dickson put the question squarely to Nordenskiöld: was he willing to change his mind and accept a decoration from Sweden this time?

Adolf Nordenskiöld replied right away, asking Dickson to assure the government that he was ready to accept all awards or honors that Sweden, or any other country for that matter, might bestow on him. In a letter he wrote to Anna at the same time, he told her his reasons for this decision. Titles and decorations were important to most people, and even rabid radicals, such as the leaders of the Paris Commune uprising of 1871, insisted that their ribbons and stars be returned to them, when they were amnestied by the government. To appear without a decoration in one's lapel at a German social function would brand a man redder then the reddest revolutionary; in Russia, he would be considered a political martyr. In any case, Nordenskiöld had plans to set economic and political forces in motion to exploit the potential of the Northeast Passage, and he was not about to sacrifice their success by insisting on a matter that he considered of little practical importance.

The news was reported by Dickson to the government, and King Oscar himself expressed his pleasure, in a hand-written letter, at this change of attitude. The King added that, if Nordenskiöld insisted on continuing his trip aboard *Vega* back to Sweden, rather than returning from Italy by train, that was quite acceptable. The King only hoped that by so doing, Nordenskiöld would not miss out on the festivities planned in his honor, since, after all, the festivities were to honor Sweden as well.

It took *Vega* nearly three weeks against cold northerly winds to sail up the Red Sea to Suez, the entrance of the Suez Canal. By the time they set foot on Egyptian soil, it turned so cold that the men had to put on winter clothes. They could hardly believe that the shores of the Red Sea are known for exceptionally high temperatures.

Suez marked another stop. The Egyptian Geographical Society having invited Nordenskiöld to visit Cairo, he and the officers and scientists went by rail from Suez to the Egyptian capital. They did the sights: visited the sphinx and the pyramids, and even explored an area of petrified trees in the desert.

After their return to Suez, *Vega* crossed the Canal to its northern, Mediterranean end at Port Said. Being in the Mediterranean felt almost like home to the men, after an absence from Europe of more than a year and a half.

Letters awaiting Nordenskiöld in Port Said spoke of a formal reception, being prepared in Naples for the arrival of *Vega.* The Italian government, Italian scientists, Rome society, all were anxious to know the exact date and time of the ship's landing. But *Vega* was a slow sailor, and Nordenskiöld knew that it would be better to wait until they had sighted Italy before he could set a date for their landing in Naples. Palander had set the ship's course from Port Said to the Strait of Messina, that separates Sicily and the Italian mainland, and he expected that when *Vega* was sighted there she would be reported directly to Rome and Naples.

But it was after dark when *Vega* approached the Strait of Messina. Time was running short, and Nordenskiöld decided to go ashore, find a telegraph office, and announce their arrival. With Lieutenant Bove as interpreter, he started out in the steam launch for Villa San Giovanni, the nearest town and telegraph office on the mainland shore of the Strait.

Bove was not familiar with the area, and the two men landed some distance from the town. Clambering ashore, they found a railroad line running on a high embankment and following the tracks, they reached the station at Villa San Giovanni. But as soon as they entered the building, looking for the telegraph office, they were surrounded by suspicious customs officers. As Nordenskiöld wrote later, they were lucky to have landed unseen, else their welcome to Europe would have been some rifle shots, since they were suspected to be smugglers.

Luckily, Lieutenant Bove wore his Italian navy uniform, and explained to his countrymen that they came from the famous ship, *Vega.* Then the telegrapher took a closer look at the sheaf of telegrams Nordenskiöld had handed him, and saw that they were addressed to the King of Sweden, the Swedish Minister in Rome, and other personages of rank. The two men were given a much more cordial reception after that, the telegrams were sent off, and a customs officer was detailed to accompany the visitors back to their boat. Holding a torch high over his head to guide them, the officer told the visitors that they had done well, having climbed all over the rough shoreline, covered with cacti and other prickly plants, and to have walked over a high railroad bridge in the dark unaware of its existence!

With the two men back on board, Palander set the ship's course for Naples. In another day or so, Nordenskiöld was thinking, he would be back on familiar territory. It wasn't going to be long before he would be home, with his family. He was certain that the Italians would organize a friendly reception for the ship in Naples, and he looked forward to spending a day or two in Rome. After that, it was to be a pleasant, uneventful cruise back to Sweden. He was not at all prepared for the honors that Italy and Portugal, England and France, Denmark and Sweden were preparing to bestow on him.

XXI. TRIUMPHAL RETURN: ITALY, FRANCE, SWEDEN – 1880

It was shortly after noon on February 14, 1880, that the low black silhouette of *Vega* appeared off the isle of Capri, at the entrance of the Bay of Naples. Two flag-decked ships were waiting to escort her into Naples harbor. The American cruiser *Wyoming*, anchored in the harbor, gave the Swedish expedition a twenty-one gun salute.

Hardly had the engines stopped, when the barge of Admiral Franklin, commanding the Naples naval district, came alongside. Led by the Italian Minister of the Navy, a glittering group of dignitaries climbed the ladder to *Vega*'s deck; among them were Swedish diplomats stationed in Italy, and the President of the Italian Geographical Society. Nordenskiöld's old friend, Commander Negri, was in the group; he had gone to Göteborg in 1878 to see *Vega* off and was on hand to welcome the expedition on their return.

Lindstrand, Swedish Minister to Italy, spoke first and extended King Oscar II's greetings to the men of *Vega* on their return to Europe. He presented the Grand Cross of the Swedish order of the 'North Star' to Nordenskiöld, other decorations to the officers and scientists of the expedition. The Italian Navy Minister added his own words of welcome next, and presented Nordenskiöld with the Grand Cross of the Order of the Italian Crown.

The officers and scientists then went ashore in Admiral Franklin's barge, while the Admiral's flagship fired a twenty-one gun salute in honor of the Swedish expedition. There was a marquee set up on the quayside, where Count Giusso, the mayor of Naples, welcomed Nordenskiöld with a sonorous Latin address.

Suites awaited Nordenskiöld and his companions in the best hotel Naples could offer. The next five days were crowded with receptions, dinners, gala concerts, and a special performance at the San Carlo Opera, where the explorers were met with a standing ovation. They visited the Phlegraean fields, that strange area of constant, low volcanic activity just outside Naples; and were also taken to Pompeii, to see the excavations of the Roman city, buried under the ashes of Mount Vesuvius.

A photograph, taken during the excursion to Pompeii, shows the officers and staff of *Vega*, with their host, Commander Negri, seated in the center of the picture. The two Swedish naval officers, Palander and Brusewitz, look ramrod straight even in mufti; one can easily recognize the young Dane, Lieutenant Hovgaard, and the scientists Kjellman, Stuxberg, Almquist, and Nordquist. Adolf Nordenskiöld sits on Commander Negri's right: he has just a shadow of a smile in his eyes. His hair had turned nearly white during the *Vega* voyage.

The next day, all went to the crater of Mount Vesuvius, and the famed volcano put on a good show for Nordenskiöld, the geologist: thick clouds of smoke rose from the crater, there was a stream of lava pouring over the rim, and masses of red-hot rocks were spewing forth. The group climbed to the very edge of the crater, over half-solidified lava flows, to get a good look at the volcanic activity.

On February 20, the officers and staff of the expedition left Naples for Rome. A distinguished delegation, headed by the mayor of Rome, Prince Ruspoli, met them at the railroad station, and escorted them, in open carriages, across the heart of the city to their hotel.

The formal dinner offered in their honor, on their first night in Rome, was at the palace of Prince Pallavicini, on the Quirinal, one of the Seven Hills of Rome. A stream of carriages came driving up to the magnificent baroque facade of the palace, where the guests were ushered into a reception room decorated with frescoes by Rome's leading painters of the 17th century, and then set down to dine in a room aglitter with chandeliers, reflected by mirrored walls. 'I met what seemed an endless number of princesses and duchesses tonight' – wrote Adolf Nordenskiöld to his wife – 'each with an old, well-known, historic title; quite a few were beautiful, all wore magnificent gowns and were covered with jewels.'

Formal dinners in the late 19th century were state occasions, lasting several hours. The guests were served soup first, then fish, then a roast, then chicken and game birds, followed by lobster or other seafood, roast capon, vegetables and salad, and topped off with dessert. Dinners such as these, consisting of twelve to fourteen courses, were washed down with a succession of wines, ranging from sherry to red burgundy, hock, claret, and port; champagne was served with dessert; and there were cigars and brandy after coffee. A cartoonist for the leading Italian illustrated weekly summed it all up in a two-panel cartoon, entitled 'The Heroes of the *Vega*'. On the left, the men are shown deep in ice and snow, and the caption reads 'At the North Pole they ran the risk of freezing to death'; on the right, the men are shown groaning at the sight of a banquet table, while someone offers a toast, and the caption reads: 'In Italy, they run the risk of dying of indigestion!'

The days Nordenskiöld and his comrades spent in Rome were filled with festivities in their honor. The Italian Geographical Society presented its gold medal to Nordenskiöld at a public meeting. At the formal dinner, given by the Society that evening, Italy's Prime Minister, Cairoli, offered a toast to King Oscar of Sweden and Norway; Prince Caetani, President of the Geographical Society, toasted Nordenskiöld; the Minister of the Navy, Admiral Acton, saluted Palander; and the toasts went on and on.

One evening King Umberto of Italy gave a state dinner, inviting the *Vega* staff to meet the leaders of Italian politics, science, and society, and also arranging a reunion for Nordenskiöld and Palander with their old shipmate, Lieutenant Parent of the Italian Navy.

On the last of their six days in Rome, the British Minister, Sir A. B. Paget, and the Scandinavian colony of Rome, both gave receptions for the explorers. Next day, Kjellman, Stuxberg, and Almquist returned to Sweden by train; Nordquist went home to Finland; and Bove took leave to visit his family in Turin. Palander was invited to the Italian naval base at La Spezia, for a cruise aboard the new Italian ironclad, *Duilio*; and Adolf Nordenskiöld had the day to himself. He spent most of it visiting bookstores, getting acquainted with the leading rare book dealers of Rome, and acquiring books, maps, and atlases for his library.

During his stay in Rome, he met at long last the Russian patron of the expedition, Alexander Sibiriakoff. The two men had been corresponding for more than four years, ever since Sibiriakoff, hearing of Nordenskiöld's speech at a banquet in Moscow, in 1875, became an enthusiast of the Northeast Passage. Though both men had travelled far and wide across Europe, they had never met, and Sibiriakoff had made a special trip from St. Petersburg, to become personally acquainted with the chief of the *Vega* expedition.

While the officers and staff were in Rome, the crew of *Vega* was kept busy in Napels. Clausen, the Swedish Consul, saw to it that the enlisted men aboard were not forgotten: they were invited to dinner by the city of Naples, went to the opera, and visited Pompeii. Each man had a turn ashore, while those on board dealt with the onrush of visitors.

A lithograph in an Italian weekly, labeled 'Everyone to the *Vega*!', shows a flotilla of rowboats lined up at the approaches to the ship's ladder. Ladies with bustle and parasol, gentlemen in top hats and cutaways, soldiers and sailors in uniform, all were being rowed out to visit the famous vessel. One day the crush was so great that one of the Swedish seamen, trying to cope with the crowd pushing and shoving its way around the ship, fell down a ladder, and broke an arm. He was the only casualty of the entire voyage.

On February 29, after a glorious fortnight in Italy, *Vega* sailed from Naples. The wardroom was half empty, only Nordenskiöld and the three naval officers, Palander, Brusewitz, and Hovgaard, remained on board. They crossed the Mediterranean, passed through the Strait of Gibraltar, and anchored in Lisbon harbor on March 11. Nordenskiöld was delighted to have this chance to visit Portugal, the land of Henry the Navigator and Vasco da Gama, the home of some of the greatest explorers in history.

The King of Portugal, a former naval officer like King Oscar of Sweden, received Nordenskiöld and Palander in private audience, and questioned them at length about their experiences. There was a formal dinner and reception at the residence of the Swedish Minister, and the visitors were special guests at a meeting of the Portuguese Geographical Society. This was of special interest to Nordenskiöld: he listened to two Portuguese explorers, recently returned from southern Africa, report on their travels and he also met Major Serpa Pinto, who only two years earlier had made headlines with his crossing of southern Africa.

Before the ship left Lisbon, the Prime Minister presented Nordenskiöld and Palander with decorations, and the Chamber of Deputies passed a special resolution, honoring the men of *Vega*.

Many years later, a distinguished British diplomat, Sir Robert Morier, was writing to Adolf Nordenskiöld, concerning matters of navigation and trade in the Siberian Arctic. Morier was British Ambassador to Russia then, but he reminded Nordenskiöld, in a postscript to his letter that they had met earlier, when Morier was British Minister to Portugal.

'I am not likely to forget the muster of those twenty splendid Vikings' – wrote Morier – 'on the deck of the little Arctic ship, scarred and cicatrized with her polar battles, but standing erect and defiant against the deep blue southern sky, like some sea creature out of a saga, coming from the furthest North to conquer the lands of the orange and the olive! That picture has gone on living in my memory, and will do so to the end, not only for its own sake, but for the vivid manner in which it visioned out to me that great and beneficent crisis in the world's history when the Northmen emerged from their mists and icefloes, to endow us with brighter brains and stouter backbones!'

On March 16, *Vega* steamed out of the wide estuary of the Tagus, Lisbon's superb natural harbor, and turned north towards England. Great preparations had been made for her arrival there: England had sent more ships and more men to the Arctic than any other European nation, and the Swedes' achievement was valued highly by Englishmen.
But weather interfered with the plans carefully made by Nordenskiöld's friends. When *Vega* sailed past Portugal and across the Bay of Biscay, winds were in her favor; but when she was approaching the English Channel, she ran into exceptionally strong headwinds. After several days of futile maneuvers, Palander decided to land at the nearest English port. *Vega* was supposed to have anchored at Portsmouth where a reception committee was waiting; instead, she made Falmouth, two hundred miles to the west, in Cornwall.
By the time Nordenskiöld and Palander reached London it was Easter Saturday morning, and people had left town for the long holiday week-end. To complicate things further, England was in the midst of an election campaign. The ruling Conservative Party had become highly unpopular, in part because of wars fought simultaneously by English troops in Afghanistan and in South Africa. Prime Minister Disraeli decided to dissolve Parliament and had appealed to the country in a general election.
The formal festivities planned for the Swedish guests in England, that included a banquet of the Royal Geographical Society, with the Prince of Wales in the chair, had to be cancelled. But there were numerous informal engagements to take their place. Adolf Nordenskiöld was the house guest of Clements Markham, Secretary of the Royal Geographical Society, who had supported polar research enthusiastically for many years. There were dinners offered by the Swedish Consul-General and by the well-known Arctic explorer, Sir Allen Young.
On Easter Monday, the Earl of Northbrook, President of the Royal Geographical Society, invited Nordenskiöld to his estate near Winchester; among other things, the visiting explorer, who had served in the Swedish parliament, was able to attend a typical election rally in the English countryside. On the way back to London, Nordenskiöld dined at the country place of the President of the Royal Society, England's most prestigious scientific body, and saw some interesting electrical experiments, designed to produce light in a vacuum tube.
Before leaving for France, Nordenskiöld and Palander were entertained for dinner by the Swedish envoy to Britain, and attended a party given

in their honor by the Scandinavian colony of London. It must have been a truly festive occasion, with innumerable toasts; Nordenskiöld merely described it as 'an occasion for happiness, in old Nordic fashion'.

The chief of the *Vega* expedition and the commander of the vessel must have welcomed the few hours of rest that the trip across the channel, by night sleeper and ferry boat, afforded them. Boulogne, where they landed, put on quite a show, welcoming the two heroes to French soil. There were speeches and festive meals, starting with breakfast and ending with a late dinner, and it was not until the next morning that the two travellers arrived in Paris.

It was seven o'clock in the morning when the train from Boulogne arrived at Paris' St. Lazare station, but this did not diminish the enthusiasm of a large group assembled to greet Adolf Nordenskiöld and Louis Palander on their arrival. A distinguished French explorer welcomed them to the city on behalf of the Paris Geographical Society, and pointed out with pride that, ten years earlier, the Society had already honored Nordenskiöld with its Roquette gold medal. The French government offered to lodge their distinguished guests in the best hotel of the city, but the two Swedes had already accepted the invitation to be house guests of Alfred Nobel.

Nobel, chemist, inventor, and future philanthropist, and Nordenskiöld, mineralogist and explorer, had known each other well for some time. The fact that Nobel was one of Europe's richest men made little impression on Adolf Nordenskiöld; it was more important that he and Nobel had shared interests in science, and the two Swedes felt that Nobel's town house, in the most elegant neighborhood of Paris, was a haven where they could rest during the festivities that awaited them.

Paris welcomed Adolf Nordenskiöld in a way that surpassed anything he and Palander had encountered before. Albert Edelfelt, an artist from Finland, whose family knew the Nordenskiölds well, was in Paris at the time, and described the atmosphere in his letters home. 'Everyone is caught up in the excitement over Nordenskiöld. You would not believe the way he is feted around here. All the papers have been talking about him and only about him, for the past four days. His name is on everyone's lips, and the welcome he received in Paris has been so grandiose that I could hardly believe it. I never thought that this immense city could concentrate its attention on just one man.'

The program of Nordenskiöld and Palander's visit to Paris was packed with festive events. The evening of their arrival, the Geographical

Society held a public meeting and hired the great circus of Paris to hold the thousands who came to see and hear Nordenskiöld. 'It was magnificent', wrote Edelfelt, 'there were thousands of people shouting his name, and there stood Nordenskiöld, calm, self-assured in the midst of this huge crowd. Admiral de La Roncière, President of the Paris Geographical Society, welcomed the two explorers, and Nordenskiöld replied in French.'

'Nordenskiöld's brother-in-law, Carl Mannerheim, asked him to practice his speech and be sure to pronounce it right. But Nordenskiöld was dead tired, having spent two nights on trains, and had a good rest instead. He spoke to the crowd with the most dreadful Swedish accent, but that did not matter in the least. People listened to every word, interrupting him constantly with their applause.'

The meeting at the Paris circus ended with the presentation of the Geographical Society's gold medal to Nordenskiöld. On the following day the French Government and the University of Paris were hosts, at a meeting held in the great hall of the Sorbonne. Representatives of twenty-eight learned societies, from all over France, mingled with ladies and gentlemen from Paris society, and listened to a formal address by the French Minister of Education. The meeting ended with the presentation of the insignia of a Commander of the Legion of Honor to Nordenskiöld, and of Officer's insignia to Louis Palander.

The dinner offered by the Scandinavian Society of Paris was one of the highlights of the Nordenskiöld celebration. It was attended not only by the ambassadors of Sweden and Denmark, but by the Russian Ambassador, too. Nordenskiöld sat next to Christina Nilsson, one of the best known opera singers of the day. When the dinner was over, Nordenskiöld, Nobel, Carl Mannerheim, and several other Swedes adjourned to a night spot beloved by all Swedish residents of Paris, until the guest of honor, overcome by fatigue, begged off and went to bed.

Next day it was the turn of the French Academy: it held a special session honoring Nordenskiöld, in the Academy building on the banks of the Seine. Afterwards, a cortège of carriages took the guests across the river to a reception organized by the City of Paris. There, the mayor spoke eloquently of *Vega*'s triumph, and presented Adolf Nordenskiöld with a gold medal specially designed for the occasion.

Dinners honoring Nordenskiöld and Palander were given by President Grévy of France and by the President of the Paris Geographical Society. Then, on the last day of their visit to Paris, Nordenskiöld was invited to luncheon in the apartment of the greatest living writer of France, Victor Hugo.

It was an intimate luncheon, only ten people were present. Hugo the poet and Nordenskiöld the explorer had both opposed tyranny and had gone in exile rather than to submit to the will of an emperor. In his toast, Victor Hugo greeted his guest saying: 'They who open the great highroads that bring the peoples of the world closer together, render the greatest service to civilization.'

Albert Edelfelt, who attended all of the functions honoring his famous countryman, continued to be impressed by the complete lack of pretense in the behavior of Adolf Nordenskiöld. 'Whether he was dining with the President of the French Republic, or at luncheon with Victor Hugo, he was just as much at ease as at a student feast. All listened carefully as he explained, in his broken French, his plans for the future, or spoke of experiences on his travels. His picture can be seen in the window of every bookstore, he is truly the hero of the day. Parisians were thrilled to find out that he was a former deputy, concerned with politics, and that he was interested in French literature. It could truly be said that no one had been so celebrated by the French newspapers in recent years as Adolf Nordenskiöld!'

Thoroughly exhausted, but carrying memories they would always cherish, as Nordenskiöld put it, he and Palander left the following day for Vlissingen, the Dutch port, where *Vega* was waiting for them. On April 15, the expedition passed once more through the Kattegat, the strait separating Denmark and southern Sweden, near the spot where Palander, nearly two years earlier, had given their destination as 'Bering Strait'.

A whole fleet of ships, bearing Swedes and Danes, greeted *Vega*, serenading her as she slowly steamed towards Copenhagen. The ship lay at anchor in the Sund, outside the Danish capital, and it was only the next morning that they entered Copenhagen harbor. *Vega* fired a nine-gun salute from her tiny cannon, and the forts at the harbor entrance replied. The reception committee, headed by the Prime Minister of Denmark, met them at the maritime customs building.

This time, the crowds lining the streets hailed not only Nordenskiöld and Palander, but their own countryman too, the *Vega* expedition's hydrographer, Lieutenant Andreas Hovgaard, of the Danish Navy. The leaders of the expedition stayed in the heart of Copenhagen, at the Hotel d'Angleterre and once more festivities occupied every waking

moment of the four days they spent in Denmark's capital.
King Christian IX of Denmark was host at a state dinner in the royal palace of Amalienborg; the Chamber of Commerce and the Danish Geographical Society gave banquets in their honor; and the crew of *Vega* were guests at a dinner organized by the merchants of the city. Many Swedes crossed over from nearby south Sweden, only a short distance away, to watch their countrymen being honored, since Nordenskiöld had to decline invitations to visit the nearby Swedish cities of Malmö and Lund. It was King Oscar's express wish that the men of *Vega* should land in the heart of Stockholm, at the royal palace, the first time they touched Swedish soil.
On Thursday evening, April 22, *Vega* anchored off Dalarö, at the southern tip of the Stockholm archipelago. The next afternoon the wives of Nordenskiöld and Palander arrived from Stockholm to spend the night before the arrival on board.
In Stockholm, *Vega* fever, as some called it, reached a high pitch. Special trains kept arriving from all parts of the country, bringing thousands who wanted to watch the triumphant arrival of the famous ship. The Stockholm newspapers carried column after column of advertisements offering seats aboard ships to meet *Vega* as she approached Stockholm harbor. Merchants, too, jumped on the *Vega* bandwagon. Sweden was flooded with cigars, tablecloths, chocolates, spectacles, stockings, collars, candles, all bearing Nordenskiöld's or *Vega*'s name. One of these articles, a seaman's cap, remained popular for decades, and in the 1920's was still known as a '*Vega*-cap'.
A grey, rainy sky dawned on Stockholm on Saturday, April 24, 1880. Out in the archipelago, the tiny resort town of Dalarö was covered with flags, honoring Vega's presence in its harbor. At noon, the warship *Sköldmön* arrived, bearing special guests: Nordenskiöld's three oldest children, Maria, Gustav, and Anna; one of his brothers and one sister; his Swedish cousins; his sister-in-law; and his shipmates, Bove, Kjellman, Stuxberg, Almquist and Nordquist. The guests toured *Vega*, then returned to the Navy vessel where Admiral Lagercrantz, personal representative of King Oscar, was host at lunch. It was mid-afternoon before *Vega* got underway, and nearly dusk when she drew up abreast the old fortress of Vaxholm, guarding the entrance to the Stockholm archipelago.
The shipping lane that leads from Vaxholm to the inner harbor of Stockholm twists and turns through the labyrinth of offshore islands

between the city and the open Baltic Sea. Since early afternoon that day, some one hundred and fifty steamers, carrying well over fifteen thousand people, had been waiting, watching for *Vega* to appear.

There were dark clouds scudding across the sky and showers pelted the decks of the waiting ships. But just as *Vega* appeared to the first of the ships, turning a corner, the setting sun broke through the clouds, and the ship shone in an intense light, that was slowly changing from brightness to gold to blue. People on shore, and on the ships, suddenly saw *Vega* pass through a magnificent double rainbow; it gave the little ship's progress the looks of a triumphal procession.

Ships fell in line as *Vega* passed by, bands were playing on deck, men and women were shouting themselves hoarse, and soon *Vega* was steaming ahead of a double column of ships that stretched several miles behind her. As darkness set in, thousands of lanterns and torches were lit on each island and in each small settlement, and by the time the parade of ships was approaching the inner harbor, the lowering clouds were bright with the reflection of the sea of lights below.

The inner harbor of Stockholm was a fairyland. Each building was outlined with lanterns, torches, and floodlights; each window had its own decoration of candles. *Vega* was to anchor in the very heart of the inner harbor, opposite the royal palace. It was there, more than twenty years earlier, that Adolf Nordenskiöld had first come ashore in Stockholm. That night, the English Consulate, in the center of the waterfront, was covered with flags, and a large sign: 'Welcome, *Vega*. Well done!'

The immense east front of the royal palace was a mass of lights: there were chandeliers in every window, torches and lanterns in the garden, *Vega*'s name was outlined in gas lights on the top floor, and a huge star, made up of lanterns, shone on the roof of the palace. A wooden staircase, built for the occasion, led from the terrace down to the water's edge; on each side of it there were obelisks with the names of the officers, scientists, and crew of *Vega*, while a triumphal arch at the top of the stairs bore the names of Nordenskiöld and Palander, and the coats of arms of Italy, Denmark, Russia and Finland.

At a quarter to ten, a rocket announced that *Vega* was about to enter the inner harbor. This was the signal for a huge fireworks display, lasting nearly half an hour, as *Vega* steamed slowly towards the royal palace. Limelights placed on three sides of the harbor clearly outlined the low silhouette of the ship, its three masts and short smokestack. A crowd estimated at one hundred and fifty thousand, who had patiently waited for the moment, shouted and hailed the explorers.

As *Vega* let go her anchor, the batteries at the naval armory on Skeppsholm fired a salute. Barges carried Nordenskiöld and Palander, the officers, and the scientists ashore. A committee composed of the governor of Stockholm, the city council, members of the governing board of the Academy of Sciences, and representatives of Uppsala University, met them under the triumphal arch. The governor spoke briefly, and presented Nordenskiöld with a formal address of welcome by the city of Stockholm, bound in a red morocco case. Then the group moved into the palace, where King Oscar and his family awaited them in the Queen's sitting room.

King Oscar spoke in a voice filled with emotion, greeting the men who had honored Sweden, as well as themselves, by their discovery of the Northeast Passage. He announced that Adolf Nordenskiöld was created a baron, and presented him with his new coat of arms, and the Grand Cross of the North Star, covered with diamonds. Louis Palander was honored with a title of nobility by the King, and presented with the Knight's Cross of the North Star, with diamonds. Oscar Dickson, absent because of illness, was also made a member of Sweden's nobility, and decorated.

All of the officers and members of the scientific staff received decorations, and the King brought the ceremony to a close by presenting the special *Vega* medal, in gold, to Nordenskiöld and Palander, as well as to Oscar Dickson and Alexander Sibiriakoff.

It was close to midnight when Nordenskiöld and his companions left the royal palace. A row of open carriages, preceded by mounted policemen, was waiting for them, to take Adolf Nordenskiöld to his home, in the Academy of Sciences building on Drottninggatan. Sven Hedin, one of the greatest explorers of the twentieth century, described the scene, nearly fifty years later.

Sven Hedin was fifteen years old at the time, he stood at the window of the family apartment on Drottninggatan, only two blocks from the Academy. The whole family was looking out on a sea of light, created by torches and lanterns that decorated every house. 'A low, continuous roar filled the night' – he wrote – 'it became stronger, it came nearer and nearer, finally it was deafening. Then we saw the carriage with Nordenskiöld and Palander, completing the last stage of their triumphal journey. I could not take my eyes off them, as they sat in the carriage, waving to everyone. Near our building, von Otter stood on his balcony. And his voice, the voice that resounded over the Arctic Ocean when *Sofia* was near sinking, could be heard over the roar below, as he called out: "Welcome, Nordenskiöld and Palander!" '

There never has been anything comparable to *Vega*'s return in the history of Stockholm, before or since that time. Sven Hedin, who earned fame with his exploration of Inner Asia, always said it was on that night, overwhelmed by the reception given Adolf Nordenskiöld, that he had decided to become an explorer himself. And the voyage of *Vega* is remembered in Sweden every year: April 24 is called '*Vega* Day' in the Swedish calendar, and it is still celebrated with a formal dinner in Stockholm's Grand Hotel, where the heroes of the *Vega* were welcomed by their friends and admirers in 1880.

On Sunday morning, April 25, the crew of *Vega* attended divine service in the chapel of the royal place. In the afternoon, King Oscar, members of the royal family, and the Minister of the Navy inspected the ship, and the King presented each crew member with the silver *Vega* medal. After the royal visit, it was the Norwegian government's turn; they were followed by Oscar Dickson, who gave each petty officer and enlisted man a savings book for five hundred kronor. That evening, members of the crew were invited to the royal palace to hear King Oscar toast *Vega*, at the formal dinner honoring the expedition's staff.

For the next three weeks, an endless series of luncheons, dinners, receptions filled Adolf Nordenskiöld's daily program. The Academy of Sciences, the Royal Swedish Sailing Society, Nordenskiöld's own favorite society 'Idun', all honored him. The students at Uppsala University put on their own show before Adolf and Anna Nordenskiöld: it was an elaborate spoof, illustrating each of the stages of the *Vega* voyage with a different skit.

The Swedish parliament expressed its thanks to the men of the *Vega*, too. Nordenskiöld and Palander were both voted a life pension of four thousand kronor a year, a sum equal to the annual salary of high-ranking civil servants. Each member of the staff and each man of the crew received a cash bonus.

For the next two weeks *Vega* remained at anchor opposite the palace, open to visitors who came by the thousands. On May 10, the night the Swedish Society for Anthropology and Geography presented their own *Vega* medal to Nordenskiöld and Palander, it was time for the ship to leave Stockholm. The crew put on a handsome fireworks display, and later that night left Stockholm, bound for the Karlskrona Navy yard.

There, on May 19, the flag was lowered from the mast, the crew dismissed, and *Vega* was turned over to the Göteborg whaling concern that had purchased her.

Other famous explorer's ships, Scott's *Discovery*, Nansen's *Fram*, Amundsen's *Gjöa*, Heyerdahl's *Kon-Tiki* and *Ra*, have been preserved for posterity, in drydock or afloat. *Vega* returned to whaling, her original vocation, and ended her days at the bottom of the Arctic Ocean. Only a few relics, her wheelhouse on the west coast of Sweden, her bell and one of the whaleboats on Nordenskiöld's old country estate, and her barge, kept outside Stockholm, survive.

Adolf Nordenskiöld had hoped that most of the celebrations would be over by late May and that he could then settle down to the task of writing the story of the *Vega* voyage. But Sweden, and the rest of Europe, felt they had first call on the celebrated explorer's time. In July, he travelled to Göteborg, to receive a special gold medal from the local Society for Sciences and the Arts. Thence he went on to Berlin, to receive a special gold medal of the Berlin Geographical Society. It was presented to him at a dinner where the discoverer of the ruins of Troy, the famous archaelogist Heinrich Schliemann, was also honored.

Getting ready to leave Berlin for home, Nordenskiöld received an invitation to dine with the Emperor of Germany, William I. 'My host in Berlin was overcome with the invitation, extended by the Emperor' – wrote Adolf Nordenskiöld to his wife. 'I tried to show him how highly I valued this honor, by exclamations in true German fashion. In fact, I was willing to stay over an extra day, for I wanted to know what the "Father of Victory", the most powerful ruler in the world, would be like when seen at close quarters. I must say that Their Highnesses were truly kind and friendly.'

Shortly before Christmas, 1880, the Russian minister in Stockholm presented Adolf Nordenskiöld with an invitation to visit St. Petersburg, as a guest of Russian scholars and businessmen. Since the way to St. Petersburg lay across Finland, Anna was anxious to accompany her husband, hoping to meet old friends on their way home from the Russian capital.

The Nordenskiölds left Stockholm on December 30, aboard a steamer specially designed to withstand the hazards of Baltic ice. The journey to Hangö, in southwest Finland, took almost two days, due to snowstorms and drifting ice; from Hangö, they travelled by train to St. Petersburg.

Alfred Nobel's brother Ludwig was the Nordenskiölds' host in the Russian capital, and the visitors were entertained by businessmen, anxious to develop the sea route to Siberia; by scientists, honoring the leader of the *Vega* expedition; and by the imperial family. The day after his arrival in St. Petersburg, Adolf Nordenskiöld was received in audience by Tsar Alexander II, who presented him with the Order of St. Vladimir. Nordenskiöld was the only Swedish citizen ever to receive this decoration, and he must have reflected on the change of heart of the Russian government, honoring a man who, many years earlier, had left his homeland under the shadow of political oppression.

On their last night in St. Petersburg, Adolf and Anna Nordenskiöld were invited to dinner by the Tsar. A sleigh, with the imperial coat-of-arms on its doors, came to call for them at the Nobel residence, in the Viborg section of the city. Drawn by matched black horses, the sleigh crossed the Alexander Bridge over the frozen Neva River and sped along the embankment, where gaslights spread their white reflection on the snow-covered pavement. Across the open parade ground, the Champ de Mars, they went, on between the elegant facades of private residences until the sleigh turned into the vast square in front of the Winter Palace.

Officers of the Imperial Guard, in white uniforms, wearing silver helmets surmounted by the imperial eagle, stood at attention with drawn swords as the guests walked up the wide staircase, to be ushered into the Empress' drawing room, and presented to the imperial household. The St. Petersburg newspapers reported the next day that the Tsar asked Adolf Nordenskiöld 'not to forget his old homeland, even though he was a citizen of another country now'.

The Nordenskiölds went directly to the Finland station after the dinner at the Imperial palace, and left by night train for Finland. Their journey across Finland was a national holiday; thousands turned out at every station to greet the Finn who had become a world figure. On their way, Adolf and Anna Nordenskiöld visited the family homestead at Frugård, before their arrival in Helsingfors.

The Nordenskiölds spent four days in Helsingfors, seeing family and friends, and were caught up in a round of festivities that lasted all day and late into the night. Tired but happy, they left by train for the ferry port of Hangö, to return to Sweden, but the short route home was impassable. Exceptionally heavy ice on the Baltic, and storms that reduced visibility to near zero, kept the ferry steamer in port, no vessel would venture out of Hangö harbor. Adolf and Anna Nordenskiöld had to take the long way home; by train to Helsingfors, thence to St. Petersburg, Berlin, Copenhagen, and Stockholm.

It was mid-January. Almost exactly a year had passed since *Vega* had steamed into Aden harbor, and Adolf Nordenskiöld looked back on that eventful year. In Aden, reading letters and telegrams from home, he expected little fanfare on his return. He was anxious to get back to his family, to start writing the story of the voyage, to pick up his work at the Museum. Instead, he had a triumphal tour across Europe from Naples to St. Petersburg. Covered with honors, he was the man of the moment.

XXII. HERO, WRITER, COUNTRY SQUIRE

The festivities celebrating the return of the *Vega* expedition were still in full swing when Adolf Nordenskiöld began to feel the pressure of his many duties. There was the matter of selling *Vega* in order to reimburse King Oscar, Dickson, and Sibiriakoff for some of the money they had invested in the expedition. Dickson used his many commercial contacts, but letters and telegrams arrived almost daily from Göteborg, through the spring and much of the summer of 1880, asking Nordenskiöld to look after details, provide the necessary documents, and check the paperwork involved in the transaction.

The mineralogy section of the National Museum had been run during Nordenskiöld's absence by his faithful assistant, Lindström, but there was correspondence to be answered, decisions on exchanges and purchases to be made. And overriding all these matters, there was the demand for publication of his story of the *Vega* voyage, and of its scientific results.

Although several Swedish publishers expressed a strong interest in acquiring publication rights, one publisher, Frans Beijer, made certain that he would get the manuscript. He went to Naples to meet Nordenskiöld as soon as he set foot in Europe, and returned to Stockholm not only with the contract to publish the story of the *Vega* voyage, but with the right to represent Nordenskiöld as his literary agent.

Frans Beijer was truly a self-made man. Apprenticed at the age of fourteen to a bookseller, he had his own bookstore in Göteborg by the time he turned twenty, and his own publishing house four years later. He was an innovator in the book business: having acquired a large stock of books from the company he bought out to start his own firm, he sold these at low prices in auction sales that were held yearly throughout Sweden and Finland. His agents went even further, and held yearly booksales in the United States in colonies of Swedish immigrants. Beijer's fortunes rose higher every year, and when he acquired the rights to the book on the *Vega* voyage he became a very wealthy man. As a result of their collaboration on the book, he and Nordenskiöld became close friends.

Realizing that it would take time for Nordenskiöld to assemble all of his material for the book, Beijer suggested a method that was very popular in the late 1880's: publication by installments. The first of these came out in October, 1880, barely six months after the expedition's return to

Sweden, and on October 10, 1881, one year later, the manuscript for the last installment was delivered.

The full title of the book: 'The Voyage of the *Vega* round Asia and Europe – with a Historical Review of Previous Journeys along the North Coast of the Old World', sets Adolf Nordenskiöld's book apart from the more romantically presented explorers' narratives of the 19th century. There is precious little drama or suspense in the story he tells; it is methodically put together, carefully documented and scientifically accurate.

Four of the twenty chapters of the 'Voyage of the *Vega*' are entirely historical. Nordenskiöld felt that he had to give a full account of the way the Northeast Passage was reconnoitered, explored, described and mapped by his predecessors. He gave full credit to the Russians who, step by slow step, had tried to accomplish a crossing of the entire Passage, and emphasized how much he had relied in planning the voyage on the observations and achievements of those who had been in the Siberian Arctic before him.

'Voyage of the *Vega*' is the story of what the Swedish expedition saw, recorded, collected, and reported, from the time of their departure to their arrival in Ceylon. The reader looks in vain for stories of dangerous escapes from the hazards of the arctic winter. If any one illustration represents the spirit of the expedition, it is the one intitled: 'An evening in *Vega*'s wardroom during the wintering.' The zoologist, Stuxberg, is reading in the foreground; Nordenskiöld and Palander are playing back-gammon; the group in the back is involved in a game of chess; while one man, wearing heavy boots, and winter outdoor clothing, holds his rifle, saying goodnight on his way to his six-hour tour of duty at the observatory. It is a drawing of a group of men at ease, perfectly equipped for facing temperatures of thirty-five degrees Celsius below zero, thirty degrees below zero Fahrenheit, in an observatory made of iceblocks, equally well prepared to ward off the boredom of the long hours of winter darkness by reading, or playing games, or working on their own scientific obser-vations.

The medical record of *Vega* remains one of the most remarkable in the annals of polar medicine. There was not a single attack of scurvy during the voyage, and Doctor Almquist, the surgeon of the expedition, had so little work on his hands that he spent most of his time collecting lichens and algae, his scientific hobby. Much of the credit for this achievement goes to the man who supervised the preparations for the expedition, and saw to it that food and drink were plentiful and well balanced, to preserve the health of the men aboard: Adolf Nordenskiöld. But equal credit belongs to Louis Palander, *Vega*'s skipper, who maintained regular naval routine throughout the entire voyage, keeping the crew occupied with their duties, carrying out periodic inspections of the ship and all of its contents, seeing to it that there were no idle hands aboard, for scurvy hits those the hardest.

The two volumes of the original Swedish edition of the 'Voyage of the *Vega*' contain almost exactly one thousand pages. There are three hundred woodcuts, many of them based on Louis Palander's excellent photographs; six reproductions of old maps, illustrating the history of attempts to traverse the Northeast Passage; a general map of the Arctic, showing the route of the *Vega*; and five handsome steel engravings, of King Oscar II, Nordenskiöld, Palander, Dickson, and Sibiriakoff.

Completing a book of a thousand printed pages, with hundreds of illustrations, in only eighteen months seems an almost impossible task for one man. It was possible, in part, because Nordenskiöld had started working on his manuscript when *Vega* left Japan, and completed nearly half of it before he became involved in the round of festivities that awaited him in Europe. But he had help, too, for his publisher, aware of the size of the job, sought to find an assistant for Nordenskiöld.

Beijer's main concern was to get the *Vega* story in print as quickly as possible. Seeking assistance for editing the manuscript, checking references, and looking after the illustrations, he turned to his brother-in-law, Elof Tegnér, for advice. Tegnér was an officer of Stockholm's Royal Library, and he suggested a young man working at the Library, August Strindberg.

Strindberg was Tegnér's choice because he had an exceptional interest in the history of discoveries. He accepted the position of assistant to Nordenskiöld with enthusiasm, and reported for duty almost immediately after *Vega*'s return to Stockholm. But he did not last long on the job. His first assignment was to call on the Secretary of the Swedish Geographical Society to pick up a manuscript Nordenskiöld had loaned the Society. When Strindberg appeared at the Society's headquarters, he was informed that the manuscript had already been returned. As on so many occasions, Nordenskiöld in his absent-minded way forgot about the manuscript, but Strindberg was so upset by what he considered a futile assignment that he resigned on the same day he had accepted the position of editorial assistant.

The publisher became alarmed at the prospect of finding someone who could cope with Nordenskiöld's moods, but a second man was suggested and he turned out to be the right one for the job. His name was Erik Dahlgren, he was of a calm disposition, and got along quite well with the famous explorer.

Not that it was an easy job to be the middleman between a demanding author and the engravers, printers, and publisher's assistants. It took a lot of time and patience to work with Nordenskiöld, Dahlgren wrote in his autobiography. There were no telephones in Stockholm in 1880-1881, and every time a problem arose – checking references, correcting errors in the manuscript, making sure that the lithographer followed the original picture faithfully – Dahlgren had to look after every detail in person.

And then there was a matter of Adolf Nordenskiöld's moods. He had a temper, and more than once he and his assistant became embroiled in argument. But these moods soon changed, and having challenged Dahlgren's judgment and competence in one moment, Nordenskiöld was just as likely to invite him to a midday meal in an elegant restaurant, and be the perfect, gracious host.

When the two elegant volumes of the first edition of 'Voyage of the Vega' appeared at Christmastime, 1881, Dahlgren found that his 'chief' paid him a handsome tribute in his preface to the book. And in the copy he presented to his assistant he wrote: 'To my friend E. W. Dahlgren, with many thanks for his hard work toward the publication of this book, and for the criticism, imagination, and knowledge he has always shown.'

The first translation of the 'Voyage of the Vega' was in Czech, published in Prague. This was followed by English, Finnish, French, Dutch, Italian, Norwegian, Russian, Spanish, and German versions. Abridged editions also were published in Sweden, Finland, Germany, England and France. 'Voyage of the Vega' was one of the most popular travel books of the time and paid handsome royalties to its author.

Within a year of the publication of his book on the voyage, the first volume of the scientific papers based on it, entitled 'Scientific Observations of the Vega expedition, by Participants of the Voyage and Other Scientists', was in print, the expenses for the work having been underwritten by the Swedish parliament. The second and third volumes of the series appeared in 1883, the fourth and fifth in 1887. By that time the original grant had already been spent, for the five volumes total nearly three thousand pages, and Nordenskiöld's old friend and supporter,

Oscar Dickson, paid for the publication of the last two volumes of the series.

Nordenskiöld contributed three essays to the series: a reprint of his reports on the voyage that he had sent to Dickson, originally published in a Göteborg newspaper; a report on the possibilities of commercial shipping in the Arctic Ocean to Siberia and the Pacific; and a study on the *aurora borealis*, the northern lights, made during *Vega*'s Siberian winter.

'Scientific Observations of the Vega Expedition' is a milestone in the literature of polar exploration. The essays in these volumes dealt with observations made, and specimens collected, of the flora, fauna, meteorology, geophysics, palaeontology, hydrography, and terrestrial magnetism of north Siberia. Not until well into the twentieth century was there such a mass of information available on the world of the Arctic and sub-Arctic of the Old World. These volumes, compiled by twenty-eight scholars from Sweden, Finland, Germany, and Great Britain, stand as a monument to the scientific achievements of the voyage that opened the Northeast Passage for mankind.

Preparation of the scientific results of the *Vega* voyage for publication occupied much of Adolf Nordenskiöld's time during 1881 and 1882. But even before the first of the bulky volumes of the scientific series appeared, Nordenskiöld's popular account of the expedition was in print, and it was a huge success.

The original version of 'Voyage of the *Vega*' sold out quickly, when first published in installments. The two bound volumes of the Swedish edition came out in 1881, all of the translations into other European languages were published in the next two years. Royalties, too, started to accumulate: just before Christmas, 1881, Nordenskiöld received a royalty check for the English edition of the book of one thousand pounds sterling, five thousand U.S. dollars

Royalties from his book allowed Adolf Nordenskiöld to realize what has been his, and his wife's, dream for many years. Early in 1882, he purchased Dalbyö, the country estate that was to be the Nordenskiölds' summer home for many years. It was close enough to Stockholm to be reached in a few hours' time, yet not too easy to get to, so as to discourage casual visitors. It reminded Adolf and Anna Nordenskiöld of the country homes they knew in Finland, it remained their most cherished possession all their lives.

There were two ways to get from Stockholm to Dalbyö in the 1880's. One could take a train to Gnesta, southwest of the capital, about an hour's journey. There, a carriage from the estate would meet the traveller, and take him to Dalbyö, a distance of twenty miles, first by country roads, then by a narrow track across the grounds. A longer, but more interesting way was to take a steamboat that left Stockholm in the morning, crossed the eastern end of Lake Mälar, passed through the narrow Södertälje Canal, and then entered one of the bays of the Baltic Sea. The trip ended at the charming resort town of Trosa, an hour or so distant by carriage from Dalbyö.

The car track across Dalbyö estate stops right behind the house. The first sight greeting the visitor is a low barn, with a tiny turret on its roof: inside the turret hangs a ship's bell that once tolled watches on *Vega*'s deck. The house on the estate is a two-story structure, built in the early years of the 19th century. There is a central hallway, where a staircase leads to the upper floor. Downstairs, the living room extends across the entire house. In Nordenskiöld's time, it was filled with mementos of Adolf Nordenskiöld's voyages: oriental rugs, Japanese scrolls, a suit of black-lacquered Japanese armor.

Upstairs were Anna and Adolf Nordenskiöld's sitting rooms and bedrooms. Anna's sitting room was centered around a chaise longue where she liked to read; next to it stood a low tea table with an inlaid mother-of-pearl top, on it a teaglass in its silver holder, a handbell, and a French novel, for she preferred French literature to all others.

Across the landing were Adolf Nordenskiöld's two rooms. The walls were covered with bookshelves, the bleached skull of a walrus occupied space between two old maps, there were mineral samples and papers all over the desk, and a huge atlas was spread open on its own stand. The inner room had a plain iron bedstead, a washstand, more books, and a huge bearskin on the floor.

But the real charm of Dalbyö reveals itself only when one walks out the front door. The house sits on a low hill, and the waters of the Baltic are only a few yards away. Two huge old oaks stand in front, and were there in Adolf Nordenskiöld's time. He liked to sit there and look out over the bay, where dark evergreens cover the tiny hillocks on each shore and the water sparkles against the clear blue summer sky.

The former owners of Dalbyö had planted a large orchard in the 1850's that took up much of the ten acres of the estate. Anna Nordenskiöld loved each and every tree of the orchard, for they reminded her of

Villnäs, her beloved childhood home in Finland. Apples and pears were the produce of the orchards of Dalbyö, and when the trees were in bloom, the Professor, as he was known at home, loved to wander about and quietly enjoy the sight of that cloud of white flowers.

There was a large kitchen garden, too, where the walks were lined with raspberry bushes, between rows of lettuce, radishes, and cucumbers. Nearer the house, flowers occupied most of the space, and there were fresh bouquets in the rooms at Dalbyö every spring and summer day.

Orchard and garden, these were Anna Nordenskiöld's domain. Her daughter's friend Hedvig Swedenborg described her in her gardening attire: 'She wore ample skirts caught up with clothespins, boots, and a curious hat, with an enormous violet bow, broad-rimmed to protect her against the sun. On her hands she wore thick gloves, and she carried a basket with pruning shears, grafting wax, and whatever else she might need. She would walk for hours in this rig, up and down between rose-bushes and fruit trees, purposeful and self-assured. And she was just as much at home in stable or chicken house.'

As for 'Uncle Adolf', he was not very much interested in garden or livestock. 'He used to walk about the place, wearing wide, soft jackets, made from linen or raw silk, extremely creased trousers, an old panama hat, and a pince-nez on a thick black string which he never could manage, praising his wife's roses, apples, poultry and calves, the latter totally incomprehensible to him. However, after the animals had been subjected to certain complicated chemical procedures in the kitchen, he very much appreciated the produce of the estate.'

Axel Klinckowström, a friend of Nordenskiöld's older son Gustav, who had often visited Dalbyö, spoke of him as 'broad shouldered, robust, with a heavy, almost bear-like walk. I remember him as a study in grey: grey haired, with a grey mustache, friendly grey eyes under bushy grey eye-brows, all grey, for I can even recall that he wore grey suits most frequently. He was kind, nearsighted, and very absent-minded.'

Klinckowström was but one of the scores of young people who had been guests at Dalbyö. At times there were so many young visitors that putting them up overnight was a problem. They played games, and when the Nordenskiöld children were still in their teens, they often dressed up and put on plays. There was an old boathouse on the place, where two whaleboats, 'Lena' and 'Yenisey', were resting from their Arctic adventures, and in the attic above a tiny playhouse beckoned to the young visitors. There was a curtain, some old backdrops, and ship's chests containing marvellous costumes and objects from all over the world, from Greenland and China, from Japan and India.

But it wasn't only the youngsters who dressed up in outlandish gear. In a letter he wrote to Anna in the fall of their first year at Dalbyö, Adolf Nordenskiöld told her that he had invited some friends for a visit, while she was in town. Three of the guests, including Nordenskiöld's old German friend, the wealthy merchant Schönlank, had arrived on Thursday; the others were to join them on Saturday, aboard a steamer the publisher, Frans Beijer, had chartered for the trip.

'A large dinner was being prepared, to be served to our guests around six or seven in the evening. We got all dressed up to greet them on the beach. Old man Schönlank put on my Persian dressing gown, and a hat complete with leaves and flowers. Gyldén wore one of the huge straw hats that hangs on the living room wall, and a grey Japanese silk robe. Stuxberg wore a Japanese suit of armour, and cut a fine figure. I was in my bathrobe, the one with the purple fringe, and put on a straw hat with flowers. Anna wore a Chinese costume and Erland had on a Ceylonese silk gown and a blue Chinese cap. At six o'clock we heard the whistle of a steamboat. We rushed down to the beach, waited half an hour, an hour, two hours in vain. Finally we trooped back, disappointed, to the house, and had our dinner.

Just as we were finishing dinner, we heard something splashing in the bay. We rushed out, but it wasn't a steamboat we saw, it was a rowboat, full of people, shipwrecked on the shore.' Frans Beijer had rented a steamboat in Stockholm to bring the rest of the group out to Dalbyö, for a small vessel could anchor at the foot of the little hill where the house stood. But several of the party, including a naval officer, insisted on having the privilege of steering the ship. They ran it aground, and had to finish the journey in a rowboat. Nordenskiöld ended his letter by describing his friend from Berlin, Schönlank, falling in love with Dalbyö, wandering around admiring the view, while humming tunes from Wagner operas.

Horace had his Tusculum in the hills near Rome, Nordenskiöld had Dalbyö overlooking the waters of the Baltic Sea. For twenty years it was Adolf Nordenskiöld's retreat, where he would invite his old friends, and many a distinguished visitor from foreign lands. To Anna Nordenskiöld, Dalbyö was a quiet haven, where she was surrounded by her children and had her husband at her side. There she could indulge in gardening, her favorite pastime: she even created new varieties of apples by cross-breeding. For her success, she was made an honorary member of the Imperial Society of Apple Growers of Russia, and the letter advising her of her election was carefully preserved in Adolf Nordenskiöld's personal papers.

In 1881, Maria Nordenskiöld, the oldest of Adolf and Anna's four children, turned seventeen. When her mother had been in her teens, she had spent several years in an exclusive girls' school in Geneva, Switzerland. There she had learned French well, and made friends with girls from all over Europe and the United States. It was only natural for her to feel that her daughter, too, should have an opportunity to see something of Europe and to learn French.

Adolf Nordenskiöld accompanied Maria on the journey to Geneva, but they first stopped to visit his favorite cousin, Countess Alma von Oertzen, in Germany. Alma's father, Count von Kothen, had been one of Finland's leaders in the mid-1800's, and the daughter maintained close and friendly relations with the highest circles in Finnish and Russian society. Thus, when Adolf Nordenskiöld and his daughter called at the Oertzen estate, north of Berlin, they were almost immediately whisked by carriage to a neighboring estate and introduced to a sister of Tsar Alexander II, the Grand Duchess Catherine, who was visiting there.

After two days at the Oertzen's, father and daughter travelled to Berlin and Munich, where they saw the sights and attended theatres and the opera, before they continued on to Geneva. Having delivered his daughter to Mademoiselle Maunoir's boarding school there, Nordenskiöld went on to visit Spain, a country he had never seen before.

His first stop in Spain was Barcelona, and his first impressions were most favorable. 'It is good to get away from a desk-bound life', he wrote Anna, 'that only gives you a potbelly and leads to distraction. Here in Spain it is sunny and warm still, like a lovely but not too warm summer at home. Nature is magnificent, with high mountains and dark green olive groves; there are many unusual and interesting buildings; the women are remarkably pretty, though almost always dressed in black; peasant costumes are picturesque, the street scenes colorful, and there is much to make life pleasant for the visitor.'

But Nordenskiöld did not visit Spain merely to enjoy the sights. He had become more and more interested in the history of exploration, and in old maps. Maps, he felt, reflect the slow and painstaking way man's knowledge of his earth had evolved through history. And as his interest in old maps and in explorers' reports grew, so did his desire to own the books and atlases and maps that had first brought the achievements of explorers to the attention of the world.

Adolf Nordenskiöld grew up among books, in his father's library. He had always collected books, but now, with a good income from his own writings and from the Swedish state, he was on his way to becoming a true bibliophile, a collector of rare books and atlases. He had already made the acquaintance of Italian dealers in rare books when he visited Rome, in 1880, and he hoped to find some valuable additions to his library in Spain.

From Barcelona, Nordenskiöld travelled south, to Valencia, Córdova, Granada, and Seville. But his enthusiasm for Spain was waning. He found little of interest in bookstores, and not too much in the libraries he visited. The countryside was brown, and only a few scattered, stunted trees would break the monotony of endless open fields. Only a few high spots of southern Spain offered any change, such as the magnificent gardens of Granada's Alhambra, and the date and palm trees of the Alcázar in Seville. It was almost with relief that he turned north again, to Madrid.

Madrid did have something of interest: libraries and archives, and a few precious, rare books. On the train from Madrid to Paris, he was recognized by his table companion, who turned out to be a gentleman-in-waiting to the dowager queen of Spain, Isabella. Excited to meet the hero of the *Vega*, the Spanish nobleman insisted on presenting Nordenskiöld to the queen, who was travelling in her private car on the same train.

Nordenskiöld's program in Paris included a dinner with James Gordon Bennett, publisher of the New York Herald, who was anxious to hear the views of the discoverer of the Northeast Passage on the probable fate of the yacht *Jeannette*, missing for over a year in the waters off East Siberia. He also met Ferdinand de Lesseps, the builder of the Suez Canal, who was then engaged in an attempt to build a similar canal at Panama; called on Hachette, publisher of the French version of his book; and had a conference with the publishers of the catalog of the collection of Japanese books, that he had presented to the Stockholm Royal Library.

From Paris, Adolf Nordenskiöld continued his journey to London, where he met with his English publishers, and after a short stay, travelled to Holland. Ostensibly, he stopped in Amsterdam to get acquainted with the firm that was publishing the Dutch translation of the 'Voyage of the *Vega*'. In fact, he was after something quite different.

At the end of the sixteenth century, the Dutch sent out two expeditions to find the Northeast Passage, in 1594 and 1595. Both had to turn back, unable to achieve their purpose, and when a third expedition was contemplated, the Dutch Government, instead of granting funds for such a voyage, offered a prize instead. On April 13, 1596, Their High Mightinesses, the Estates General of the United Netherlands, resolved that 'if some merchants adventures should attempt, either as a company or separately, to make such a journey at their own risk and expense, without requesting either a vessel or funds for it, then the said adventurers, if they had completed the journey and brought true and faithful evidence of this feat, shall be awarded the sum of twenty-five thousand guilders.'

It had been Nordenskiöld's hope that his success in completing the Northeast Passage, would earn him the Dutch prize, even though two hundred and eighty years had gone by since it was first posted. Thanks to the world-wide publicity given to the voyage of the *Vega*, Adolf Nordenskiöld received the award of twenty-five thousand guilders, and a gold medal, too.

It was December by the time Nordenskiöld returned to Stockholm. Winter had closed in on the Swedish capital, snow covered the streets and parks and there was ice floating in the harbor. A few days after he had come home, Nordenskiöld attended a dinner in the Grand Hotel. It was dark when he came to the front door of the hotel, in fur hat and heavy fur coat, to take a cab back to his apartment. But a look at the world outside made him change his mind, and he decided to walk, at least part of the way.

Snow was falling over Stockholm, and fine, powdery flakes were swirling around the gaslights. He looked across the harbor, at the silent, stony mass of the royal palace, where *Vega* had once lain at anchor; down to where the ships, plying to Finland, were barely visible as a heavy snow squall swept across the view. It was a winter night, it reminded Adolf Nordenskiöld of nights in the Arctic.

He had achieved much in the North. True, he did not get to the North Pole, but he made Spitsbergen as well known as Sweden itself, and he opened a new seaway for the ships of the world. But there were still many things to look for in the Arctic, and in the Antarctic, too, for that matter. Adolf Nordenskiöld was not yet ready to become an armchair traveller. He wanted to return to the Arctic once more.

When Nordenskiöld brought up the idea of another voyage to the Arctic,

Oscar Dickson was a good listener, as he had been on past occasions. He was willing to provide support. A detailed plan was submitted to the government, and by the end of 1882, Adolf Nordenskiöld was getting ready for his tenth trip to the North; this time to Greenland.

The subject of further voyages to the polar regions was often discussed in *Vega*'s wardroom during the forced wintering, and on the long journey home. Nordenskiöld himself wrote later on that while all aboard were fascinated by the possibility of reaching the North Pole, they were convinced that other problems in the Arctic were equally interesting and, from a scientific point of view, far more important for further study. The men of *Vega*, after many an argument, concentrated on two possible projects for further polar voyages: Antarctica, and a continuing exploration of the sea north of the Lena delta.

Finding funds for a major expedition to Antartica seemed too great a task even for Adolf Nordenskiöld to tackle. As for explorations in the Arctic Ocean off Eastern Siberia, several expeditions were active in those waters between 1879 and 1882. The *Jeannette* had been there, in 1879-1881; she was lost, but Commander De Long's journal of observations was saved. In 1882, both a Russian group and a Danish group, commanded by Hovgaard who had served on the *Vega*, were scheduled to work in the area, in connection with the first International Polar Year.

But there was another part of the Arctic that was of special interest to Nordenskiöld, Greenland. He had gone there in 1870, with the purpose of finding out how well dogteams would perform on ice, hoping to use dogs on his attempt to reach the North Pole. While in Greenland, he tried to explore the interior, to find out whether all of Greenland was covered by ice, as was generally believed. Lack of supplies and equipment limited his trek, on that first attempt, to thirty miles, and he was anxious to try once more, this time with a team of men and with enough equipment and food to make certain that he could penetrate the Greenland ice cap far enough to find out its true nature.

There was a second reason for Adolf Nordenskiöld's interest in a voyage to Greenland. The Danish settlements on the island were all on the west coast. Most of the east coast, hemmed in by what was believed to be an impenetrable barrier of offshore ice, was virtually unknown. Nordenskiöld wanted to land on the east coast, make a detailed study of its geology and animal life, and look for any possible traces of early Norse settlements there.

A plan setting forth in detail what the expedition hoped to accomplish along both the west and east coast of Greenland and on the icecap, was presented to Dickson. Dickson offered to cover all of the costs of the expedition, if the Swedish government provided a vessel. *Sofia*, the ship Nordenskiöld had used in 1868, was still in service as a mail steamer. The government was authorized by parliament to make *Sofia* available for the expedition, without charge, and with full insurance. Captain Nilsson, who had commanded the *Fraser*, one of the tenders that had accompanied *Vega* part way in 1878, accepted Nordenskiöld's invitation to serve as *Sofia*'s skipper. The Swedish geologist Alfred Nathorst, two zoologists, a physician, a hydrographer, and a surveyor-photographer made up the scientific staff. In May, 1883, *Sofia* was ready to start for Greenland.

Adolf Nordenskiöld was convinced that somewhere in the remote interior of Greenland he would find ice-free ground, and demonstrated, by using arguments based on climatic observations, that this had to be the case. His detailed plan for the voyage was published in 'Ymer', the journal of the Swedish Society for Anthropology and Geography, early in 1883. The plan was carefully read by earth scientists everywhere and shortly before *Sofia* left Sweden, Nordenskiöld received a letter from Ferdinand von Richthofen, the dean of German geographers.

'Hearty greetings and best wishes to you' – wrote Richthofen – 'on the eve of your new, and boldly planned enterprise. "Do not ever stand still and tired", that is the principle of your life, as you go on from one great feat to the next. You have barely returned from an epochal voyage, when you turn your hand to creating a literary masterpiece, and barely have you laid down your pen, when you are off once more, to where nature is at its most grandiose, and where laurels are hardest to get. But you have never avoided a challenge, and none of your enterprises has failed. May good luck accompany your energy, your careful plans, your wide experience. You have spoken with courage against currently held views, and you shall act boldly to find out whether your views are right, whether Greenland bears its name by right and is only surrounded by a barrier of ice. Were this to be the case, it would be a triumph for scientific deduction. In any case, I know that you shall bring back results of the highest interest to science.'

XXIII. THE LAST TRIP TO THE ARCTIC: THE SECOND EXPEDITION TO GREENLAND 1883

On May 23, 1883, *Sofia* left Göteborg harbor, bound for Greenland. It was Adolf Nordenskiöld's tenth voyage to the Arctic; judging by his account of it, it was the one he had enjoyed most. His fame as a polar explorer had spread around the world, he was recognized as the leading authority on all matters related to the Arctic. The scientific staff aboard *Sofia* was as enthusiastic about exploration as their leader. There was general agreement on the goals of the voyage, too: the group was going to try and find out the nature of Greenland's interior, and attempt to identify early Norse settlements on the island's east coast.

The scientists of the time had believed that all of Greenland was covered by ice, and that all early Norse settlements on the island were on the west coast. Adolf Nordenskiöld set out to disprove both theories. It was not the first occasion that he had held an opinion totally opposed to that of his colleagues, and he liked scientific controversy. Everyone in scientific circles was convinced that the Kara Sea, north of Siberia, was an impassable mass of ice most of the year. Nordenskiöld had proven, in 1875 and 1876, that a ship could get through the Kara Sea. All experts also claimed that no ship could sail past Cape Chelyuskin. *Vega* had accomplished that feat, and went on to Bering Strait, first to cross the Northeast Passage. Going to Greenland, Nordenskiöld had deliberately set out to demolish a widely held belief by exploring Greenland's interior, something no one had ever attempted before.

When Nordenskiöld and his companion, Berggren, made their short trip on the Greenland icecap in 1870, their journey was cut short by lack of equipment. This time, everything was carefully planned and enough food, tents, and instruments were aboard *Sofia* to ensure success. There was only one doubt on Nordenskiöld's mind: would the rough terrain of the interior allow the exploring party to proceed at sufficient speed to penetrate very far? If the party could not move fast enough, he had planned to send scouts ahead as far as they could go. For that difficult task, he had recruited two Lapps, men who were able to move fast and over long distances on skis.

The two Lapps who were aboard *Sofia*, Pava Lars Tuorda and Anders Rossa, came from the province of Lapland, in northernmost Sweden. Both were known to be outstanding hunters and fast skiers. Success or failure of the trek to the interior of the Greenland icecap was likely to depend on their skill and endurance.

Oscar Dickson had made arrangements for coal to be available for *Sofia* en route, in Scotland, Iceland, and Greenland. The ship made her first stop in Thurso, on the north coast of Scotland, took on bunker coal, and set her course for Iceland. Besides the staff of the expedition, there were three passengers aboard, travelling to Iceland: a geologist, a botanist, and a student of the Icelandic language.

At first, the weather was sunny and clear, and the ship steamed past the Danish-owned Faeroes Islands over a calm sea. But next day a violent storm swept across *Sofia*'s path, and she was driven far to the east. When the storm abated, the expedition found itself off Iceland, but there weren't any lighthouses or buoys to show them the way to the nearest harbor. In fact, the available charts were so poor that *Sofia* had to speak to a French fishing smack to find out where they were. At last they made port at the east coast settlement in Reydarfjordr. The three passengers on board, bound for Iceland, left the ship to start their studies right away, while *Sofia* set course for the west coast of Iceland, and came into Reykjavik harbor on June 6.

The weather was cold and rainy during the four days the expedition spent in port, while coal and fresh food were put aboard. Adolf Nordenskiöld went for long walks around the city of Reykjavik. On one such walk, he came across a furrier's shop, where he bought eight handsome blue fox skins, and sent them to Anna, suggesting that they should be made into a theatre cape. He also found an old Icelandic silver necklace; he planned to give it to his oldest daughter as a birthday present.

On June 10, *Sofia* left Iceland, bound across Denmark Strait for the east coast of Greenland. At five o'clock in the morning on June 12, the lookout called from his crow's nest on the mainmast: 'No ice in sight! Clear water all the way to the coast!' For a moment, Nordenskiöld believed that he was about to accomplish what no one had been able to do for centuries: land on the south-east coast of Greenland. Tall mountains appeared on the horizon, but as the ship steamed in their direction, they remained as distant as ever. 'This land must be bewitched,' said one of the Lapps. 'No matter how close we get to it, it is still far away!' The clear northern air had played another optical trick on the men: they could see the high peaks clearly, but the sea ice along the shore was invisible. Soon, though, *Sofia* came up against an impenetrable mass of drift ice and her course had to be set to the southwest, for Cape Farewell, Greenland's southernmost point.

On June 17, *Sofia* was approaching Julianehaab, the principal town in southern Greenland, when a small schooner, one of the vessels engaged in trade between the settlements along the coast, came into view. The captain offered to pilot *Sofia* to Julianehaab, an offer that was promptly accepted, since navigation through the narrow passages among the many offshore islands is difficult.

It was off Julianehaab that the expedition first encountered a group of Eskimo, piloting their kayaks across the waters of a narrow fjord. Nordenskiöld devotes a long passage in his book on the Greenland expedition to a description of the kayak. He calls it 'the most elegant vessel ever constructed either by primitive or by civilized men. No other one-man boat can rival its speed. In it, an experienced rower can defy storm and the highest of waves with incredible safety. The smallest detail of a kayak, its shape, its construction, its paddles and harpoons, the bone buttons securing its cover, the special clothing used by the paddler, all have been brought to perfection by the work of many generations. It is an admirable piece of work and the European, with all his inventiveness, cannot add anything to it. It is truly an Eskimo invention; the manner in which it is made and the materials that are used to build it make it different from small boats made by other primitive peoples. The kayaks I saw used by the Chukchi were poor, clumsy imitations. The canoes of the American Indian are quite different. They are built for travel on lakes and rivers, and are hardly capable of facing the billowing ocean.'

Nordenskiöld not only admired the way a kayak was built, he was also impressed by the skills of the paddlers. Kayaks are always paddled by men, but once in a while an Eskimo will take his girl friend for a ride. The girl will kneel behind the paddler, holding on with her arms. Another, safer way to carry a passenger is to tie two kayaks together for greater width and stability. Nordenskiöld, in 1870, rode across a lake in Greenland that way, kneeling behind the paddlers. The Eskimo can cover great distances at high speed in their kayaks going as fast as a long-distance runner on land: until the introduction of motorboats and aircraft, mail was carried to outlying settlements in Greenland by 'kayak men'.

Sofia spent two days at Julianehaab; her boilers had to be cleaned, and the steam engine overhauled before continuing on her way north. The next stop was to be at Ivigtut, the world's only source of cryolite, a mineral used in the manufacture of aluminum. On the way, they passed a sailing ship, and when *Sofia* raised the Swedish flag to the mast, according to custom, the other vessel failed to respond by showing her colors. The incident puzzled everyone on board, but it was not until they reached Ivigtut that they found out what had happened.

The ship they had met was an American sailing vessel bound for Greenland to take on a cargo of cryolite at the Ivigtut mine. Approaching the Greenland coast, the ship was caught in drift ice and the pressure became so great that she sprang a leak. There was a ballast of two hundred tons of stone aboard, and the captain, concerned about the ship's safety, had the pumps manned at once, since water was rapidly flooding the hold. But pumping was of no avail, the water kept rising, and the captain, certain that the ship would sink, ordered the lifeboats to be put out. The men dragged the lifeboats over the ice, and after they reached open water, started to row towards the nearest settlement.

A short time after the ship was abandoned, a party of sixteen Eskimo, out seal hunting, came across the ship, which was caught in an ice floe. They immediately climbed onto the ice and ran to the ship, hoping to chat, to get a drink, a cup of coffee, or some other tidbit, as was the custom when a ship encountered kayaks off the Greenland coast. Much to their surprise, they found the ship deserted, but there were supplies of all sorts on board, and the Eskimo made themselves at home.

Their next move was to decide how they would get their prize to port. The most courageous climbed the masts and hoisted sail, except for the mainmast, too high for anyone. The rest started pumping water from the hold. Gradually the pack began to come loose, the pressure of the ice slackened, the leak in the hull began to close up; by the time the ship was out of the pack ice, the Eskimo had pumped out so much water that she was afloat. With favorable winds, they set sail for the missionary settlement of Frederiksdal.

In the meantime, the captain and crew of the ship had their share of trouble, finding their way amidst the offshore islands, and reached the Frederiksdal mission. They were given food and dry clothing, and had just settled down to tell their hosts of the shipwreck, when a lookout shouted that a ship was coming towards the settlement. This was a major event in any Greenland outpost, especially since this ship was the first of the season. Everyone came running to the shore, including the American captain and his crew. The Eskimo, having excellent eyesight, were certain that it was not one of the usual coastal schooners; everyone was guessing what ship might be approaching, when suddenly the American

captain let out a whoop: 'Goddammit, I think that is my ship!'
The captain jumped in a boat tied up at the pier, and rowed as fast as he could, trying to find out what magic could have brought his ship, given up for lost, straight into port, sailing under full sail. As he climbed aboard, he found everyone busy at work. One Eskimo was in the kitchen, watching a huge pot of porridge and vegetables. Another was handing out generous portions of coffee to his shipmates. A third was making a list of the ship's carpenter's tools. The captain quickly took command again, and the Eskimo departed, seemingly content with a small payment for having pumped the ship dry.
But once ashore, the improvised crew found out that, according to the law of the sea, they were entitled to an altogether different kind of reward for salvaging the ship. The captain told Nordenskiöld, when they met at Ivigtut, that he sent in a full report to the owners and, presumably, the Eskimo received a large sum as their reward from the insurance company in America.
It was on the way to Ivigtut that the men aboard *Sofia* first saw the Greenland icecap. The weather was perfectly clear, the ship was making her way among the icebergs floating offshore, when the *inlandsis*, the icecap, suddenly came into view, shining like a giant wall of blue glass. 'It shouldn't be too hard to march on that', said one of the sailors. 'You'll find out about it when you get there,' replied one of the Lapps.
Slowly *Sofia* steamed north towards the settlement of Egedesminde. It was near there that Nordenskiöld had started out on his trek to the icecap in 1870, and there he intended to start this time. But first they made a stop on Disko Island, near Egedesminde. The island is known for fossils showing the vegetation of Greenland in earlier geological times, and the expedition's geologist intended to spend several days there collecting specimens.
Disko Island is separated from Greenland by a narrow strait that the Dutch whalers christened 'The Blowhole', due to its sudden, violent storms. But the day *Sofia* sailed through it, the strait was calm, and filled with icebergs. 'The weather was magnificent' – wrote Nordenskiöld – 'and nature surrounding us grandiose. To the east, we could see the crest of the icecap, shining with a blue-white light. In a few days, we shall try to solve its mysteries. Is there ice, only ice, beyond that blue-white wall, all the way to the mountains of the east coast? Or does that wall of ice shelter oases that are free of ice, with some greenery? That was one of the questions the expedition set out to solve.

'North of us rose the high, dark basalt cliffs of Disko Island. They, too, present many an unsolved mystery to the researcher; they hide remains of a past so remote that, in comparison, the pyramids of Egypt are but the children of yesterday. The sea around us was smooth as a mirror, covered with hundreds of giant icebergs. Their magnificent shapes were enlarged and made even more beautiful by a mirage, stronger than any I have ever seen in Arctic seas. Islands that lay below the horizon became clearly visible, some appearing in a double image, one right side up, the other upside down. Some icebergs could be seen doubled or tripled; their vertical dimensions became so exaggerated that even a small berg might appear from a distance like a giant cathedral, crowned with tall towers. The icebergs changed shape constantly, their towers rose and sank down again in unpredictable ways. Just as they were at their biggest and most beautiful, a new image appeared on top of the old one, exactly like it down to the smallest detail, but standing upside down, with its highest peak on top of the peak in the original image. But if the tiniest puff of a cold breeze blew across the water, the whole magnificent double edifice disappeared, or it shrank to the dimensions of a small iceberg, floating on the horizon. In another instant, that iceberg started to rise, to sprout roofs and towers, only to shrink back, moments later, to its former insignificance.'

On July 1, *Sofia* anchored at the head of Tasiusarsoak Fjord, located at 68 degrees north latitude on the west coast of Greenland. It was a landscape of stone and rock that greeted the explorers, the coast range rose almost immediately above the shore. But small streams, carrying meltwater from the nearby glaciers, ran to the sea, and their valleys were covered with a carpet of moss and lichens, that supported a vast variety of wildflowers, and even an occasional dwarf birch or dwarf willow.

Nordenskiöld organized a cache of food, fuel, and dry clothing, that was left in charge of a small band of Eskimo at the place where *Sofia* landed the party. It was agreed that *Sofia* would continue north along the coast as far as ice conditions would allow, to carry out geological and paleontological studies. The ship was to return to Egedesminde not later than August 16 to pick up Nordenskiöld and his party.

Nordenskiöld did not believe that either reindeer or dogs could be useful to an expedition on the icecap; he was going to rely on the men, to drag the heavily loaded sleds that were to carry food and equipment. Fortunately the crew of *Sofia*, anxious to take a close look at the icecap, came ashore and helped the group going on the ice to get the sleds up the steep slopes of the coastal mountains to the edge of the icecap. The crew then returned to the ship, and the shore party of ten men got ready to start out, to explore the mysteries of Greenland's interior.

Nordenskiöld was in charge, and though he had celebrated his fiftieth birthday the previous fall, he was still in excellent physical shape and not at all concerned with the hardships that lay ahead. The others on the ice party were Doctor Berlin, the expedition's physician, who was an experienced botanist as well; Lieutenant Kjellström, cartographer and photographer; one of *Sofia*'s quarter-masters; two Swedish sailors; two Norwegian whalers; and the two Lapps.

Everyone slept under a single, large tent, in sleeping bags laid on top of rubber air mattresses. They carried enough food for forty days; an alcohol stove to cook warm meals; a good supply of brandy, cigars, and chewing tobacco; the best available ice climbing equipment, including special crampons sent to Nordenskiöld by the German-Austrian Alpine Club; and, in case they encountered a deep glacial stream, paddles to get across, using the air mattresses as improvised rafts.

As on all of his Arctic expedition, Nordenskiöld took precautions to make food not only plentiful but palatable as well. For animal proteins, he relied on Australian corned beef, Swedish smoked ham, liver sausage, canned sardines, butter, and cheese. There was plenty of bread, about 20 ounces per person per day; a ration of brandy for those who drank alcoholic beverages; coffee, and tea. Coffee was prepared twice daily, and warm meat was served in the evening.

North of the Arctic Circle, there is no darkness during the month of July. Lest the men try and keep going too many hours a day, Nordenskiöld had insisted on a strict daily routine. He sounded reveille at eight in the morning, woke up the cook – one of the Norwegians – and wound up the chronometers. Breakfast was ready within half an hour, then all cleaned up their tin cups, plates, and utensils, rolled up sleeping bags and mattresses, took down the tent, bundled everything on sleds, and the expedition was on its way. At noon, the group stopped only long enough to have a cold meal of sandwiches, washed down with a shot of brandy. There was always a cold wind, and since the men were perspiring from their work, the noon break was short so that no one could catch cold. In the evening, the tent was set up as soon as the expedition came to a halt; the cook started supper going, Dr. Berlin collected tiny algae from the snow, Kjellström took photographs and sketched the surrounding terrain.

When the group stopped for the night, the two Lapps went out on skis to take a look at what lay ahead for the next day's march. Nordenskiöld came to rely more and more on Lars Tuorda: in that wilderness of snow and ice, devoid of any landmarks, he managed to retrace his steps without a single mistake the next day. Instead of the ordinary ski pole everyone was using, Lars carried a lance, with twenty-five notches on its shaft, one for every bear he had killed on the high slopes of his native Lapland. He would have been most pleased to add a polar bear to his lists of kills, but none were to be found on the icecap.

The expedition's progress was slow. The weight of food and equipment amounted to nearly two thousand pounds at the start; each sled carried about three hundred pounds. The surface of the icecap is far from uniform, and the men had to struggle over small hillocks; up the steep slopes of ice pyramids, some over twenty feet high; through wet snow, and over snow ridges shaped like sand dunes. Worst of all obstacles were the streams carrying meltwater to the coast, flowing swiftly between steep banks. If the stream was narrow, the men would lay three ski poles across, to improvise a bridge, and wrestle the sleds over it. Some streams were far too wide to be bridged in this fashion, and long detours had to be made to move ahead.

Moving ahead across the icecap, the expedition also kept climbing higher every day. Starting from sea level, they reached 1300 feet on the fifth day. At the end of the first week, they were at 2500 feet. Under these circumstances, the distance covered each day never exceeded eleven miles, and on particularly difficult terrain the group advanced only two or three miles a day.

Sunlight was so intense on clear days that the men became severely sunburned, and the skin tended to break down into open sores. The wind was blowing constantly, whipping across the ice, and caused constant irritation and pain. Though everyone was issued protective glasses, the light was so brilliant that several men suffered from snow blindness, and had to be treated by the surgeon. But these were the only health problems the expedition had to cope with.

On July 21, the seventeenth day of the trek, rain began to fall and the ground was rapidly covered with slush. Daily progress was now measured by hundreds of yards. When the group stopped to camp, they had covered seventy-two miles from the coastline, and climbed to an altitude of 4950 feet.

Immediately after supper, Lars left to look over the terrain that lay ahead. His report was most discouraging: though he covered nearly fifteen miles on skis, he had to struggle with slush of ice and snow everywhere. Nordenskiöld had to make a decision. Should he push ahead, risking the men's lives if they were caught in a storm, or turn back? He decided to return to the coast, but before starting on the return journey, he sent the two Lapps eastward, for a report on what the land looked like.

The Lapps started out on July 22, striking eastward across the ice. They were instructed to follow as straight a route as possible, to read the barometer and record their compass heading every eighteen miles, to note what the terrain looked like, and to bring back specimens of any vegetation they found. After forty-eight hours they were to turn back; the expedition was going to wait for them at the last camp site until July 28, giving them two extra days for their return journey in case they ran into difficult terrain or stormy weather. At the end of six days, however, the expedition had to start for the coast, lest they run out of supplies. If the Lapps had not returned by then, Nordenskiöld told them, he was going to leave a cache of food, brandy, sleeping bags and mattresses at the camp site.

For their four-day journey, the two Lapps carried six pounds of bread, two cans of sardines, six pounds of corned beef, two pounds of butter, a pound of cheese, half a bottle of brandy, twelve cigars, and six twists of chewing tobacco. They also carried two compasses, an aneroid barometer, and an accurate watch.

The last camp site of the expedition was in a low spot, and Nordenskiöld, concerned lest a sudden rain would transform it into an impenetrable morass of sludge, told Lars that the group would move back westward, to the previous night's camp. It was there that the party waited for the Lapps' return. And back they came, after an absence of fifty-seven hours, on July 24th.

Had it not been that they were afraid of running out of drinking water, due to the absence of meltwater streams and the lack of fuel to melt snow, Lars thought they would have gone even further east. As it was, their accomplishment still stands as one of the great ski runs of all time: the two men covered a total of 460 kilometers, 286 miles, in fifty-seven hours. Since they only stopped once, for a four-hour rest, they averaged eight kilometers, five miles an hour. At the point where they turned around, they were at an altitude of 6,387 feet above sea level.

Lars' report described what they had found, having reached the midpoint of the Greenland icecap. 'After we covered about 48 kilometers, 30 miles from the last camp site, we could not find any more water. Further on, the icecap was perfectly flat and smooth, with low snowhills spaced 40 to 50 kilometers, 25 to 30 miles apart. The temperature at that point was five degrees below zero, Celsius, twenty-three degrees Fahrenheit. I have never seen a better surface for skiing, we went ahead easily but were very thirsty. At our turning point we made a fire using part of our ski poles, and melted water in a can. The snow was even there, well packed down by storms, we couldn't see any trace of open land, only ice and very fine snow. The top seven feet of it was loose snow, below that was a nearly open space wide enough for one's hand, walled with ice crystals, below that coarsely grained ice. The icecap was shaped like a set of stairs: first a low slope, then a wide level space, then another slope.

'We stopped once, during the second night, for about four hours, in a hollow formed in the snow while a storm passed overhead. The first day out we did not encounter any wind. The second evening the wind came from the south, and kept coming from that direction until we turned around. About 40 kilometers, 25 miles west of our turning point the wind veered to the west. On our way back, about 85 kilometers, 53 miles from the last camp we saw two crows, coming from the north. We stopped, the crows landed on our tracks, then took off again for the north.'

The two Lapps established beyond doubt that the icecap extended across all of Greenland. Yet Lars was so convinced, even after their reconnaissance, that there was open country somewhere, that he dreamt about it. Nordenskiöld was struck by the fact that the Lapps, ordinarily stolid and unimaginative, had unusual dreams. Anders Rossa, who was always quiet and serious in his waking hours, often woke up the rest of the group during the night, choking with laughter in his sleep. One morning, Lars reported that he dreamed of continuing eastward on skis, and meeting a fellow Lapp. 'He said to me: "Cousin from far away, why do you keep going on the ice? Why don't you come down to the wooded valley, near the tent? It follows the foot of the mountains, and extends far to the south".'

The dream of Lars the Lapp matches, strangely enough, an Eskimo legend that insists on the existence of a stream that runs across all of Greenland in the area explored by the Nordenskiöld expedition. In fact, a map of Greenland, made in 1788, shows such a stream, but it is now fully proven that all of the island's interior is ice-covered.

It was late in July when the expedition started back towards the west coast, the weather had turned stormy, and there were flights of birds overhead, practicing for their southward migration. On August 3, the men had reached the coast and were greeted enthusiastically by the Eskimo who had guarded the cache of food and clothing left behind for emergencies. The party returned to the settlement of Egedesminde, a short distance north, to wait for *Sofia*.

The expedition's ship appeared on August 16, on schedule, to pick up the ice party. While they were exploring the ice cap, *Sofia* sailed as far north as Cape York, 76 degrees north latitude. They made several landings and Nathorst, the expedition's geologist, brought back an outstanding collection of fossil plants. They included tropical species now found in mid-Pacific islands, such as breadfruit, briars and ferns, and midlatitude species of the Sequoia family.

While they had been waiting for *Sofia*, Adolf Nordenskiöld found out that a ship was leaving Egedesminde for Denmark, and took advantage of the opportunity to mail a letter home. 'All is well,' he wrote Anna, 'the exploration of the icecap was successful, although I did not find any land free of ice. Perhaps it was because the conditions upon which I built my theory of such open land simply did not exist. You'll find out more about our journey from the enclosed draft of my letter to Dickson.'

'This was the first time that the interior of Greenland was the subject of careful field research. But you need not worry because I suggested that other attempts should be made to explore the icecap from places further north and further south. *My Arctic travels have now ended.* (Underlined in the letter!). I have lost quite a bit of weight, but otherwise feel fine. Even my feet held up during the long trek . . . From here we shall sail south to Ivigtut, to Julianehaab, around Cape Farewell to the east coast, then on to Reykjavik and home.'

On their way south, *Sofia* steamed into Igaliko fjord, to visit a group of ruins attributed to the early Norse settlers of Greenland. There was a tradition that Erik the Red, the first Norsemen to come from Iceland to Greenland, built his homestead, Brattahlid, on Igaliko fjord. Nordenskiöld handled the question of the location of Norse settlements with caution: he was willing to concede that the ruins on Igaliko fjord represented homes, stables and sheep folds built by settlers of the 10th and 11th centuries, but would not accept the tradition that this particular settlement was the first European outpost on Greenland. Before leaving the site, Lieutenant Kjellström took photographs of the ruins, against the stark backdrop of the mountainous rim of Greenland.

The last task that Nordenskiöld had set for the expedition was to try to find traces of early Norse settlement on Greenland's south-east coast. No modern explorer has been able to land on that icebound shore-line, yet Nordenskiöld believed that in an earlier, warmer climatic phase Norsemen might well have established outposts there. From his knowledge of earlier reports, he was certain that there were Eskimo living along the east coast, and he hoped to find out something about old ruins from them. The problems Nordenskiöld had faced in this last endeavour were, first, getting his ship through the ice barrier to a landing place on the east coast, second, to search out and find Eskimo and third, to find someone to act as an Eskimo interpreter for the expedition.

There were very few Danes living in the area of south Greenland, but Nordenskiöld knew that the Moravian church of Germany ran a mission station at Frederiksdal, near the southern tip of the island. *Sofia* stopped at the mission station, and Nordenskiöld persuaded the Reverend Brodbeck, one of the German missionaries who spoke the Eskimo language fluently, to accompany the expedition as an interpreter.

From Frederiksdal the ship followed the southernmost part of the west coast of Greenland and once past Cape Farewell, attempted to find a way to the eastern coast. But heavy ice prevented any progress, and the ship turned northward until, at latitude 66 degrees, they found the offshore ice was not as thick as along the rest of the coast. Nordenskiöld climbed to the crow's nest, took a long look towards the shore, and decided that the icepack could be crossed. *Sofia* turned her prow to the ice, and with her engine working at full steam, forced her way to a deep, sheltered bay that Nordenskiöld named King Oscar's Harbor. It was the first time since the Middle Ages that a European vessel anchored on the east coast of Greenland, south of the Arctic Circle; further north, other explorers had landed during the 19th century.

As soon as the anchor reached bottom, boats were lowered and the scientists hastened to explore the land. Several small valleys opened onto the fjord, their floors were covered with grassy meadows and small willows grew by the streams. In one of the valleys the bottom was sandy and it showed footprints, but a careful search failed to find any Eskimo nearby. There were several cairns on the low hills facing the sea, and the ruins of a small stone building at the head of the fjord: Nordenskiöld thought it possible that these were constructions dating to the time of Norse occupance.

There were many vestiges of the Eskimo in King Oscar's Harbor, ruins of dwellings, stone circles, traps, and several tombs. The most moving of the finds was a child's grave, where the explorers found miniature models of hunting and fishing tackle, and the head of a dog. Paul Egede, an eighteenth century Danish settler in Greenland, wrote that the Eskimo frequently placed a dog's head in children's graves: the dog, able to find his way anywhere, was to guide the child through the land of the dead.

Frustrated by the absence of any natives who might have provided information on Norse remains, and concerned lest *Sofia* be caught in the ice by a storm, Nordenskiöld reluctantly decided to give up any further investigations. On September 6, the expedition left Greenland, arriving in Iceland three days later, just ahead of a violent storm. The passage from Iceland to Sweden was uneventful. On September 27, *Sofia* anchored in Göteborg harbor. All returned safe and well from their summer in the Arctic.

The Reverend Brodbeck's services as an interpreter were never required since the expedition could not find any Eskimo on the east coast of Greenland, so he returned to Germany for a short vacation. He was on his way back to the Greenland mission in the spring of 1884, aboard the pride of the Greenland fleet, when the vessel was hit by a storm off the Shetland Islands. Pastor Brodbeck, and most of the others aboard the ship, lost their lives in that shipwreck.

The results of the 1883 expedition to Greenland satisfied Adolf Nordenskiöld. Though he himself was still not completely convinced, he did report that as far as he could find, the island's interior was indeed covered with ice. Little room was left for doubt, and subsequent expeditions only confirmed his findings. As for early Norse settlements on Greenland's east coast, the short stay of the expedition in that area had prevented any detailed investigations. But Nordenskiöld insisted in his report that such outposts did exist in medieval times and, once more, later field investigations did confirm his intuitive, though informed, guess.

The most important results of the expedition consisted of the magnificent collections of fossils and of rare minerals, gathered along the west coast of Greenland from Ivigtut in the south as far north as Cape York. These fossil remains of an earlier vegetation contributed a great deal to our knowledge of climates prevailing in earlier geological periods in the Arctic regions.

In the eyes of the general public, the most spectacular achievement of the expedition was the reconnaissance carried out by the two Lapps that took them to the center of the Greenland icecap. For men to have covered 460 kilometers, nearly three hundred miles, in fifty-seven hours seemed unbelievable. Nordenskiöld was the first to admit that while he had full faith in the Lapps' report, he knew of no previous long-distance ski run to compare with the Lapps' performance.

To convince the public that the two Lapps did indeed accomplish what seemed a superhuman performance on the Greenland icecap, Nordenskiöld persuaded Oscar Dickson to organize a long-distance ski race in Lapland in April, 1884, during the spring following the expedition's return.

The race was to take place on April 3 and 4, 1884. Winter was nearly over in Lapland by then, though nights were cold, and snow was still deep on the ground. The starting point was at the Lapp village of Purkijaur; the course was laid out across a number of lakes and rough country as well, to the village of Kvikkjokk. There the runners had to turn around and go back to the starting point. The length of the course was 110 kilometers from the start to the turn-around point, 68 miles; the total distance to be covered was 220 kilometers, 137 miles. The rules of race stated that time out for rest or refreshment was counted as part of the runner's total time for the course.

Sixteen men started out on April 3, at four in the afternoon. The start was delayed because of heavy snowfall and, later, a sudden thaw. Some of the participants were Lapps, the others Swedes who had settled only recently in Lapland. Many of the Lapps came from distant villages, and one participant had made what he called 'a short run' of 160 kilometers, 100 miles, the day before the race, to borrow a special pair of skis that would run smoothly on wet snow.

Lars Tuorda, who was with Nordenskiöld in Greenland, was first off at the start. The skiers were going at a good pace: one of the judges had planned to follow the group in a sleigh, driving the fastest horse in the district, but was left far behind within an hour. It was dark by the time the runners arrived at the half-way point of the course, where the local Lapps had lit a bonfire, and had coffee ready.

Lapps are known to drink more coffee than almost anyone else: all coffeepots were quickly emptied, and after a half-hour break, the skiers were once more on their way. By the time the end of the course was reached, six of the sixteen runners gave up – the pace was too fast for them. Seven Lapps and three Swedes were still in the race. At the village of Kvikkjokk, the turn-around point, a tent was set up on the frozen lake. There was a fire going, one of the judges was sleeping in the tent, while the other two were making coffee. Later, a meal of roast reindeer meat was to have been prepared.

The runners weren't expected until the afternoon, due to poor weather. But shortly after four o'clock in the morning there was a rustle in the snow, and moments later the first four runners gathered around the fire. Lars Tuorda, the Greenland veteran, was first; the next three followed him at intervals of a few seconds. Lunch was not ready for them, but they were content with having coffee, squatting around the fire, smoking and talking. Having had his fill of coffee, Lars decided to visit a friend in the village. While he was gone, the man who came in second, Per Olof Ländta, took advantage of his absence, and started out on the homeward stretch of the race. He had a jump of sixteen minutes on his rival, but when Lars returned and found him gone, he put on a mighty spurt, and within a few miles caught up and took the lead.

Shortly after three in the afternoon on April 4, less than twenty-four hours after the race had begun, a lookout signalled that two skiers had appeared at the end of the lake furthest from the finish line. Lars and Per Olof covered the last mile and a half in ten minutes in a final spurt, and completed the course in twenty-one hours and twenty-two minutes. Per Olof Ländta lost out by five seconds, and received second prize. 'That fellow has a lot of strength left in him,' said Ländta, speaking of his victorious rival, 'he could run quite a few more miles today.'

The two winners completed the race at an average speed of 6.4 miles per hour. This was even faster than the speed claimed by Tuorda and Rossa for the run on the Greenland icecap, and silenced the critics of Nordenskiöld's statement about the Lapps' penetration of interior Greenland.

Even the London Times carried an account of the Lapland ski race, written by Oscar Dickson, and to this day that unusual sporting event is called the 'Nordenskiöld Ski Race'. Other long-distance meets for skiers are held yearly in Scandinavia, but the race of 1884, organised by Nordenskiöld and Dickson, remains the first and longest of all.

When Nordenskiöld returned from Greenland in the fall of 1883, reports on the expedition were published in all the newspapers. One evening in October, 1883, a young Norwegian naturalist, Fridtjof Nansen, was listening as his father read the newspaper to his family. Suddenly,

Nansen's attention was caught by a dispatch, reporting Nordenskiöld's observations on Greenland. 'The expedition did not find any oases, only endless snowfields, over which the two Lapps were supposed to have covered an unbelievable distance in a very short time, and found the skiing excellent.' On hearing the report, Nansen decided to organize an expedition to cross Greenland on skis.

It took nearly four years for Nansen to work out the details of his plan, but in November, 1887, he had it all on paper, and went to Stockholm to ask Nordenskiöld for advice. He was introduced to the great explorer with these words: 'This is Dr. Nansen, Curator of the Bergen museum; he wants to cross the Greenland icecap.' 'Well, I'll be . . .', said his host; but the two men got along so well that at the end of that first talk, Nordenskiöld insisted that the young Norwegian borrow his snow boots. 'It is most important to look after your feet,' was Nordenskiöld's advice to the novice in Arctic exploration. Later that week, Nansen was his guest at the 'Idun' society, and when he left for Norway, Nordenskiöld promised to support his application for funds to Oslo university.

In June of 1888, Nansen set out with five companions, to cross Greenland on skis. Starting from the east coast of the island, they made it to one of the Danish settlements on the west coast, accomplishing what most experts called an impossible feat. The group was too late to catch a ship back to Denmark that year, and had to spend the winter in Greenland. But Fridtjof Nansen was anxious to let the world know of his success, and sent a dispatch to the man he always considered the dean of polar explorers, Nordenskiöld.

The telegram announcing Nansen's success is preserved in Adolf Nordenskiöld's papers. Dated October 4, 1888, it begins with the words: 'I have the great pleasure to inform you that Greenland was crossed from east to west. I cannot give you a detailed report now; I have just scribbled these lines and gave them to a "kayak man". He is taking it to Ivigtut, and shall give it to the captain of the steamer *Fox*, asking the captain to forward it to you on his arrival in Denmark.'

After his return from Greenland, Nordenskiöld followed progress in polar research from the quiet haven of his study. But he kept in close touch with younger men who were still active explorers, and was always generous with his advice and support for new projects. His own interests had been gradually changing, even before his Greenland expedition, and much of his time and energy for the remaining years of his life was devoted to work on the history of geography and of maps.

XXIV. PUBLIC SUCCESS, PRIVATE TRAGEDY – 1883-1895

Waiting for his ship on the coast of Greenland, in August of 1883, Adolf Nordenskiöld wrote his wife that his Arctic travels had ended. He considered himself an Arctic veteran, retired from active duty. Yet once more he was called to return to the polar regions, in 1887.

All of Nordenskiöld's travels had been to the regions surrounding the North Pole. But the call of 1887 came from the opposite end of the earth, from Australia, asking him to lead an expedition to the unknown continent of Antarctica. A group of Australian scientists, inspired by the success of the *Vega* expedition, and supported by local businessmen, had decided that the time was ripe for an exploration of Antarctica and cabled Nordenskiöld, informing him of their plans and asking him to take command of the enterprise. The cable arrived in Stockholm in May of 1887, asking whether Nordenskiöld could travel to Australia during the summer and start out for Antarctica in October. Time was far too short to make the necessary preparations, the funds subscribed in Australia were insufficient to cover even minimal expenses, and Nordenskiöld declined the offer.

But the Australians continued to work on the project, collected more funds, and by suggesting that the expedition be a joint Swedish-Australian venture, even managed to obtain Oscar Dickson's promise to make a sizable financial contribution to their cause. Early in 1890, it had seemed to Nordenskiöld as if the project might become a reality. Writing to the president of the Royal Australasian Geographical Society in Melbourne, Australia, he stated his ideas about the goals for such a venture. 'My intention,' he wrote, 'is to adopt for our Antarctic expedition the same plan as for the Vega expedition, i.e., to make it not an exclusively geographical undertaking, but the commencement of an exploration of the geology, natural history, hydrography, meteorology, etc., of the south polar region compared with the regions round the northern pole . . .' Nordenskiöld felt that careful scientific study of the margins of the Antarctic continent must precede any serious attempt to reach the South Pole itself.

The joint Swedish-Australian expedition did not materialize, mainly for the lack of adequate financial support. As to the order of priorities that Nordenskiöld had suggested, they were reversed in later years, and detailed scientific observations in Antarctica had to wait until the South Pole was conquered.

The Antarctic venture was Nordenskiöld's last attempt to return to active exploration. But he continued to counsel men who sought fame and applause through Arctic exploration, and he was sought out by commercial interests and by governments eager to get the views of the dean of Arctic exploration on schemes of trade and navigation in northern waters. Attempts to exploit the seaway to Siberia were made during the 1880's by Englishmen, but the unpredictable weather of the Kara Sea, the refusal of Siberian businessmen to cooperate with foreign merchants, and the difficulties of navigation on the Ob and Yenisey Rivers rendered these ventures unprofitable. The first time the northern seaway was used on a large scale for shipments to the interior of Siberia was in the early 1890's.

In the spring of 1891 construction had started on the Trans-Siberian railroad, the link between European Russia and the Pacific. Crews began laying track in several places and the problems of moving supplies to the far-flung construction sites were immense. The Russian Navy decided to prove that it was possible to ship rails and other supplies to Siberia by using the northern seaway and the Yenisey River. Early in 1893 the Russian Navy Department approached Nordenskiöld for help. Could he, the Undersecretary of the Navy wrote, suggest where ships could be chartered to transport rails from England to the mouth of the Yenisey? Could he also indicate, the letter continued, where the Russian Navy should turn for pilots who knew the Kara Sea and, since Nordenskiöld was familiar with the problems of north Siberia, what would be the best way to transfer the freight from ocean-going to river vessels on the lower Yenisey?

Nordenskiöld replied within a matter of weeks, and in the summer of 1893 a large shipment, consisting of some six thousand pieces of steel rail, was loaded in England and sent on to Siberia. These rails reached the town of Krasnoyarsk on the upper Yenisey and were the first to be laid on the middle section of the Trans-Siberian railroad.

The Russian government sent a generous check to Nordenskiöld for his services as a consultant. The Minister of the Navy added his personal thanks and wrote: 'If we accomplish our goal and the seaway to the mouth of the Yenisey will be opened to regularly scheduled shipping, your name will be attached to this great enterprise by yet another link, for you will be remembered as the man whose moral support did so mightily contribute to a decision in its favor, and whose counsel had such a large part in its success.'

As it turned out the Minister was overly optimistic in his forecast of the future of the northern seaway. To ship supplies for the Trans-Siberian Railroad by sea and river was far too expensive, and the project had to be abandoned. But once more Nordenskiöld had the right idea: when several very large hydro-electric plants were being built on the Siberian rivers in the 1960's, the machinery for these plants was shipped to the construction sites by the northern seaway.

The failure of the Navy to persuade the Russian Government to use the Arctic Ocean as a shipping route to Siberia was due not only to the high cost involved; there was also continuing doubt about merchant ships being able to make the passage when floating ice in the Kara Sea would endanger the vessels. The answer to those who believed in the usefulness of the northern seaway was in building icebreakers, ships with powerful engines that could break the ice with their reinforced steel prow, or, riding up on the ice, crush it with their weight. Shipyards in Finland and in Scotland had begun to design and build icebreakers, and Nordenskiöld had served as consultant to the leading Finnish designer. It was only natural that the Russian Navy's foremost advocate of the use of icebreakers, Admiral Stepan Makarov, turned to him for advice.

Having corresponded with Nordenskiöld for several years, Admiral Makarov came to Stockholm during the summer of 1897 to meet the great explorer in person and get his views on the future of icebreakers in Arctic navigation and discovery. Makarov was in excellent spirits, the Russian Navy had yielded to his urging and the first Russian icebreaker, the *Yermak*, was ready for sea trials. *Yermak* had a 10,000 horsepower engine, and Nordenskiöld recalled that *Sofia*, the ship he had in 1868 when he extablished an Arctic record, had only a 270 horsepower engine under her deck. It was quite obvious to both men that icebreakers were destined to play a major role in the Arctic.

Four years later, in June of 1901, *Yermak* was ready to leave for a first attempt to attack polar ice off Spitsbergen. Admiral Makarov was commanding the ship, which was waiting for him in Tromsö. On his way to Norway, Makarov stopped in Stockholm to visit Nordenskiöld, and the two men spent an entire afternoon discussing the future of the northern seaway. Makarov foresaw a major change in Russia's naval strategy as well as in her seaborne commerce: how much faster could ships reach the Pacific coast of Siberia by the northern route than by the long and tedious sea lanes through the Suez Canal. But the northern cruise of *Yermak* did not satisfy the Russian Admiralty, and the ship ended up with the duty of keeping Russia's Baltic harbors open during winter months.

The notion of using icebreakers to keep ships moving, whether in the wintry Baltic between Sweden and Finland, or in the Arctic Ocean off the rivermouths of Siberia appealed to Nordenskiöld. He was practical and openminded all his life, always willing to employ new tools and new techniques to achieve results. When balloons were suggested for the use of the planned Swedish-Australian expedition to Antarctica in 1890, Nordenskiöld took to the idea at once but insisted that 'until we will be able to steer the balloons it would be wasted expense to thus equip an expedition to advance to the South Pole'. Within three years' time a Swede, S. A. Andrée, started a series of experiments to prove that balloons could be steered and navigated.

Salomon August Andrée was an engineer, working for the Swedish patent office, who had become convinced that balloons, lighter-than-air vehicles, not only offered a means for fast and reliable transportation but could also be used as aerial platforms for scientific observations. In 1893, Andrée had received a grant from a Swedish foundation to purchase a balloon, and the following year had made nine ascensions with it, including a journey across southern Sweden when he had proved that he could steer the balloon and reach his destination regardless of prevailing winds.

Nordenskiöld had followed Andrée's experiments closely and one evening in the spring of 1894, at the close of a meeting of the Swedish Geographical Society that both men had attended, invited Andrée to accompany him on his walk home. Nordenskiöld talked at length about his own ideas on the use of balloons for scientific exploration in such inaccessible regions as Antarctica, and then asked Andrée what his plans were. Andrée said that he hoped to use a balloon to reach the North Pole, and the great explorer agreed enthusiastically with the idea.

Andrée's plan, presented to the Academy of Sciences in 1895, proposed that a large balloon, with an open gondola, be shipped to northern Spitsbergen, and there be filled with hydrogen gas. He had hoped to start his journey north in early summer, steering his balloon to take every advantage of winds, and after reaching the highest possible latitude, return to Spitsbergen or to the archipelago of Franz Josef Land. The plan was supported by Nordenskiöld and the funds for the balloon expedition were covered by public subscription. King Oscar, Alfred Nobel, and Oscar Dickson were among the principal subscribers.

On July 11, 1897, Andrée and two companions lifted off in their balloon, christened *Örnen*, 'Eagle', from an island off the northwest corner of Spitsbergen. Andrée had calculated carefully the course he wanted to follow, but within moments of their liftoff things went wrong. Struck by a sudden gust of wind, the balloon dipped so close to the sea that the men became panicky and threw out a large portion of the ballast they were carrying in the form of sandbags. Seconds later, as the balloon was slowly rising again, the heavy ropes that were to be used for steering got caught in ice crevasses and tore loose. In less than five minutes, the 'Eagle' lost most of its capacity for steering and was a prey to the winds of the Arctic.

The balloon disappeared from sight very quickly. Two days later one of the carrier pigeons the men had with them was shot by Norwegian fishermen; it carried a message giving the balloon's position and reporting that all was well. After that, there was only silence.

All Scandinavia waited for word from the Andrée expedition. Nordenskiöld felt personally responsible for their fate; it was because of his strong support of Andrée that the expedition had sufficient financial backing. The mineralogy division in the Stockholm Museum of National History became headquarters for the search for Andrée and his companions. Nordenskiöld personally plotted every report and kept in contact with newspapers all over the world to keep the search going. For reports kept coming in during the summer and early fall of 1897 of the balloon being sighted in Northern Siberia, over the islands north of Japan, over Alaska. The following year an expedition, financed by contributions from all over Sweden, searched the tundra off the mouth of the Lena River in northernmost Siberia, but no trace of Andrée was found.

More than thirty years went by before men stumbled across Andrée's last camp. In August, 1930, a Norwegian expedition investigating the waters between Spitsberg and Franz Josef Land went ashore on a small island, called White Island. A short distance inland two sailors found a canvas boat, a sled, guns, and scientific instruments, all marked 'Andrée Polar Expedition – 1897'.

As soon as word of the discovery reached Scandinavia a joint Swedish – Norwegian search party went out to White Island. It was the end of summer then, more of the area had thawed out, and the search party had found the remains of Andrée and his companions, most of the equipment they had carried, their logbooks, and a roll of photographic film. The log and the photographs, developed after they had lain thirty-three

man, administering a major division of the Museum of Natural History, continuing his research in geology and mineralogy, serving as a consultant to enterprises at home and abroad. But he considered all these activities as routine, and devoted much of his time and of his inexhaustible energy to what had become his major interest, the history of mapmaking.

Erik Dahlgren, who assisted Nordenskiöld in the preparation of his book on the *Vega* voyage, summed up the great explorer's views on the importance of the history of geography and of mapmaking in these words: 'All through his works there runs, like a red thread, an idea he had often discussed: that the discoveries and the victorious march of the civilized nations across the earth cannot be fully understood, nor its causes and effects grasped, without the knowledge of the conceptions of lands and seas of earlier times, and of the groping attempts of our forefathers to visualize these conceptions on maps of the world.'

To carry on his studies in the history of cartography, Nordenskiöld collected books, atlases and maps over a period of nearly thirty years, and built one of the world's leading private libraries of rare works on the subject. In the years following his return from the *Vega* voyage his income was, by the standards of the time, quite substantial: in addition to his salary at the Museum of Natural History he also received a generous annual grant authorized by Parliament, as a special reward for his discovery of the Northeast Passage. The royalties from his book on the *Vega* voyage went to the purchase of his country place, Dalbyö, much of the rest of his income he devoted to the buying of books.

He knew and loved rare books. Travelling a great deal, he visited the leading libraries, consulting their holdings and comparing them with his own. At the same time, he called on booksellers who specialized in rare books, and in turn received a steady stream of catalogues and special offers from the most prominent of these dealers: Henry Stevens, Quaritch, and Maggs in London; Fr. Muller in Amsterdam; Rosenthal in Munich; Harassowitz in Leipzig; Olschki in Florence.

Adolf Nordenskiöld's library became one of the leading private collections of rare items on the history of discovery and mapmaking in all Europe. He enjoyed showing his treasures to friends, and often said that he never regretted any purchase he had made, no matter how high the price. That he knew how valuable his collection had become is evident from a letter he wrote to Muller, the noted Amsterdam dealer in rare books, in December, 1900.

Nordenskiöld was seriously thinking at that time of selling his library, and the letter contains his own evaluation of his collection. He was convinced that, except for the leading national libraries of Europe, no other library could rival his own for its wealth of printed maps of the 15th, 16th, and 17th centuries. 'The library contains about five thousand books' – he went on – 'not counting pamphlets and single maps, and some of these are most valuable. I have a nearly complete collection of the *Geography* of Ptolemy, with only one 16th century edition missing; between eighty and ninety volumes of the Bibliotheca Americana Vetustissima (the basic list of books on the discovery of America published prior to 1551); a large number of editions, most of them first editions, of the works of Reisch, Münster, Waghenaer, Ortelius, Mercator, Apianus, Honter, Franciscus Monachus, Bordone, Wytfliet, Herrera, Grynaeus; a large collection of marine charts published in the 16th and 17th century; a superb copy of the Lafreri Atlas and another, less complete, collection of 16th century Italian maps; a collection of printed gores for celestial and terrestrial globes; one hundred and forty incunabula, generally not on theological subjects and several containing maps, for example Sonnetti of ca. 1470, Schedel's Nurnberg Chronicle in both the 1493 and 1497 editions, Berlinghieri, the 1475, 1478, 1482, 1486 and 1490 editions of Ptolemy; a set of globe gores of ca. 1515-1520, valued at 8,000 Marks by Rosenthal; three 15th-century manuscripts of Dati's 'La Sfera', whose importance for the development of portolan charts I have recently demonstrated; two manuscript charts of the North Pacific, prepared by officers of Vitus Bering's expedition; and nearly complete sets of the facsimile collections of old maps published by Jomard, Santarem, Kohl, Muller, Kretschmer, Ghillany and others.'

To Adolf Nordenskiöld these books and maps were tools he used constantly, preparing the many articles he wrote on the history of maps and the two books that are his greatest contributions to the subject.

The first of those books, entitled 'Facsimile Atlas to the Early History of Cartography', was published in both Swedish and English versions in 1889. It describes the history of map-making from Greek and Roman times to the mid-sixteenth century, and includes a set of superb full-size photographic reproductions of important and rare maps. 'Facsimile Atlas' was the first book to make such accurate reproductions available to the scholar; joined to Nordenskiöld's commentary it remains a standard item on the shelves of research libraries the world over. And while some of Nordenskiöld's views on early maps and their sources are no longer accepted, the 'Facsimile Atlas' remains, nearly a century after its publication, indispensable to librarians, collectors, and scholars. More than half of the 153 plates in the volume were photographed from books and atlases in Nordenskiöld's own library.

'Facsimile Atlas' deals with printed maps only, and Nordenskiöld felt that there was a need for a companion volume dealing with manuscript maps, especially the sailing charts used in late medieval times and during the Age of Discovery. His researches in libraries and his wide-ranging correspondence with scholars and specialists resulted in the publication, once more in Swedish and English versions, of his second major work, 'Periplus: an essay on the early history of charts and sailing directions'. 'Periplus' is a Greek word that describes sailing directions used by Greek mariners. The book traces the history and development of marine charts and pilot books to the seventeenth century and, like its predecessor, it is superbly illustrated. There had been other collections of reproductions of rare old maps before the publication of 'Facsimile Atlas' and 'Periplus', but none based on such careful scientific inquiry, none accompanied by so great a store of relevant detail as these milestones in the history of science.

Besides his scholarly interests, Nordenskiöld had always been passionately concerned with politics, and served five terms in the lower house of the Swedish parliament. He always thought of himself as a Liberal, and was elected to parliament on the Liberal ticket. But his career as a Member of Parliament was due as much to his fame as an explorer as to his devotion to the Liberal cause. In fact, he was accused by his opponents of being an opportunist, for having been a frequent guest at the royal palace, and a close friend of some of the wealthiest businessmen of Sweden.

Nordenskiöld was a conscientious Member of Parliament and tried to be present whenever important bills were voted on. His own bills, few in number, dealt mostly with matters of scientific interest, such as support of universities and research institutes. It was on the issue of national defense that he found himself in opposition to his own party.

Sweden was a neutral nation and the Liberal party insisted on reducing the length of compulsory military service and on cutting the defense budget. Nordenskiöld did not share these views; he had worked with naval officers who had commanded the ships of his most successful Arctic expeditions, and he valued the Navy highly. When the defense budgets came before Parliament, Nordenskiöld refused to follow his Liberal colleagues and supported the Services' point of view. Thus when the elections of 1893 were about to be held, the Liberals were no longer willing to endorse his candidacy and his parliamentary career came to an end.

It was about that time that he remarked to one of his friends: 'I have been nominated and appointed Sweden's national celebrity, and that is not going to be an unmitigated pleasure.' He was called upon to preside over meetings and congresses dealing with both scientific and non-scientific subjects, and distinguished foreigners visiting Stockholm insisted on meeting the hero of the *Vega* voyage. But he was recognized as a world figure, too: fifty-four scientific societies from all over the world had elected him to membership, an equal number made him an honorary member, and he was decorated by governments from all over Europe. As a young man Nordenskiöld had little use for decorations; later, he seems to have enjoyed them almost as curios. Attending a formal wedding in Germany, he walked from the church to the reception with two young German officers: 'My name meant nothing to these young men', he wrote his wife, 'but they tried to find out through rather leading questions who I was, since I wore the highest decoration the Emperor of Germany could award!'

Though he travelled a great deal, Adolf Nordenskiöld always enjoyed returning to his family. He and Anna had four children: Maria, Gustaf, Anna, and Erland. Erland, the youngest boy, was born in 1877, the year before the *Vega* voyage. Whether in Stockholm or at their country place in Dalbyö, Nordenskiöld managed to spend many hours with his children, taking them for walks, to the theatre, to the opera. In his letters written during his travels he often spoke of sights he knew his family would be interested in; a luncheon at the home of a Grand Duke in Saint Petersburg, watching the papal nuncio ride to the imperial palace in Vienna accompanied by outriders in gorgeous uniform, a formal dinner in Berlin the day Chancellor Bismarck was dismissed from office.

The Nordenskiöld's home in Stockholm was the center of Adolf Nordenskiöld's life whenever he was in town. There he had his superb collection of old and rare books and maps, there he and Anna had often entertained friends at luncheon or dinner, and across the courtyard was the mineralogical collection and laboratory where he worked with specimens and attended to the business of the museum.

In the mid-1880's tragedy struck the family. Maria became seriously ill with tuberculosis, and died at the age of twenty-two. The loss of their eldest child was a hard blow for Anna and Adolf Nordenskiöld; their only consolation was that their older son Gustav was an outstanding student and his rapid progress at school and at the university promised a brilliant career. He graduated from Uppsala university in 1889 at the age of twenty-one, and delighted his father by his intense interest in chemistry and mineralogy, the favorite subjects of both his father and grandfather.

The following year, Gustav Nordenskiöld sailed to the Arctic, accompanied by two of his friends, to study the geology of western Spitsbergen. He brought back a remarkable collection of petrified plants and his father, who had always encouraged and supported younger men on their Arctic adventures, was as proud of Gustav's achievements as his own.

Within a month of his return from Spitsbergen Gustav became ill and his father, remembering the loss of his daughter a few years earlier, insisted that he go to Berlin, ostensibly to continue his university studies. The elder Nordenskiöld kept his fears a secret even from his wife, but wrote the world's leading authority on tuberculosis, the German physician and bacteriologist Robert Koch, asking him to examine, and if necessary, to treat his son.

Koch's diagnosis was positive and Gustav remained in Berlin for treatments through the winter of 1890-91. But the fact that Nordenskiöld's son was in Berlin and was a patient of Professor Koch was reported in the newspapers and Gustav was concerned lest the news reach his family. He sent a telegram to his father, addressed to 'Baron Nordenskiöld, personal', and asked him either to tell his mother about his illness, or try and keep the news out of the Stockholm papers.

In the spring of 1891 Gustav returned to Sweden in much better health, but his father, concerned that the cold climate of Stockholm might worsen his condition, decided that a change of climate and the excitement of travel would be a real tonic for him. Gustav first visited Italy, then France, and in May of 1891 sailed for the United States. He travelled around the East at first, but the part of the country he really wanted to see was the Southwest.

As a university student Gustav had read about prehistoric Indian dwellings having been discovered in canyon cliffs in southwestern Colorado. He went by train to Denver, thence to Durango, and rode on horseback to Mancos, a small settlement in the southwest corner of Colorado. The ruins he wanted to see were only a few miles away, in a place called Mesa Verde, now a National Park. Gustav spent the summer in Mancos, explored Mesa Verde, took many photographs, and his letters home conveyed the mounting excitement he felt digging in the cliff dwellings. In the fall he visited the Navajo and Hopi Indian reservations in Arizona, and enjoyed the sights and sounds of the Indian pueblos, the clear desert air, the spectacular scenery. The months he spent in the Southwest agreed with him and he returned to Stockholm at Christmastime, in excellent spirits and apparently excellent health.

Back in Sweden Gustav went to work on his collections of Indian artifacts from the Mesa Verde, and prepared a long report on his excavations at the site. 1892 was the four hundredth anniversary of Columbus' discovery of America, and a special celebration took place in Spain. The elder Nordenskiöld was one of the guests of honor at the Columbian Congress in Spain and Gustav went along to arrange a Swedish exhibit that included some of his own finds of early American Indian civilizations. There were many enthusiastic comments on his work and when his book, 'The Cliff Dwellers of the Mesa Verde' was published in 1893, it was praised as a major contribution to the archaeology of America.

All seemed to be going well for Gustav. He had made a name for himself in the world of science, he was feeling well, and he fell deeply in love. After a whirlwind courtship, he married Anna Smitt, daughter of one of Sweden's most prominent businessmen. He was strikingly handsome, successful, and the future looked very bright to him and to those around him. The following year, 1894, Adolf and Anna Nordenskiöld rejoiced over the birth of their first grandchildren, Eva Nordenskiöld and Gunhild Swedenborg.

In the fall of 1894, S. A. Andrée had invited Gustav for a ride in his balloon. The flight was successful, but Gustav caught a bad cold and had a relapse of his tuberculosis. The doctors recommended an extended stay at a sanatorium north of Stockholm. Accompanied by his wife and his parents, Gustav set out for the sanatorium, but the strain of the journey was too much, and he died on the train only minutes before arriving at his destination. He was twenty-seven years old.

Had Gustav lived he might well have rivalled his father as a versatile and brilliant scientist. His father never recovered from the cruel blow of Gustav's early death and he did not live to see his younger son Erland become a distinguished scholar in his own right.

XXV. THE SUNSET YEARS – 1895-1901

The death of Gustav brought about one important change in the life of the Nordenskiöld family. Seeing his two older children, Maria and Gustav, both die of tuberculosis, Adolf Nordenskiöld became convinced that they contracted in the disease in the old family apartment in the Museum. He had insisted on moving and had found an apartment in a recently erected building, close to the heart of downtown Stockholm. The new place had a fine view of a park next door, it was open to sun and fresh air, and Nordenskiöld had hoped that by leaving the old place he and his wife would not be haunted so much by the memory of Marie and Gustav.

Anna, the younger of Nordenskiöld's daughters, had married in 1893; Erland, the younger son, was finishing high school and hoping to enter Uppsala University. Adolf Nordenskiöld was as busy as ever, running his mineralogy division at the Museum, writing articles, presiding at meetings. He travelled a great deal, and during his absences his wife spent most of her time at their country place, or visiting her daughter.

The loss of Gustav never ceased to trouble the Nordenskiölds. But they had renewed hope that yet another Nordenskiöld would continue the family tradition of scholarship. Erland graduated from Uppsala University in 1898, and the following year participated in an expedition to Patagonia, in southern Argentina. Returning to Sweden, he published his first scholarly paper, dealing with his excavations in South America, in the Transactions of the Swedish Academy of Sciences.

Adolf Nordenskiöld took great pride in his younger son's achievements. Yet he was equally proud to see the children of his and of his wife's family grow to adulthood and take their place in society. His sister's oldest son, Otto Nordenskjöld, became a geologist and followed in his uncle's path by becoming a polar explorer. One of Anna Nordenskiöld's nephews, Gustav Mannerheim, had graduated from military school in Finland and was serving in one of the elite regiments of the Russian army, the Horse Guards. He had married a wealthy young Russian woman, and in 1893, Nordenskiöld wrote to his wife of seeing 'Gustav and his lovely bride' at a horse show in the imperial riding stables, in Saint Petersburg. Years later, Gustav Mannerheim became the first head of state of Finland and led Finnish forces in two wars against the Soviet Union.

It was during the closing years of the nineteenth century that Nordenskiöld's attention turned once more to his native Finland. Things had changed in Finland since he had gone into exile: Emperor Alexander II had reaffirmed the country's autonomous status, and the Finns were prospering under the liberal rules allowed by the central government of the Russian Empire. But the strong current of nationalism within the Empire that prevailed at the court in St. Petersburg in the late 1880's and the 1890's, and the central government's increasing tendency to ignore Finland's traditional self-government, were gradually leading to open conflict. In February, 1899, Emperor Nicholas II revoked the Finnish constitution that, on his accession to the throne five years earlier, he had sworn to uphold. Finland was to be subject to Russian laws and the appointment of a martinet soldier, Bobrikov Governor-General of Finland had signalled the Emperor's intention to Russianize the country. The response to the Emperor's actions was swift, both in Finland and throughout Europe. Hundreds of thousands of Finns had signed an appeal to the Emperor that was to be presented to him by a special delegation of leading Finns. At the same time, another appeal on Finland's behalf was circulated throughout Europe, and over one thousand of the best known scholars, artists, writers, and statesmen signed that document. A delegation of eight distinguished Europeans had journeyed to St. Petersburg in late June, 1899, to request an audience with the Emperor and present the petition to him. Senator Trarieux of France, former Minister of Justice, headed the delegation, but its best known member was Nordenskiöld.

Few non-Russians had such close connections with Russian court and scientific circles as Nordenskiöld: he had been honored and decorated by the reigning Emperor's grandfather, Alexander II; on his frequent visits to St. Petersburg he was often a guest of the Emperor's uncle, Grand Duke Constantine; he was honorary member of the principal Russian scientific societies and was serving on a Russian-Swedish commission charged with the survey of Spitsbergen. Like many a Finn, Nordenskiöld had believed that the pressure of European public opinion and the views of men close to the Emperor and favorably inclined towards Finland would bring about a change in the Emperor's policy.

It was in late June, 1899, that the delegation carrying the appeal of European writers, scholars, and artists had arrived in St. Petersburg. Sven Hedin, Swedish geographer and explorer who had been a classmate of Gustav Nordenskiöld and a close friend of the family, was in the Russian capital then and had registered in the same hotel where

Nordenskiöld was staying. The delegation had just left for the Emperor's summer palace at Peterhof, and Hedin, anxious to find out what the Emperor's attitude was, decided to wait for Nordenskiöld at the hotel.

Later in the afternoon the delegates returned, and Hedin ran downstairs to look for Nordenskiöld. He found him sitting on the bench outside the hotel entrance, leaning on his cane, staring at the sidewalk. He told Hedin that the delegation was met by the Imperial Chamberlain who had made them wait, and then returned to say that the Emperor had refused to receive them. Nordenskiöld was depressed, concerned about Finland's future.

Hedin could hardly believe the news. He had just been given every facility for a journey to Central Asia by the Russians: free passage by rail to Siberia, free cavalry escort while on Russian territory, customs clearance for all of his luggage and equipment. Yet at the same time Nordenskiöld, who had opened a whole new world for the Russians and pioneered new routes to Russia's Siberian territories, was refused an audience by the Emperor because he wished to speak on behalf of Finland, a domestic matter in Russian eyes.

Nordenskiöld and his colleagues of the European delegation left St. Petersburg to return home by way of Finland. A large crowd met their train in Helsingfors; all sang 'Our Land', Finland's national anthem, and Senator Trarieux and Nordenskiöld addressed the people massed in front of the railway station. Life seemed to have come full circle for Nordenskiöld that day. More than forty years after he had fled, he was back in his beloved Finland, speaking once more 'of the days to come, if only they are not to bring an end to Finland . . . of the hope that lingers on.'

Nordenskiöld returned to Stockholm with a heavy heart, for there seemed to be little hope of improvement in Russia's policy of putting an end to Finland's right to self-government. He sought out the peace of Dalbyö, the trees and rocks and water that he loved so much. Later that year, Erland returned from Patagonia full of tales about his experiences, anxious to take off for another expedition as soon as possible.

The first year of the twentieth century saw Nordenskiöld continue the round of work he had established years before. He contributed an article on minerals to a geological journal, and discussed a set of drawings, including an early picture of the mariner's compass, which he had found on the margins of a medieval manuscript in his library. He was deeply troubled by the fact that his close friend Beijer's publishing house ran into serious financial trouble and had to declare bankruptcy. It was in a depressed mood that he wrote to the Amsterdam firm of Muller, one of Europe's leading dealers in rare books. He had told them that he was thinking of leaving Stockholm and retiring to his country place, where there was no adequate room for his library. He had asked the book dealer about the chances of selling his library as a single unit; it represented a lifetime of book collection, and he did not want to see it dispersed by an auction sale.

Nordenskiöld even set a price on his library: he considered it worth two hundred thousand Swedish kronor, about a quarter of a million dollars in present-day terms. But the Dutch dealer reported that there was little chance of selling the library as a whole, and Nordenskiöld abandoned the idea. He continued to work all through the winter of 1900-1901, but had a bad bout with influenza, the first time he had been ill in more than forty years.

On August 10, 1901, Nordenskiöld entertained several friends at lunch in his apartment in Stockholm. One of the guests, the noted mathematician Mittag-Leffler, turned the conversation to the third centenary of the death of the great astronomer Tycho Brahe, that was to be celebrated later in the year. Nordenskiöld listened carefully, and seemed to be strongly impressed when his guest quoted Brahe's last words: 'May I not seem to have lived in vain!' He asked Mittag-Leffler to write down the phrase in its original Latin version. It seemed to express his own hope that his work would survive, even if his contemporaries chose to ignore it at times.

On August 12, 1901, Nordenskiöld returned to Dalbyö. He had a severe coughing spell that evening after supper, and died in his study, of a heart attack. In three months' time he would have celebrated his sixty-ninth birthday.

The news of his death travelled swiftly around the world. Every newspaper in Europe, in the Americas, in the Far East reported it; many papers printed not only the obituary notice but reminiscences too, by people who knew Nordenskiöld well.

Burial was to be in the small country churchyard at Västerljung, the parish church where the Nordenskiölds had worshipped and where Marie and Gustav Nordenskiöld were laid to rest. But Västerljung was a small place, and Anna Nordenskiöld gave in to the request of her husband's many friends that the formal funeral ceremony be held in Stockholm.

Laid in an oaken coffin, Nordenskiöld's body was carried by six men who had worked on the estate of Dalbyö, from the house to the landing stage on the bay, beyond the great oak trees. Accompanied by wreaths from the family, the coffin was put on board a small steamer, for the journey back to Stockholm. The flag of the steamer was at half mast, and when it reached Lake Mälar and the heart of Stockholm, ships and pleasure craft all lowered their flags in tribute.

The funeral was held in St. Jacob church, a somber baroque structure facing Stockholm's Opera House. King Oscar and his queen were at their summer residence in southern Sweden; the royal family was represented by Prince Eugen. The church was packed, and the coffin was barely visible under the scores of wreaths sent by friends, by dignitaries, by scientific societies from all over the world. Nordenskiöld's old shipmates were there – Palander, Kjellman, and many others; so were members of government, representatives of the universities, of the Academy of Sciences. At the end of the funeral service, eight men stepped forward to lay wreaths on the coffin – they represented Nordenskiöld's beloved Finland. Afterwards, Anna Nordenskiöld's brother, Carl Robert Mannerheim, spoke briefly to express the family's thanks to those present. The next day, Adolf Nordenskiöld's body was laid to rest in Västerljung cemetery.

In the fall of 1901, Anna Nordenskiöld offered her husband's library for sale. Oscar Dickson had died four years earlier; there was no one in Sweden willing to purchase the collection and make a gift of it to the nation, nor was the government interested in the matter. There were several offers from abroad, but Anna Nordenskiöld had insisted that the library should be bought as a single unit. It was one of Nordenskiöld's Finnish friends, Professor Palmén from Helsingfors University, who had convinced his colleagues that the library, a monument to one of Finland's greatest sons and a superb research collection, should become part of Finland's national heritage. Finland's treasury could not meet the purchase price, and it was the government of imperial Russia that had provided the necessary funds. As an expression of thanks for the support of the Russian government that acted on orders from the Emperor himself, Helsingfors University had sent Nicholas II one of the treasures of the Nordenskiöld collection, a geography of the world printed in Switzerland in 1538, containing the earliest known printed map of Russia. The Nordenskiöld collection is now part of Finland's National Library.

Anna Nordenskiöld spent her remaining years at Dalbyö, surrounded by the treasures her husband and her sons had collected. She seldom visited Stockholm; her children and grandchildren came to see her in the lovely setting of trees and orchards and seashore. She died in 1924, at the age of eighty-four.

Erland Nordenskiöld was in South America when his father died, and returned to inherit the title of Baron, and the family tradition of scholarship. He became one of the world's leading authorities on the Indian civilizations of South and Central America; his superb Amerindian collections are part of the Göteborg Museum. His books on the aboriginals of Latin America remain standard works of reference, and his work as an ethnographer was recognized when a special chair was created for him at the University of Göteborg, where he taught until his death in 1932.

In 1920 Sweden celebrated the fortieth anniversary of the *Vega* voyage, and someone asked about Sibiriakoff, who, together with King Oscar and Dickson, had made the discovery of the Northeast Passage possible. Alexander Mikhailovich Sibiriakoff was nearly seventy years old when the whirlwind of the October Revolution destroyed his whole world. Like many another Russian of the former *bourgeoisie*, Sibiriakoff had fled Russia and settled down in Nice, on the Mediterranean coast of France. He had known Nice in former days when he was one of the wealthy men of the Russian Empire, he returned there as a penniless but still proud man.

The officers of the Swedish Geographical Society found out that Alexander Sibiriakoff was living in France, in dire poverty. They convinced the leaders of Sweden's three political parties that the nation owed a debt of honor to the man who so generously supported Adolf Nordenskiöld in his most famous adventure. A special bill, introduced by the three party leaders, was promptly acted upon by the Swedish parliament early in 1921 and Sibiriakoff was voted a yearly pension of three thousand kronor. The President of the Swedish Geographical Society went to France in person to carry the good news, and Alexander Sibiriakoff lived out his days in peace. He died in Nice in 1933.

Adolf Nordenskiöld made it a practice to remember his friends and his benefactors on his expeditions, naming islands and capes and harbors after them. King Oscar II, Oscar Dickson, his good ship *Vega* are in this way immortalized on maps, but Nordenskiöld refused to use his own name for any geographical feature of an unknown coast. It was on the initiative of geographical societies from all over Germany that the waters of the Arctic Ocean east of Cape Chelyuskin were called the

Nordenskiöld Sea, and maps in Russia and abroad showed it with that name until the 1930's. It is now called the Laptev Sea, but a small group of islands off the Siberian coast is still called the Nordenskiöld Islands.

When Sweden celebrated the fiftieth anniversary of the return of the *Vega*, it was decided to erect a monument in memory of that ship and of the men who sailed her. The Vega monument stands in the garden of Stockholm's new National Museum: it is a slender obelisk, with a model of the *Vega* on its peak, and medallions of Nordenskiöld and Palander on its sides, the only memorial bearing the likeness of the great explorer.

April 24 is called Vega Day in the Swedish calendar. The Swedish Geographical Society holds a special meeting that day. It had done so every year since 1880, honoring explorers and scientists who carry on the tradition that Adolf Nordenskiöld stood for, the free spirit of scientific inquiry. He fought for that tradition, he made it part of all voyages of exploration, it is his greatest and most lasting memorial.

INDEX

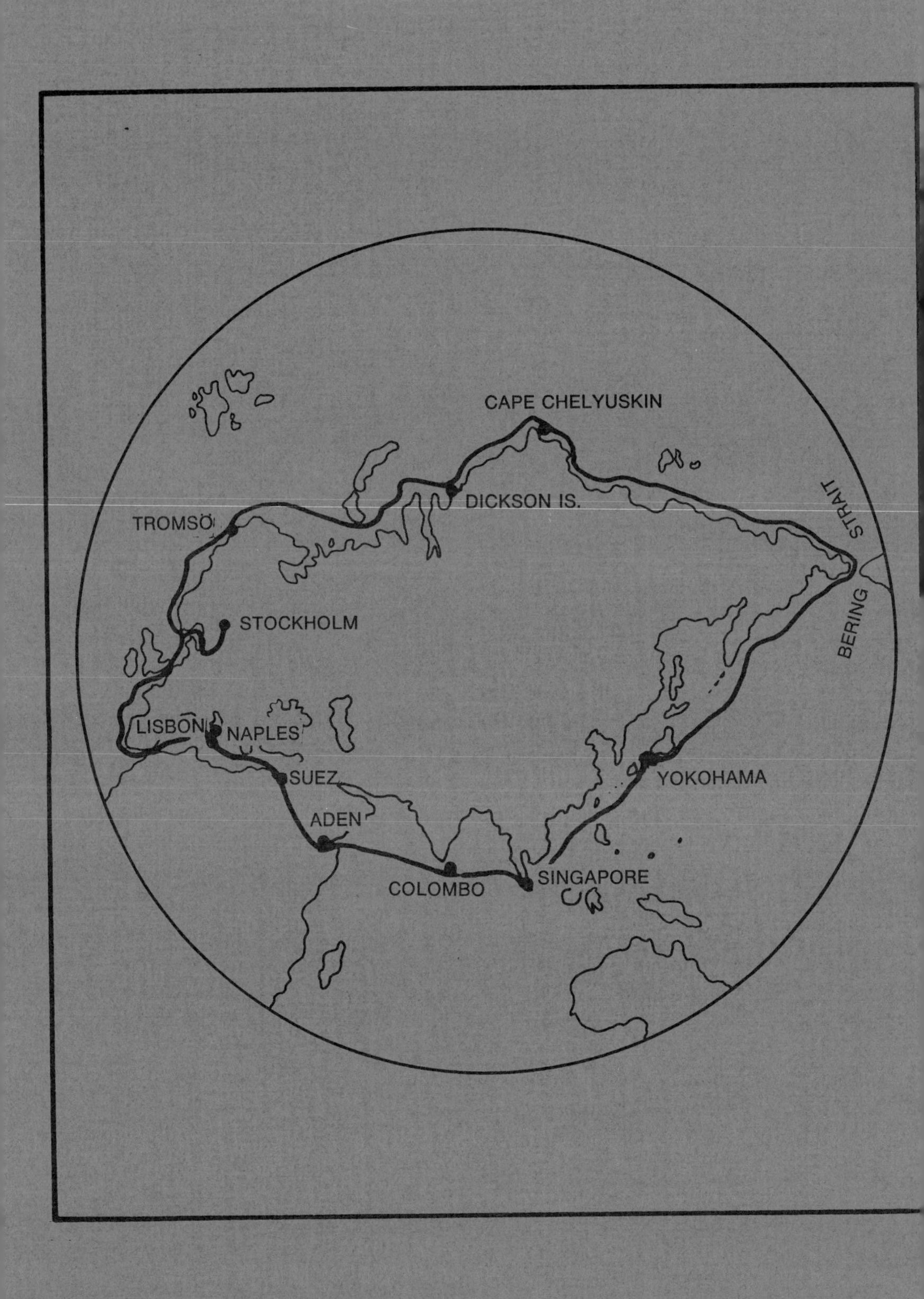
CAPE CHELYUSKIN
DICKSON IS.
TROMSÖ
BERING STRAIT
STOCKHOLM
LISBON
NAPLES
SUEZ
ADEN
YOKOHAMA
COLOMBO
SINGAPORE